THE ESSENCE OF

LOGIC

THE ESSENCE OF COMPUTING SERIES

Forthcoming titles:

THE ESSENCE OF

LOGIC

John J. Kelly

Prentice Hall
LONDON NEW YORK TORONTO SYDNEY TOKYO SINGAPORE
MADRID MEXICO CITY MUNICH PARIS

First published 1997 by
Prentice Hall Europe
Campus 400, Maylands Avenue
Hemel Hempstead
Hertfordshire, HP2 7EZ
A division of
Simon & Schuster International Group

Typeset from author's disks
by Dorwyn Ltd, Rowlands Castle, Hants

Printed and bound in Great Britain by
Redwood Books, Trowbridge, Wilts

Library of Congress Cataloging-in-Publication Data

Available from the publisher

British Library Cataloguing-in-Publication Data

A catalogue record for this book is available
from the British Library

ISBN 0-13-396375-6

1 2 3 4 5   01 00 99 98 97

Contents

Series Preface

As the consulting editor for the Essence of Computing Series it is my role to encourage the production of well-focused, high-quality textbooks at prices which students can afford. Since most computing courses are modular in structure, we aim to produce books which will cover the essential material for a typical module.

I want to maintain a consistent style for the Series so that whenever you pick up an Essence book you know what to expect. For example, each book contains important features such as end of chapter summaries and exercises, and a glossary of terms, if appropriate. Of course, the quality of the Series depends crucially on the skills of its authors and all the books are written by lecturers who have honed their material in the classroom. Each book in the Series takes a pragmatic approach and emphasises practical examples and case studies.

Our aim is that each book will become essential reading material for students attending core modules in Computing. However, we expect students to want to go beyond the Essence books and so all books contain guidance on further reading and related work.

An understanding of the basic principles of logic underpins many important topics in computing, ranging from basic hardware concepts to Artificial Intelligence. *The Essence of Logic* sets out to explore the fundamental concepts and techniques of logic, illustrating their usefulness with practical examples. This book draws on a wealth of teaching experience accumulated over many years and explores many facets of logic in an interesting and illuminating way.

Computing is constantly evolving and so the teaching of the subject also has to change. Therefore the Series has to be dynamic, responding to new trends in computing and extending into new areas of interest. We need feedback from our readers to guide us – are we hitting the target? Are there 'hot' topics which we have not covered yet? Feedback is always welcome but most of all I hope you find this book useful!

Ray Welland
Department of Computing Science
University of Glasgow
(e-mail: ray@dcs.gla.ac.uk)

Dedication

To the memory of John J. Kelly, the author.
He is deeply missed.

Preface

My father, Dr. John Kelly, lectured in Computer Science for 16 years. Prior to that he taught Maths and Physics in second level schools from the time he graduated with his degree in Physics. He was a born educator. I attended his courses as part of my degree in Computer Science. And, in spite of an obvious bias, I had to admit that I enjoyed his courses both for the content and the presentation.

He based this book largely on a course in Mathematical Logic that he has developed and taught for many years. As an educator he understood clearly that material such as Mathematical Logic must be very well motivated if the student is going to get anything out of it. He constantly strove to find clearer ways of explaining the difficult concepts without restricting the scope of the course. Having searched for years for a book that he could recommend he was disappointed when he could not find one that dealt with the full range of topics he was covering in a grounded enough fashion to maintain the students' motivation. So he was finally persuaded to write this book.

The fundamental philosophy of this book is that, while much of the area of Logic is not easy to comprehend, particularly initially, with practice and concentrated effort one can achieve a useful understanding. To that aim, the book is littered with exercises that serve the dual purpose of allowing the readers to practice what they have just learned and teaching the readers by enabling them to discover the concepts for themselves. Motivation is maintained throughout by grounding the ideas in examples that (hopefully) mean something to everybody.

The book is intended as an introductory text on Logic. It tackles the subject matter from a practical point of view. Throughout, the so-called 'tricks of the trade' are exposed in the forms of heuristics (or 'rules of thumb') and guiding principles for tackling problems in Logic. The reader is shown how to express problems in formal terms. And the various paths, including 'dead ends', down which a logician can be led in proving logical theorems are illustrated. The exercises are designed to allow the reader to practice what she has just learned and also to teach some of the ideas in the time-honoured Aristotelian tradition of dialectic. The reader is strongly advised to tackle the exercises as she comes across them, rather than ignore them or leave them until the end. Often, points that are made in later sections will involve solutions to previous exercises.

Having been developed from a course which is presented as part of a Computer Science degree, the areas of Logic tackled are chosen to represent those that are most useful and most used in Computer Science. The examples that are presented come largely from the fields of theoretical and applied computing. However, this book would also be of benefit to students of Mathematics, Philosophy, Engineering, and Science in general. It can be used for the study of logic as a subject in its own right within Mathematics or as a preparation for the analysis and application of logical techniques in Science and Philosophy. It was a firm belief of the author that a study of logical technique and an understanding of logical reasoning and argument are of great benefit to every thinking person.

For use as part of a course in Computer Science, ideally, the student should have a basic competency in Mathematics and some exposure to the fundamental topics of computing – architecture and programming. As part of an introductory course in Logic, presented during the first or second semester of a Computer Science degree, chapters 1, 2 and 3 should be used. Following such a course the students would have some of the necessary mental tools for studying the Theory of Computation and an introduction to Formal Methods. For a higher level course in Logic presented during the second or third year of a Computer Science degree, chapters 1–4, 6, 7 (sections 7.1 to 7.4) and 8 should be used. This would prepare the student for a study of topics in Formal Language and Automata Theory, Formal Semantics and Formal Methods of Software Development. At advanced level, the areas covered in chapters 5, 7, 8 (sections 8.6 onwards) and 9 would lead students into AI techniques, Logic programming and Automated Theorem Proving.

The following diagram shows the chapter dependencies in the book

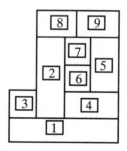

The earlier chapters – most of 1, 2 and 3 – use a relatively informal and relaxed style to introduce logic. This gives the newcomer the chance to become acquainted with the essential concepts without being overwhelmed by the necessity for exactness that formal logic demands. Having thus familiarised the reader with these basics, the book turns to a more formal study of logic as required by the subject matter. The reader should not be put off by the change in tone but should concentrate, rather, on seeing the necessity for such formality and the power it brings.

Throughout the book the feminine pronoun 'she' is used to indicate either 'he or she'.

As an introductory text in Logic this book leaves many questions unanswered. It describes only classical systems, leaving out notable topics such as Modal, Temporal and Intuitionist Logics. However, it is written to provide the sort of base from which the reader can confidently strike out in any of a number of directions in the general universe of Logic.

My father, the author, died on April 13th, 1995, before this book was finished. Undoubtedly he would have made some changes to improve the book before grudgingly admitting that it may have been ready to go to print. As was his wont, he would still have grumbled that it could have been better. I have learned a lot from reading it.

Stephen Kelly

Acknowledgements

In expressing gratitude on behalf of my father I am unable to name all those who helped him as he wrote this book. All I can do is say thank you, from him, to everyone who gave him support and advice.

There are a number of people I myself would like to thank for helping me to bring this book to completion.

First, my gratitude, and that of my father, to Prentice Hall for accepting the book initially and for agreeing to continue with it. In particular, I thank Jacqueline Harbor, the editor, for her support and encouragement.

My father's colleagues in University College Dublin were a tremendous help in ensuring the completion of the book. I would like to mention specifically Frank Anderson and Patricia Geoghegan who helped me greatly. Also, in particular, I owe a great deal to the help and support of Joseph Carthy.

I would not have been able to complete this book for my father without the constant assistance of Kevin Hely – my sincerest thanks for all he did. I also want to thank Karen Doyle whose emotional and practical support got me through some hard moments.

Finally, my father would have finished by expressing his deep gratitude to his family for their patience and support, so for him I express his gratitude to Lillian, John, Stephen, Paul, Clare, Jo Ann and Barbara.

Stephen Kelly

CHAPTER 1

Truth Tables

Chapter Aims

(1)   To introduce the basic ingredients of formal logic.
(2)   To define the important logical operators through truth tables.
(3)   To show how the truth of a logical formula may be established by means of a truth table.
(4)   To apply truth tables to simple logical problems.
(5)   To apply truth tables to the construction of logic circuits.

Having studied the chapter you should have
(a)   a basic understanding of some of the fundamental notions of formal logic – syntax, semantics, truth, validity, logical connectives, arguments, logical consequence, models.
(b)   developed the ability to construct truth tables for logical formulae.
(c)   developed the ability to apply truth tables to simple logical problems.
(d)   developed the ability to use truth tables in the construction of logic circuits.

1.1 What is Logic about?

In general, logic is about reasoning. It is about the validity of arguments, consistency among statements (or propositions, as they're called in logic) and matters of truth and falsehood. In a formal sense logic is concerned only with the *form* of arguments and the principles of valid inferencing. It is not science – it is not concerned with the *content* of reasoning. It deals with the notion of truth in an abstract sense. Thus the following two examples would generally be conceded to be cases of valid argument, even though the conclusions are in direct conflict:

(1)   All humans have 2 eyes   (2)   All humans have 4 eyes
       John is a human   John is a human
       Therefore John has 2 eyes   Therefore John has 4 eyes

In each case we have two premises from which a *valid* conclusion is drawn by a principle of valid reasoning. What do we mean when we say that a piece of reasoning is valid? We mean that the conclusion is *true* in every situation in which the premises are true. But the fact that the conclusion has been validly deduced says nothing about its actual truth. Whether it is true or not in a given case depends on the truth of the premises, and that is a matter for science, not for logic. What is of concern in logic is that *true conclusions should be drawn from true premises by acceptable rules of reasoning*. Or, to put it more strongly, that *it is never the case that a false conclusion is drawn from true premises*.

The distinction between the *form* and the *matter* of arguments is an important one, and one with which we shall be concerned throughout the text. The difference is usually expressed through the use of the terms *syntax* and *semantics*. In dealing with form we are interested in syntactical issues; in dealing with matter, or what arguments may be about, we are involved in semantics. Syntax relates to form, semantics to meaning. Although logic is mainly about the form of arguments and the construction of formal systems, it is also centrally concerned with the possibility of constructing models through which formal systems can be interpreted. It is thus also concerned with truth and falsity, with properties of mathematical relationships, with validity; in short, with semantics.

As in most areas of study, the best way to get to know logic and to become skilled in its application is to do it, rather than philosophise about it. In this book we are not going to be concerned about the wider philosophical aspects of logic – about its scope or limitations or relevance to the full range of human reasoning. We will mainly engage in a solid study of so-called classical logic because it serves as a secure foundation for an investigation of all of logic and because of its application to problems and issues in computer science, in mathematics, in philosophy, indeed to problems of reasoning wherever they arise.

1.2 Truth Tables

Although, as indicated above, logic is mainly concerned with valid deductions, and with truth only in the abstract, we begin our study with a very concrete look at how the basic ingredients of logical expression link up with the notions of truth and falsity to give some immediately practical applications.

What are the basic ingredients of logic?

They are the so-called logical connectives, *and, or, not, if… then … , if and only if*, etc. We are concerned with expressions involving these connectives. We want to know how the truth of a compound sentence like 'The cat sat on the mat *and* the dog barked' is affected by, or is determined by, the truth of the separate simple sentences 'The cat sat on the mat', 'The dog barked'. Similarly, we ask what is the truth value (i.e. is it true or false?) of the proposition '*If* it rained, *then* Stephen got wet' when the component part 'it rained' is true and the component part 'Stephen got wet' is false.

Note carefully that we are not concerned with the reasons why Stephen did not get wet (fascinating though they may be!), with whether he carried an umbrella or travelled in a car or whatever. We don't even care whether the parts of the compound sentence are really true or false. We are only interested in how the truth value of the whole is determined by the truth value of the parts. We abstract from the real-life or scientific conditions of the context.

Neither will we get involved in a discussion about the relation between the logical use of the connectives *and*, *or*, etc. and the ordinary, everyday, very flexible use of these words in natural language. For example, in a sentence such as 'The driver hit the cyclist and drove on' there is a time aspect to the use of 'and' which makes this sentence different from 'The driver drove on and hit the cyclist'. We will not be concerned with such subtle aspects of a rich natural language. For us, *and* and *or* will be taken as commutative (or symmetric) connectives, and thus the above two sentences will be treated as expressing the same proposition.

In general it is important to remember that the uses of *and*, *or*, *not*, *implies*, etc. in mathematical logic are not the same as their uses in ordinary language. How, then, are their uses within logic determined?

One simple way is through the use of *truth tables*. Truth tables give us operational definitions of the important logical connectives, separate from and independent of their use in ordinary language. They also provide a mechanism whereby the truth values of complicated expressions may be worked out.

Truth table definitions are not, of course, entirely independent of natural language. After all, logic is not usually pursued as merely an abstract game played out according to interesting and imaginative, but unrealistic, rules. It is intended to capture and formalise as much as possible of the processes of human reasoning. Consequently, the rules and mechanisms of logic are drawn up with the objective of providing a fit between formal reasoning and the real world, particularly as expressed through the medium of natural language.

Let us look then at the truth table definitions of the elements of logic. First, the following symbols are used to represent the logical connectives or operators:

and	$\wedge$
or	$\vee$
not	$\neg$
if ... then ... (implies)	$\rightarrow$
... if and only if ...	$\leftrightarrow$

Figure 1.1

These operators are used to connect components (symbolised by letters) together to form expressions or logical forms. We will be concerned with the truth values of these logical forms.

Now for the truth tables.

We start with $\wedge$ *(conjunction)*, and we use the letters F and T to stand for false and true respectively.

A	B	A∧B
F	F	F
F	T	F
T	F	F
T	T	T

Figure 1.2 : ∧ truth table

What information does the truth table give us?

It tells us that the conjunctive operator ∧ is being treated as a *binary* logical connective – it operates on two logical arguments. The letters A and B are *propositional variables*, i.e. they stand for any propositions. (Again, we will not go into a philosophical analysis of propositions. For us, a proposition is simply something that can be true or false). The table tells us that the compound proposition A∧B is true only when both A and B are true separately, otherwise it is false. Note that A and B stand for any propositions, simple or compound. Ultimately, however, the truth value of a compound proposition is built up from the truth value of simple component propositions. The truth table tells us how to do this for the ∧ operator. A∧B is called a *truth function* of A and B, as its value is dependent on and determined by the truth values of A and B. The basic truth tables we discuss essentially provide definitions of truth functions.

Truth tables present an exhaustive enumeration of the truth values of the component propositions of a logical expression. The information embodied in them can also be usefully presented in tree form.

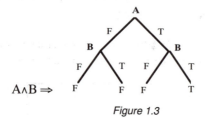

A∧B ⇒

Figure 1.3

The branches descending from the node A are labelled with the two possible truth values for A. The branches emerging from the nodes marked B give the two possible values for B for each value of A. The 'leaf' nodes at the bottom of the tree are marked with the values of A∧B for each truth combination of A and B.

The tree could also be presented in the form:

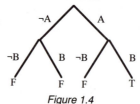

Figure 1.4

where instead of using F to label the branch where A is false we use ¬A; similarly for ¬B.

Exercise

1.1 Does the above truth table 'definition' tell us anything about the value of B∧A? Is the value of B∧A the same as the value of A∧B? What about the value of A∧A?

Armed with the above truth table for ∧ we can work out the value of more complicated conjunctions.

Example 1.1

Take, for example, (A∧B)∧C:

A	B	C	A∧B	(A∧B)∧C
F	F	F	F	F
F	F	T	F	F
F	T	F	F	F
F	T	T	F	F
T	F	F	F	F
T	F	T	F	F
T	T	F	T	F
T	T	T	T	T

Figure 1.5

First, the value of A∧B is worked out using the binary definition. Then, this value is combined with the value of C to give the final result, which tells us that (A∧B)∧C is true only if the values of all three components are true.

Exercise

1.2 Work out the truth value of A∧(B∧C) under all possible truth values of A, B and C. What do you conclude?

Let us continue, now, with the other logical connectives.

∨ *(Disjunction)*

A	B	A∨B
F	F	F
F	T	T
T	F	T
T	T	T

Figure 1.6 : ∨ truth table

The truth table for the *disjunctive* binary operator ∨ tells us that the compound proposition A∨B is false only if A and B are both false, otherwise it is true. This is the inclusive use of the operator *or*. It contrasts with the more usual exclusive use of *or* in ordinary natural language. For example, in 'I was in Dublin or London at 8.00 yesterday', it was physically impossible for me to be in both places. Our logical ∨ disregards such physical inconvenience! It always allows for the possibility that both terms of the operator may be simultaneously true.

The tree for ∨ is:

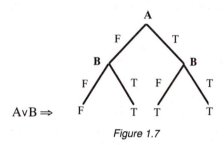

Figure 1.7

Exercise

1.3 Is the value of B∨A the same as the value of A∨B? What is the value of A∨A? Work out the value of (A ∨B)∨C for all possible truth values of A, B and C. Is the value of (A ∨B)∨C the same as the value of A∨(B∨C)?

¬ (*Not*)

The negation operator is a *unary* operator (i.e. it operates on one argument), rather than a binary operator like ∧ and ∨.

Its truth table is:

A	¬A
F	T
T	F

Figure 1.8 : ¬ truth table

The table presents ¬ in its expected role, i.e. the negation of true is false, and the negation of false is true.

Exercise

1.4 What is the value of ¬ ¬A?

→ (*Implication*)

Implication in logic can be treated in different ways. The type of implication indicated by → is called *material implication*.

The truth table is as follows:

A	B	A→B
F	F	T
F	T	T
T	F	F
T	T	T

Figure 1.9 : → truth table

In tree form:

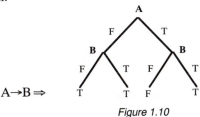

A→B ⇒

Figure 1.10

The only time that A→B evaluates to false is when the antecedent A is true and the consequent B is false. The truth table for implication (→) gives rise to the biggest clash with the intuitions derived from natural language. For example, both the following propositions would have truth value true:

> *If* 2+2 = 4 *then* fish swim   (i.e. 2+2 = 4 implies fish swim)
> *If* 2+2 = 7 *then* fish swim

This appears rather strange. To illustrate the reasoning consider the statement '*If* it rains *Then* I will carry an umbrella'. Clearly, if it rains and I do not carry an umbrella I will have falsified my statement. However, if it doesn't rain I can carry an umbrella or not without being called a liar.

One could disagree with the reasoning behind this interpretation, but we will avoid philosophical tangles and simply remark that this definition of → provides a coherent and ultimately fruitful element in the formalisation of classical logic.

Exercise

1.5   Has B→A the same truth value as A→B? i.e. is A→B equivalent to B→A? Is (A→B)→C equivalent to A→(B→C)?

↔ (*If and only if*)
Finally we have the truth table for if and only if:

A	B	A↔B
F	F	T
F	T	F
T	F	F
T	T	T

Figure 1.11: ↔ truth table

In tree form:

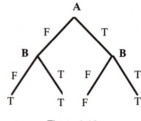

$A \leftrightarrow B \Rightarrow$

Figure 1.12

$A \leftrightarrow B$ is true whenever A and B have the same truth value – true or false.

As well as providing effective definitions of the logical operators, truth tables give us a method of working out the truth value of complex propositions.

Example 1.2

Consider the following:

> If I look into the sky and I am alert then either I will see the flying saucer or if I am not alert then I will not see the flying saucer.

Somewhat difficult to take in on a first reading! Let us see if we can express its structure in a clear symbolic way and determine its truth value.

Let   A stand for 'I look into the sky'

        B stand for 'I am alert'

        C stand for 'I will see the flying saucer'

A reasonable representation might then be: $(A \wedge B) \rightarrow (C \vee (\neg B \rightarrow \neg C))$

Now we use a truth table to determine its truth value.

A	B	C	A∧B	¬B	¬C	¬B→¬C	C∨(¬B→¬C)	(A∧B)→ (C∨(¬B→¬C))
F	F	F	F	T	T	T	T	T
F	F	T	F	T	F	F	T	T
F	T	F	F	F	T	T	T	T
F	T	T	F	F	F	T	T	T
T	F	F	F	T	T	T	T	T
T	F	T	F	T	F	F	T	T
T	T	F	T	F	T	T	T	T
T	T	T	T	F	F	T	T	T

Figure 1.13

Notice how we gradually build up to the value of the full expression by evaluating larger and larger subexpressions. Notice too that, no matter what the truth values of A, B and C are, the value of the final expression is always true. When this happens we call the expression a *tautology*. This was probably not so easy to determine from the original English sentence. Well, this is what logic is partly about, making things clearer! Tautologies assume a central importance in logic, as we will see.

A very simple tautology is $A \lor \neg A$. Check it out for yourself.

Incidently, notice how we chose the (sub-)sentences to represent propositions.

Heuristic for formalising English

Pick the smallest statements without *and, or, if ... then ...*, etc. about which you could answer the question 'Is it true or false?'. Using propositional variables to stand for these statements connect them with the relevant logical connectives $\land$, $\lor$, $\rightarrow$, etc.

Exercise

1.6 Which of the following logical forms represent tautologies?

- (i) $A \rightarrow A$
- (ii) $A \rightarrow (B \rightarrow A)$
- (iii) $(B \rightarrow A) \rightarrow A$
- (iv) $A \land \neg A$
- (v) $A \land A$
- (vi) $\neg \neg A \rightarrow A$
- (vii) $(\neg A \rightarrow \neg B) \rightarrow (B \rightarrow A)$
- (viii) $(A \rightarrow (B \rightarrow C)) \rightarrow ((A \rightarrow B) \rightarrow (A \rightarrow C))$

If you examine carefully the expression whose truth table was presented in Table 1.13 you will realise that, with a little thought, we could have simplified our task and reduced the amount of work involved. Remember that an implication has the value T if the antecedent is F, no matter whether the consequent is T or F. In the above the antecedent of the main implication is $A \land B$ and it will be F if either A or B (or both) are F. Therefore in those cases (6 out of the eight possible cases) the whole expression will turn out to have the value T. Therefore we need to examine in detail only the cases where A and B are both true – the last two lines of the truth table.

A	B	C	$A \land B$	$\neg B$	$\neg C$	$\neg B \rightarrow \neg C$	$C \lor (\neg B \rightarrow \neg C)$	$(A \land B) \rightarrow$ $(C \lor (\neg B \rightarrow \neg C))$
T	T	F	T	F	T	T	T	T
T	T	T	T	F	F	T	T	T

Figure 1.14

See if you can use similar considerations to simplify your truth tables for the last exercise.

1.3 Equivalences

From some of the exercises above you will have determined that B∧A always takes on the same truth value as A∧B. We say that B∧A is *logically equivalent* to A∧B and we can write this as follows:

$$B∧A ≡ A∧B \qquad \text{Commutativity}$$

Definition   In general, two expressions are *logically equivalent* if each one always has the same truth value as the other.

Also

B∨A ≡ A∨B	Commutativity
A ∧ (B∧C) ≡ (A∧B) ∧ C	Associativity
A ∨ (B∨C) ≡ (A∨B) ∨ C	Associativity

These equivalences reveal ∧ and ∨ to be *commutative* and *associative* operators.

But these are not the only important equivalences that hold between logical forms. Consider the following two truth tables:

A	B	A→B
F	F	T
F	T	T
T	F	F
T	T	T

Figure 1.15

A	B	¬A	¬A∨B
F	F	T	T
F	T	T	T
T	F	F	F
T	T	F	T

Figure 1.16

Notice that the last two columns in the tables have exactly the same sequence of truth values. So A→B ≡ ¬A∨B. Thus, we could do without the → operator.

For example, consider the two statements:

If you don't study *Then* you will fail.   A→B
Study *or* you will fail.   ¬A∨B

Clearly, they say the same thing. The logical versions of these two statements are equivalent under our original definition of → .

So, everywhere → occurs it could be replaced by a combination of ¬ and ∨.

Now, consider the following two truth tables:

A	B	A∧B
F	F	F
F	T	F
T	F	F
T	T	T

Figure 1.17

A	B	¬A	¬B	¬A∨¬B	¬(¬A∨¬B)
F	F	T	T	T	F
F	T	T	F	T	F
T	F	F	T	T	F
T	T	F	F	F	T

Figure 1.18

From these tables we see that $A \wedge B$ is logically equivalent to $\neg(\neg A \vee \neg B)$. Thus $\wedge$ could be replaced by a combination of $\neg$ and $\vee$.

Similarly we could show that $\leftrightarrow$ can be replaced by a combination of $\neg$ and $\vee$.

Exercise

1.7 Show that

  (i) $A \vee A \equiv A$

  (ii) $A \wedge A \equiv A$

  (iii) $A \wedge (A \vee B) \equiv A$

  (iv) $A \vee (A \wedge B) \equiv A$

  (v) $A \wedge (\neg A \vee B) \equiv A \wedge B$

  (vi) $A \vee B \equiv \neg (\neg A \wedge \neg B)$

  (vii) $(A \wedge B) \vee (A \wedge \neg B) \equiv A$

  (viii) $A \vee (B \wedge C) \equiv (A \vee B) \wedge (A \vee C)$

  (ix) $A \wedge (B \vee C) \equiv (A \wedge B) \vee (A \wedge C)$

  (x) $A \leftrightarrow B \equiv (A \rightarrow B) \wedge (B \rightarrow A)$
  $$\equiv (\neg A \vee B) \wedge (\neg B \vee A)$$
  $$\equiv \neg(\neg(\neg A \vee B) \vee \neg(\neg B \vee A))$$

The equivalences $A \wedge B \equiv \neg (\neg A \vee \neg B)$ and $A \vee B \equiv \neg (\neg A \wedge \neg B)$ are known as *De Morgan's Laws*.

We have used the term tautology for a logical form that is always true. We will use the symbol **1** to represent a tautology – where **1** occurs we mean *a proposition that is always true*.

An expression that always has the truth value false is called a *contradiction*. We will use **0** to represent a contradiction – where **0** occurs we mean *a proposition that is always false*.

Take a look at the following truth tables:

A	1	A∧1
F	T	F
T	T	T

Figure 1.19

A	0	A∧0
F	F	F
T	F	F

Figure 1.20

From these truth tables we see that $A \wedge 1 \equiv A$ and that $A \wedge 0 \equiv 0$.

Exercise

1.8 Show that $A \vee 1 \equiv 1$ and $A \vee 0 \equiv A$.

1.3.1 Simplification

The various equivalences between logical forms provide us with a means of simplifying expressions. For example, we can simplify the logical form $(A \vee 0) \wedge (A \vee \neg A)$ as follows:

$$(A \vee 0) \wedge (A \vee \neg A) \equiv A \wedge (A \vee \neg A)$$
$$\equiv A \wedge 1 \text{ (since } A \vee \neg A \text{ is a tautology)}$$
$$\equiv A$$

Similarly

$$(A \wedge \neg B) \vee (A \wedge B \wedge C) \equiv A \wedge (\neg B \vee (B \wedge C))$$
$$\equiv A \wedge ((\neg B \vee B) \wedge (\neg B \vee C))$$
$$\equiv A \wedge (1 \wedge (\neg B \vee C))$$
$$\equiv A \wedge (\neg B \vee C)$$

It is useful at this point to gather together a list of important equivalences.

$A \wedge 0 \equiv 0$	Zero of $\wedge$
$A \wedge 1 \equiv A$	Identity of $\wedge$
$A \vee 0 \equiv A$	Zero of $\vee$
$A \vee 1 \equiv 1$	Identity of $\vee$
$A \wedge A \equiv A$	Idempotence
$A \vee A \equiv A$	Idempotence
$A \wedge \neg A \equiv 0$	Law of contradiction
$A \vee \neg A \equiv 1$	Tautology
$\neg \neg A \equiv A$	Law of double negation
$A \wedge B \equiv B \wedge A$	Commutativity
$A \vee B \equiv B \vee A$	Commutativity
$A \wedge (B \vee C) \equiv (A \wedge B) \vee (A \wedge C)$	Distributivity
$A \vee (B \wedge C) \equiv (A \vee B) \wedge (A \vee C)$	Distributivity
$A \wedge (A \vee B) \equiv A$	Absorption
$A \vee (A \wedge B) \equiv A$	Absorption
$A \vee (\neg A \wedge B) \equiv A \vee B$	Absorption
$A \wedge (\neg A \vee B) \equiv A \wedge B$	Absorption
$\neg (A \wedge B) \equiv \neg A \vee \neg B$	De Morgan's law
$\neg (A \vee B) \equiv \neg A \wedge \neg B$	De Morgan's law
$(A \wedge B) \vee (A \wedge \neg B) \equiv A$	
$A \rightarrow B \equiv \neg A \vee B$	
$A \rightarrow B \equiv \neg (A \wedge \neg B)$	

These equivalences give us the basis for an algebra of expressions. This algebra is an instance of a class (or type) of algebras called *Boolean algebras*.

Exercise

1.9 (i) Show that each of the above equivalences holds.

(ii) Simplify the following logical forms:

(a) $A \wedge A \wedge A \wedge A \wedge A \wedge A \wedge A$

(b) $A \wedge (\neg A \vee B) \vee B \vee (A \wedge (A \vee B))$

(c) $\neg A \rightarrow \neg (A \rightarrow \neg B)$

1.4 Sufficiently Connected

As we have indicated, there is room for considerable philosophical discussion about whether the logical connectives we have been using reflect ordinary reasoning in any proper or adequate sense. Be that as it may, the connectives *and*, *or* and *not* can be shown to be adequate for classical propositional logic as we have been presenting it. In fact, we don't even require all three. We know, for example, that ∨ can be expressed in terms of ∧ and ¬. Consequently, ∨ can be eliminated from logical forms, thus giving us a complete representation in terms of ∧ and ¬.

But, we can go one better! We can identify a single connective that is sufficient to represent all propositional logic forms. It is not one of our familiar *and, or, not*. Neither is it *if ... then ...* or *... if and only if ....* It is a connective called *nand* (sometimes called the Sheffer stroke), symbolised by a vertical stroke |. It can be defined by means of the following truth table:

A	B	A|B
F	F	T
F	T	T
T	F	T
T	T	F

Figure 1.21

A nand B is false only when both A and B are true. Clearly, this is the opposite of A *and* B, which reveals why the connective is called nand, i.e. *not and*.

To show that nand is sufficient on its own we would have to show that *and, or* and *not* can all be expressed in terms of nand alone. In fact, we need only show that *and* and *not* can be so expressed, since *or* can be converted into these two.

Consider then the truth table for A|A:

A	A	A|A
F	F	T
T	T	F

Figure 1.22

A|A has precisely the same values as ¬A.
Now consider the truth table:

A	B	A|B	(A|B) | (A|B)
F	F	T	F
F	T	T	F
T	F	T	F
T	T	F	T

Figure 1.23

Figure 1.23 shows that the values of (A|B) | (A|B) are the same as those for A∧B. Thus, both ∧ and ¬ can be expressed in terms of nand alone, so we conclude that nand is a sufficient logical function on its own.

It is not the only such sufficient operator. The operator *nor*, defined as ¬(A∨B), can also be proved to be sufficient. Nor is sometimes called the Peirce arrow (after the 19th century American logician and philosopher C. S. Peirce) and is symbolised by ↓ .

Exercise

1.10 (i) Find expressions, using only nand, which are equivalent to (a) A∨B and (b) A→B. Show the equivalences using truth tables.

(ii) Express ∧, ∨ and ¬ and in terms of nor only.

(iii) Express ↓ in terms of |.

(iv) Express | in terms of ↓.

Historical Notes

Truth tables present a systematic exhaustive enumeration of the possible truth values of combinations of simple propositions. The modern form of truth table was popularised by Emil Post (1897–1954) and Ludwig Wittgenstein (1889–1951) in the 1920s, but truth tables had been used (in a somewhat awkward notation) by Gottlob Frege in developing Boole's theory of elective functions (i.e. truth functions). The notion of truth function had been anticipated in ancient times by the Greek philosopher and logician Philo of Megara in his treatment of implication.

George Boole (1815–64)
Boole was born into a poor family in England. From an early age he was a keen scholar and taught himself Latin and Greek before he was twelve years old. He learned Mathematics from his father who had himself advanced beyond the level to which he had been taught in school.

In 1831, when he was 16, Boole got a job as a teacher in an elementary school. Four years later he opened his own school and extended his mathematical studies with renewed vigour. He wrote a number of papers on different aspects of mathematics. In 1949, he was appointed Professor of Mathematics at Queen's College, Cork. He died at the regrettably early age of 49 from pneumonia contracted from a wetting he received while keeping a lecturing appointment.

Boole, along with Gottlob Frege (see Chapter 7), may justifiably be considered to be the founder of modern logic. His seminal contribution was the development of an algebra of logic, which he expounded first in his *Mathematical Analysis of Logic*. His ideas are again presented, along with applications to the calculus of probabilities and some metaphysical discussions, in his most famous work *An Investigation of the Laws of Thought on which are founded The Mathematical Theories of Logic and Probabilities*.

1.5 Language to Logic

1.5.1 Consistency

The techniques of truth tables and Boolean algebra are inadequate to deal with the rich complexities of natural language. Nevertheless, it is possible to handle some situations.

Example 1.3

Consider the following:

Sales of houses fall off if interest rates rise. Auctioneers are not happy if sales of houses fall off. Interest rates are rising. Auctioneers are happy.

The question is: are these statements consistent with each other?

Consistency is an extremely important notion in mathematical logic and we will deal with it more formally in later chapters. For the moment we will use a less formal definition:

Definition   A collection of statements is *consistent* if the statements can all be true simultaneously.

In this case, without resorting to heavy logical apparatus, we can easily see that they are not consistent! However, let us see how to express the situation in logical form and use our truth tables to come to some conclusions.

Let   S stand for 'sales of houses fall off'
R stand for 'interest rates rise'
H stand for 'auctioneers are happy'

We can now symbolise our statements.

$$R \rightarrow S, S \rightarrow \neg H, R, H$$

To see if these are mutually consistent we will ascertain if the conjunction $(R \rightarrow S) \wedge (S \rightarrow \neg H) \wedge R \wedge H$ can have the value true. We set up a truth table.

S	R	H	R→S	S→¬H	(R→S) ∧ (S→¬H) ∧ R ∧ H
F	F	F	T	T	F
F	F	T	T	T	F
F	T	F	F	T	F
F	T	T	F	T	F
T	F	F	T	T	F
T	F	T	T	F	F
T	T	F	T	T	F
T	T	T	T	F	F

Figure 1.24

From the truth table (Figure 1.24), we see that under no circumstances is the propositon (R→S) ∧ (S→H) ∧ R ∧ H true. Hence we conclude that the statements are mutually inconsistent.

1.5.2 Arguments

Example 1.4

Consider the following argument:

If the violinist plays the concerto, then crowds will come if the prices are not too high.

If the violinist plays the concerto, the prices will not be too high.

Therefore, if the violinist plays the concerto, crowds will come.

Is this argument valid, i.e. does the conclusion (the third statement) follow logically from the premises (the first two statements)?

In order to determine whether the argument is valid we will adopt a very common and powerful strategy. We will see if the 'opposite' of the conclusion is incompatible with the other information. So, we will check to see if the negation of the conclusion is inconsistent with the premises.

Let   P stand for 'the violinist plays the concerto'

          C stand for 'crowds will come'

          H stand for 'prices are too high'

The statements are $P \rightarrow (\neg H \rightarrow C)$

                          $P \rightarrow \neg H$

                  $\therefore$ $P \rightarrow C$

We negate $P \rightarrow C$ and check the consistency of $(P \rightarrow (\neg H \rightarrow C)) \wedge (P \rightarrow \neg H) \wedge \neg(P \rightarrow C)$ using a truth table.

$$(P \rightarrow (\neg H \rightarrow C)) \wedge (P \rightarrow \neg H) \wedge \neg(P \rightarrow C)$$

P	C	H	¬H	¬H→C	P→ (¬H→C)	P→¬H	P→C	¬(P→C)	
F	F	F	T	F	T	T	T	F	F
F	F	T	F	T	T	T	T	F	F
F	T	F	T	T	T	T	T	F	F
F	T	T	F	T	T	T	T	F	F
T	F	F	T	F	F	T	F	T	F
T	F	T	F	T	T	F	F	T	F
T	T	F	T	T	T	T	T	F	F
T	T	T	F	T	T	F	T	F	F

Figure 1.25

From our final column we indeed see that the negation of the conclusion is incompatible with the premises. In other words it cannot be the case that the premises and the negation of the conclusion are true together. Therefore the conclusion is always true when the premises are true. Therefore we conclude that the argument is correct.

The strategy of negating the conclusion and seeing if the result is inconsistent with the premises is called a *refutation strategy*. Although it is a very powerful one, and one to which we will come back again and again throughout the text, it's perhaps a little extravagant here. We are really only interested in seeing if the conclusion is true whenever the premises are all true. Thus we are interested in the situations when the 6th and 7th columns of the above truth table have simultaneous values T. This happens in the 1st, 2nd, 3rd, 4th and 7th rows. We ask ourselves: is P→C true in these circumstances? And the answer is clearly seen to be yes. So, the whole truth table is not needed. In this particular problem we do not save a whole lot. But in other situations we may be able to economise quite a bit. Truth tables are very good at presenting a survey of all the truth possibilities in a given situation, but they do not go directly to the heart of the problem. In the next chapter we will study a more direct method.

We could also eschew the drawing up of the truth table and reason as follows:

Could P→C be F and at the same time both P → (¬H→C) and P→¬H be T? For P→C to be F, P must be T and C must be F.

If P is T then ¬H→C must be T in order for P → (¬H→C) to be T.

Hence ¬H must be F, as we have already determined that we need C to be F.

But then P→¬H will be F, since P must be T.

So we conclude that it is impossible for P→C to be F and both P → (¬H→C) and P→¬H to be T.

Hence, we say that P→C is a *logical consequence* of P → (¬H→C) and P→¬H.

We abbreviate this to: {P → (¬H→C), P→¬H} ⊨ P→C

We also say that every *model* of {P → (¬H→C), P→¬H} is a model of P→C. In the present context we define a model of a set of statements as follows:

Definition   An assignment of truth values to the basic components of the statements will produce truth values for the statements; some assignments may result in all statments being true; we chose, as a *model*, one such assignment, if it exists.

Example 1.5

Consider now the following argument:

> If Static Rovers win the league, their supporters will be happy.
>
> The supporters will drink too much if they are not happy.
>
> Therefore if the supporters do not drink too much Static Rovers will win the league.

Let   W stand for 'Static Rovers will win the league'

H stand for 'the supporters will be happy'

D stand for 'the supporters will drink too much'

The argument is

$$W \rightarrow H$$
$$\neg H \rightarrow D$$
$$\therefore \ \neg D \rightarrow W$$

Suppose ¬ D→W is F. This requires ¬D to be T and W to be F, i.e. v(D) = F and v(W) = F (using v(A) as an abbreviation for value of A).

Then, for ¬H→D to be T we need ¬H to be F (since v(D) = F) and therefore H to be T.

Also, since v(W) = F, v(W →H) = T.

Hence, there is a set of values of W, H and D which render the premises W→H and ¬H→D true and the conclusion ¬ D→W false. This set of values v(W) = F, v(H) = T and v(D) = F provides a counter example, or countermodel – a model for the premises which is not a model for the conclusion – which makes the argument invalid.

Example 1.6

Finally, consider the following argument:

If Jack takes a holiday then Jill will be happy and she will not cry.
Jack will take a holiday and if Jill is happy she will cry.
Therefore Jack will take a holiday.

Let J stand for 'Jack will take a holiday'
H stand for 'Jill will be happy'
C stand for 'Jill will cry'

The argument is

$$J \rightarrow (H \wedge \neg C)$$
$$J \wedge (H \rightarrow C)$$
$$\therefore \ J$$

Let us construct a truth table to check the validity of the argument.

J	H	C	H ∧ ¬C	J → (H ∧ ¬C)	H→C	J ∧ (H→C)
F	F	F	F	T	T	F
F	F	T	F	T	T	F
F	T	F	T	T	F	F
F	T	T	F	T	T	F
T	F	F	F	F	T	T
T	F	T	F	F	T	T
T	T	F	T	T	F	F
T	T	T	F	F	T	T

Figure 1.26

We notice that J → (H∧¬ C) and J ∧ (H→C) are never true at the same time, i.e. the premises of the argument have no model. What can we conclude about the validity of the argument?

We conclude that it is valid! Why?

Because, as there is no model for the premises, there can be no countermodel, i.e. there is no situation where the premises are true, but the conclusion is false. We accept validity by default.

In fact, no matter what the conclusion was we would say the argument was valid, because we cannot have a situation where the premises are true and the conclusion is false – we have no situation where the premises are true.

It may appear strange to ascribe validity in a situation like this, but it is in harmony with the requirement that for a valid argument there should be no circumstance where the premises are all true and the conclusion is false. It is essentially in line with the classical logic property that from a contradiction anything follows. In the argument above, the premises contradict one another. Any conclusion follows! It is another example of how formal logic may run counter to ordinary intuitions. Of course, you are not compelled to accept the conclusion.

1.6 Applications to Circuit Design

One of the most important applications of Boolean algebra is to the design of electronic circuits and especially to the design of computer logic. The basic logic functions *and, or* and *not* can be realised by electronic devices called gates and these can be combined together to form complicated circuits. These can then be used to provide arithmetic, logical, timing, storage, control and other important functions for computers. In this section we take a brief look at the ideas behind the use of logic elements in circuit design.

The *and* connective is realised by an *and-gate* which is symbolised as follows:

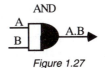

Figure 1.27

The idea is that if the *and-gate* receives input signals on both the A and B input lines then there will be an output signal on the line marked A.B (standing for A∧B). If there is no input on either A or B or both, there will be no output signal.

Similarly, an *or-gate* is symbolised as follows:

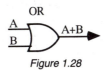

Figure 1.28

In Figure 1.28, if there is an input signal on either A or B or both, there will be an output signal on A+B (standing for A∨B).

Finally, a *not-gate* (or inverter) looks like:

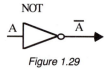

Figure 1.29

In this case, if there is an input A, there will be no output; if there is no input A there will be an output. The input is said to be inverted or negated.

To see how these components can be put together we look at some examples.

Example 1.7

First, consider a circuit to implement the logical function A↔B, i.e. a circuit which will give an output true exactly when A and B have the same truth values, whether they are both false or both true.

Let us look at the truth table again.

A	B	A↔B
F	F	T
F	T	F
T	F	F
T	T	T

Figure 1.30

Looking at this carefully we see that A↔B can be represented by ($\neg A \wedge \neg B$) $\vee$ (A∧B). In other words ($\neg A \wedge \neg B$) $\vee$ (A∧B) is logically equivalent to A↔B. The lines to look out for in the truth table are those where the desired result is true. In the present case these are the first and last lines, i.e. when A and B are both false, and when A and B are both true. It is clear that if we negate those values which are false and leave the others alone in any given line we will have only values which are true. If these are 'anded' together, the result will be true.

Think it through for yourself!

Now we can realise our desired equivalence function with the basic *and, or* and *not* building blocks. If we go through the expression ($\neg A \wedge \neg B$) $\vee$ (A∧B) from the left we see that we need to negate both A and B and feed the outputs through an *and-gate*. We also need to feed A and B directly through an *and-gate*. Finally we must take the output of the two *and-gates* and feed them through an *or-gate* to get the result.

The required circuit is:

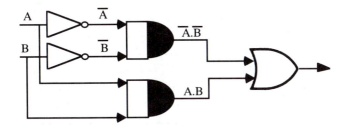

Figure 1.31

Example 1.8

As another example let us take a function known as the *exclusive-or (XOR)* function which has the following truth table:

A	B	A XOR B
F	F	F
F	T	T
T	F	T
T	T	F

Figure 1.32

We see that A XOR B has exactly the opposite truth value to A↔B, i.e. A XOR B is false when A and B are the same and true when they are different. In order to implement A XOR B then we could simply use the circuit, in Figure 1.32, for A↔B and invert the output. However let us determine an equivalent function using *and*, *or* and *not* directly from the truth table and implement a function accordingly. The important lines are the middle two, and the function is (¬A∧B) ∨ (A∧¬B). The corresponding circuit is:

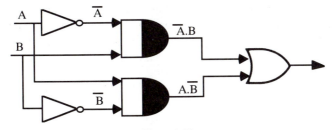

Figure 1.33

Example 1.9

As a final example, consider the truth function R expressed in the following table:

A	B	C	R
F	F	F	F
F	F	T	T
F	T	F	T
F	T	T	T
T	F	F	T
T	F	T	T
T	T	F	T
T	T	T	F

Figure 1.34

If we construct a logical form for R from the rows where R has the value T we get the following expression:

$(\neg A \wedge \neg B \wedge C) \vee (\neg A \wedge B \wedge \neg C) \vee (\neg A \wedge B \wedge C) \vee (A \wedge \neg B \wedge \neg C) \vee (A \wedge \neg B \wedge C) \vee (A \wedge B \wedge \neg C)$

To implement this form as it stands would require 26 gates – 9 *not-gates*, 12 *and-gates* and 5 *or-gates*. If we could simplify this expression we might economise on the number of gates and also make it easier to implement.
We can simplify it by using our Boolean algebra equivalences – essentially, in this case, the commutative and distributive rules, i.e. $B \wedge A \equiv A \wedge B$ and $A \wedge (B \vee C) \equiv (A \wedge B) \vee (A \wedge C)$. We make use of the distributive rule to do some factoring, e.g. we factor A out of $(A \wedge B) \vee (A \wedge C)$ to get $A \wedge (B \vee C)$.

So, we proceed as follows:

$(\neg A \wedge \neg B \wedge C) \vee (\neg A \wedge B \wedge \neg C) \vee (\neg A \wedge B \wedge C) \vee (A \wedge \neg B \wedge \neg C) \vee (A \wedge \neg B \wedge C) \vee (A \wedge B \wedge \neg C)$

$\equiv (\neg A \wedge C) \wedge (\neg B \vee B) \vee (B \wedge \neg C) \wedge (\neg A \vee A) \vee (A \wedge \neg B) \wedge (\neg C \vee C)$

From 1st & 3rd	From 2nd & 6th	From 4th & 5th
components above	components by	components by
by 'factoring' out	factoring out	factoring out
$\neg A \wedge C$	$B \wedge \neg C$	$A \wedge \neg B$

$\equiv (\neg A \wedge C) \wedge 1 \vee (B \wedge \neg C) \wedge 1 \vee (A \wedge \neg B) \wedge 1$

$\equiv (\neg A \wedge C) \vee (B \wedge \neg C) \vee (A \wedge \neg B)$

If we examine this expression carefully, we see that we require only 8 gates to implement it – 3 *not-gates*, 3 *and-gates* and 2 *or-gates*.
A suitable circuit would be

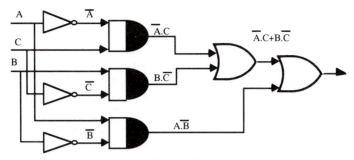

Figure 1.35

Exercise

1.11 Draw suitable circuits using only the *and-gate*, *or-gate* and *not-gate* to implement the logical functions given by the following truth tables:

A	B	R
F	F	T
F	T	F
T	F	F
T	T	F

Figure 1.36

A	B	C	R
F	F	F	F
F	F	T	T
F	T	F	F
F	T	T	T
T	F	F	F
T	F	T	T
T	T	F	F
T	T	T	T

Figure 1.37

A	B	C	R
F	F	F	F
F	F	T	F
F	T	F	F
F	T	T	T
T	F	F	F
T	F	T	T
T	T	F	T
T	T	T	T

Figure 1.38

1.7 Summary

- Logic is the study of some methods of reasoning and is concerned with such issues as the validity of arguments, consistency and formal aspects of truth and falsehood.
- Important logical operators are ∧ (and), ∨ (or), ¬ (not), → (implies), ↔ (if and only if), | (nand) and ↓ (nor).
- The effect of the logical operators in determining the truth or falsity of statements may be defined by means of truth tables which present a systematic exhaustive enumeration of the possible truth values of combinations of simple propositions.
- The pair of operators ∧ and ¬, or the pair ∨ and ¬, is sufficient to express the full range of propositional forms. Further, nand is sufficient on its own, and nor is sufficient on its own.
- A tautology is a logical expression which always takes on the value true.
- A contradiction is a logical expression which always has the value false.
- There are a number of important equivalences between logical expressions which are useful in practice. These equivalences afford a means of effecting simplifications of logical forms in many cases.
- Truth functional logic may be implemented in the form of electronic circuits.
- Truth tables may be used in assessing consistency of statements and validity of arguments.
- An argument is valid if it is never the case that the premises are true and the conclusion is false.
- A model of a set of statements is an assignment of truth values to the basic components of the statements for which the statements are all true.

In this chapter we have

- introduced some of the basic notions of formal logic – syntax, semantics, truth, validity, logical connectives, arguments, logical consequence, models.
- defined the important logical connectives through truth tables.
- shown how the truth of a logical formula may be established by means of a truth table.
- applied truth tables to the construction of logic circuits.
- applied truth tables to simple logical problems.

   In the next chapter we will try to get around the awkwardness and limitations of truth tables by exploring a different, more direct, approach to determining the validity of arguments.

Miscellaneous Exercises

1. Draw up truth tables for each of the following propositional forms:
    (i) $\neg(A \wedge \neg A)$
    (ii) $\neg(A \vee \neg A)$
    (iii) $A \rightarrow (\neg A \rightarrow A)$
    (iv) $A \rightarrow (\neg A \rightarrow B)$
    (v) $\neg A \rightarrow (A \rightarrow B)$
    (vi) $A \wedge B \wedge C \wedge D$
    (vii) $A \vee B \vee C \vee D$
    (viii) $A \rightarrow (B \rightarrow (C \rightarrow D))$
    (ix) $(A \rightarrow B) \rightarrow (C \rightarrow D)$
    (x) $(A \rightarrow B) \rightarrow ((A \rightarrow \neg B) \rightarrow \neg A)$

2. Which of the expressions in Exercise 1 represent tautologies?

3. Which of the following pairs of expressions are logical equivalences?
    (i) $A \rightarrow B$ and $\neg(A \wedge \neg B)$
    (ii) $A \leftrightarrow B$ and $(\neg A \vee B) \wedge (\neg B \vee A)$
    (iii) $A \rightarrow (\neg A \rightarrow B)$ and $\mathbf{1}$
    (iv) $(A \vee \neg B) \rightarrow C$ and $(\neg A \wedge B) \vee C$
    (v) $A \rightarrow (B \rightarrow C)$ and $(A \rightarrow B) \rightarrow C$
    (vi) $A \downarrow A$ and $\neg A$
    (vii) $A \downarrow (B \downarrow A)$ and $\neg A \wedge B$
    (viii) $A \downarrow (B \downarrow B)$ and $\neg A \wedge B$

4. Simplify each of the following logical forms:
    (i) $A \wedge (\neg A \rightarrow A)$
    (ii) $(A \rightarrow B) \rightarrow ((A \rightarrow \neg B) \rightarrow \neg A)$
    (iii) $(A \rightarrow (B \vee \neg C)) \wedge \neg A \wedge B$

5. Construct a logical form for the functions expressed in each of the following truth tables and implement the function as a circuit.

(i)

A	B	R
F	F	T
F	T	T
T	F	T
T	T	T

(ii)

A	B	C	R
F	F	F	F
F	F	T	F
F	T	F	F
F	T	T	F
T	F	F	T
T	F	T	T
T	T	F	T
T	T	T	T

(iii)

A	B	C	R
F	F	F	F
F	F	T	F
F	T	F	T
F	T	T	T
T	F	F	F
T	F	T	F
T	T	F	T
T	T	T	T

6. Draw up a truth table to represent the function implemented by the following circuit:

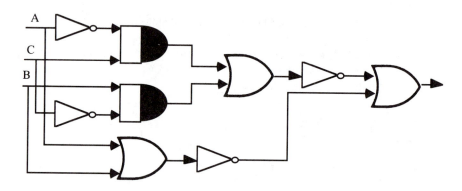

7. Are the following arguments valid?
   (i) If m is negative then q is negative. If p is positive then q is negative. Therefore if m is negative or p is positive then q is negative.
   (ii) If m is negative then q is negative. If p is positive then q is negative. Therefore if m is negative and p is positive then q is negative.
   (iii) If Murphy copied the examination then the invigilator was negligent, or the lecturer was intimidated. If the lecturer was not intimidated, then the invigilator was not negligent. The lecturer was intimidated. Therefore Murphy copied the examination.

CHAPTER 2

Semantic Tableaux

Chapter Aims

(1) To show why truth tables are inadequate in practice.
(2) To study the construction and use of semantic tableaux.
(3) To understand why semantic tableaux rules are reasonable.

At the end of this chapter you should
(a) know the rules for constructing semantic tableaux in propositional logic.
(b) understand the reasons for the rules.
(c) be able to construct semantic tableaux.
(d) be able to resolve arguments through the use of semantic tableaux.

2.1 Exponential Growth

In the last chapter we concentrated on truth tables as an intuitively easy method of getting to know some of the basics of logic. We found that they could be usefully employed in designing electronic circuits using basic components, and in evaluating the consistency of sets of sentences and the validity of arguments. The validity of arguments is a central theme in logic, and in this chapter we concentrate on this problem and study an alternative method of dealing with the issue.

The problem with truth tables is that they can get very large very quickly, and I mean VERY large. You will have noticed that a table involving two propositional variables, say A and B, has four rows, and that a table involving three propositional variables has eight rows. If you attempted some of the exercises at the end of the last chapter you will have seen that when four variables are involved the truth table has sixteen rows. So it seems as if the number of rows of a truth table doubles every time a new propositional variable is added. And that is exactly what happens. Therefore, a truth table with just ten variables would have 1024 rows! In general, a truth table with n propositional variables has 2^n rows.

When we keep doubling a number the answer gets awfully big awfully fast. For example, if you took a thin sheet of paper and doubled it 64 times, the resulting thickness would take you billions of miles out into space!! We have what is called an exponential explosion. Whenever a function grows in size in accordance with a positive power of a number greater than 1, it is said to grow exponentially.

Another problem with the truth tables we have used in assessing the validity of arguments is that we have looked at all possible values of the propositional variables involved, whether or not those values are relevant to or possible in the particular circumstances of the argument. With a little thought we could reduce the size of the tables in some circumstances. However, rather than attempting to tailor the truth tables to the requirements of argument validation, we will turn to a different and more direct method.

2.2 Semantic Tableaux

The use of semantic tableaux is based on the important strategy which we identified in section 1.5.2, namely, negating the conclusion of an argument and checking if the result is inconsistent with the premises. The idea is to see whether it is possible for a supposed conclusion to be false when all of a set of premise statements are true. If this is not possible, i.e. if the conclusion must be true when the premises are true, we say that the conclusion is *semantically entailed* by the premises.

What is a semantic tableau?

Essentially it is a sequence of propositional forms constructed according to certain rules, and usually laid out in the form of a tree. Let us begin by taking a look at those rules.

Rule (1): A∧B

If a tableau contains A∧B it can be extended to form a new tableau by adding both A and B to the branch containing A∧B. This can be expressed compactly as follows:

$$A \wedge B$$
$$A$$
$$B$$

Rule (2): A∨B

If a tableau contains A∨B it is extended to form a new tableau by adding two new branches, one containing A and the other containing B, thus:

A∨B

A   B

From now on we shall simply state the rule in diagrammatic form, because that shows most clearly how a tableau is extended.

Rule (3): A→B

$$A→B$$
$$\diagup \quad \diagdown$$
$$¬A \qquad B$$

Rule (4): A↔B

$$A↔B$$
$$\diagup \quad \diagdown$$
$$A∧B \qquad ¬A∧¬B$$

Rule (5): ¬ ¬A

$$¬ ¬A$$
$$A$$

Rule (6): ¬(A∧B)

$$¬(A∧B)$$
$$\diagup \quad \diagdown$$
$$¬A \qquad ¬B$$

Rule (7): ¬(A∨B)

$$¬(A∨B)$$
$$¬A$$
$$¬B$$

Rule (8): ¬(A→B)

$$¬(A→B)$$
$$A$$
$$¬B$$

Rule (9): ¬(A ↔ B)

$$¬(A↔B)$$
$$\diagup \quad \diagdown$$
$$A∧¬B \qquad ¬A∧B$$

Rule (10):

Finally, and most importantly, whenever a logical form A and its negation ¬A appear in a branch of a tableau, an inconsistency is indicated in that branch and it is said to be 'closed', i.e. it is not further extended. This is because A and ¬A cannot both be true at the same time.

If all the branches of a semantic tableau are closed then the logical expressions from which the tableau was 'grown' are mutually inconsistent, i.e. they cannot all be true simultaneously.

Before commenting further on the reasons for the rules for semantic tableaux, let us take a look at an example of a semantic tableau in action.

Example 2.1

Are the following logical expressions mutually consistent?
¬(A→B) and ¬A∨B

Our semantic tableau is

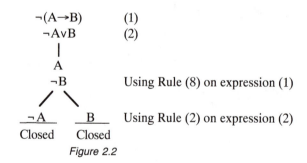

¬(A→B)	(1)	
¬A∨B	(2)	
¬A B	Using Rule (2) on expression (2)	
A A		
¬B ¬B	Using Rule (8) on expression (1)	
Closed Closed		

Figure 2.1

We see that both branches of the tableau in Figure 2.1 are closed: the left branch as it contains ¬A and A, the right one as it contains B and ¬B. We conclude, that the original expressions are mutually inconsistent.

The tableau in Figure 2.1 is not the only one we could have used to prove the incompatibility of the given expressions. The following one would also do.

¬(A→B)	(1)
¬A∨B	(2)
A	
¬B	Using Rule (8) on expression (1)
¬A B	Using Rule (2) on expression (2)
Closed Closed	

Figure 2.2

This is a slightly better tableau. Why?

Because we expand ¬(A→B) into A and ¬B only once, instead of twice as in the first tableau. Why is this? Because we chose to expand the 'branching' expression ¬A∨B after the 'non-branching' expression ¬(A→B). In general it is better to leave the expansion of expressions giving rise to two branches as late as possible in the development of the tableau.

So, we have the following heuristic (rule of thumb):

Heuristic for applying rules in Semantic Tableaux

Apply non-branching rules before branching rules.

Let us consider another example.

Example 2.2

Are the following logical forms mutually consistent?
$\neg A \vee B$, $\neg(B \wedge \neg C)$, $C \rightarrow D$ and $\neg(\neg A \vee D)$

We construct the following sequence of semantic tableaux.
First the formulae are written under one another.

(1)	$\neg A \vee B$
(2)	$\neg(B \wedge \neg C)$
(3)	$C \rightarrow D$
(4)	$\neg(\neg A \vee D)$

Figure 2.3

Develop (4) using Rule (7) to get

(1)	$\neg A \vee B$
(2)	$\neg(B \wedge \neg C)$
(3)	$C \rightarrow D$
(4)	$\neg(\neg A \vee D)$
	|
(5)	$\neg \neg A$
(6)	$\neg D$

Figure 2.4

Develop (5) using Rule (5) to get

(1)	$\neg A \vee B$
(2)	$\neg(B \wedge \neg C)$
(3)	$C \rightarrow D$
(4)	$\neg(\neg A \vee D)$
	|
(5)	$\neg \neg A$
(6)	$\neg D$
	|
(7)	A

Figure 2.5

Unfortunately, we now have only branching options, so we are forced to apply a branching rule to extend our tableau. We choose to expand (1).

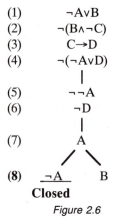

(1)	¬A∨B
(2)	¬(B∧¬C)
(3)	C→D
(4)	¬(¬A∨D)
(5)	¬¬A
(6)	¬D
(7)	A

(8)   ¬A   B
Closed

Figure 2.6

Luckily the left branch is closed immediately because the route it is on contains A and ¬A. Therefore we do not have to worry about it anymore. Let us now expand (2).

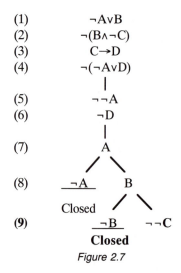

(1)	¬A∨B
(2)	¬(B∧¬C)
(3)	C→D
(4)	¬(¬A∨D)
(5)	¬¬A
(6)	¬D
(7)	A

(8)   ¬A   B
Closed

(9)   ¬B   ¬¬C
Closed

Figure 2.7

Again the left branch closes.

Extend the right branch by adding C to get the tableau shown over.

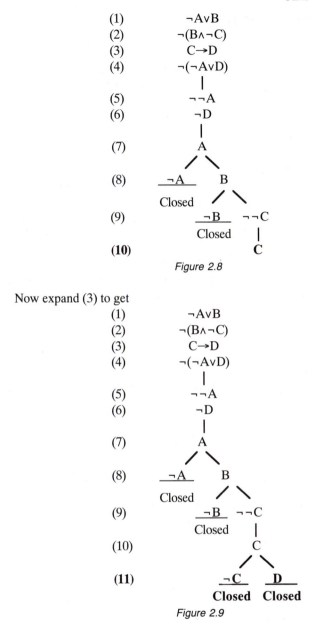

(1)	¬A∨B
(2)	¬(B∧¬C)
(3)	C→D
(4)	¬(¬A∨D)
(5)	¬¬A
(6)	¬D
(7)	A
(8)	¬A B
	Closed
(9)	¬B ¬¬C
	Closed
(10)	C

Figure 2.8

Now expand (3) to get

(1)	¬A∨B
(2)	¬(B∧¬C)
(3)	C→D
(4)	¬(¬A∨D)
(5)	¬¬A
(6)	¬D
(7)	A
(8)	¬A B
	Closed
(9)	¬B ¬¬C
	Closed
(10)	C
(11)	¬C D
	Closed Closed

Figure 2.9

Careful inspection of Figure 2.9 reveals that both remaining branches can be closed. We have now fully developed our semantic tableau and all branches are closed.

Therefore, we conclude that the original expressions were mutually incompatible.

2.3 Rules of Right Reason

What justification have we for using these semantic tableau rules? Well, we could just treat them as the rules of an interesting game, with no compulsion to interpret them other than as having a role in the game. In a purely formal sense this is what they are. They can be thought of as the rules of a purely deductive system (or proof system) with no attempt to interpret them in any other context. They can be viewed purely *syntactically*.

However, a more fruitful view is provided by thinking of the rules in *semantic* terms. We view them as providing us with the means of constructing models of the statements symbolised by the logical expressions. In particular, we attempt to show that there is no model (or interpretation) in which the premises of an argument are all true, while at the same time the conclusion is false. Our understanding of semantic tableaux will, therefore, be in terms of *model theory* rather than *proof theory*. We are not *merely* interested in playing the formal game of logic. We want to capture at least some aspects of human reasoning in contexts ranging from the everyday to the scientific. Consequently our rules should be reasonable and realistic. Let us examine them one by one.

Rule (1)

$$A{\land}B$$
$$A$$
$$B$$

Essentially, this rule reflects the fact that if A∧B is true then both A and B are true. So, in a branch of a tableau tree all these expressions can be true together.

Rule (2)

In this case, if A∨B is true then either A is true or B is true. So one or other branch will reflect a possible, consistent, state of affairs.

Rule (3)

We know from Chapter 1 that A→B is equivalent to ¬A∨B. Consequently the reasoning that we used to justify the ∨ branching applies here also.

Rule (4)

A↔B is equivalent to (A∧B) ∨ (¬A∧¬B). (Check this out using a truth table.) So again we have a disjunction and therefore a branching of the tree.

Rule (5)

$$\neg\,\neg A$$
$$A$$

This rule is justified by virtue of the fact that $\neg\neg A \equiv A$.

Rule (6)

$$\neg(A∧B)$$

$$\neg A \qquad \neg B$$

By one of De Morgan's laws $\neg(A∧B) \equiv \neg A∨\neg B$, thus branching again.

Rule (7)

$$\neg(A∨B)$$
$$\neg A$$
$$\neg B$$

By another of De Morgan's laws $\neg(A∨B) \equiv \neg A∧\neg B$. So both $\neg A$ and $\neg B$ will be true if $\neg(A∨B)$ is true, and so we add both to the existing branch.

Rule (8)

$$\neg(A→B)$$
$$A$$
$$\neg B$$

Because $\neg(A→B) \equiv \neg(\neg A∨B) \equiv \neg\neg A∧\neg B \equiv A∧\neg B$.

Rule (9)

$$\neg(A↔B)$$

$$A∧\neg B \qquad \neg A∧B$$

Because

$\neg(A↔B)$	$\equiv \neg((A∧B) ∨ (\neg A∧\neg B))$	
	$\equiv \neg(A∧B) ∧ \neg(\neg A∧\neg B)$	By De Morgan's law
	$\equiv (\neg A∨\neg B) ∧ (\neg\neg A∨\neg\neg B)$	By De Morgan's law
	$\equiv (\neg A∨\neg B) ∧ (A∨B)$	By double negation
	$\equiv (\neg A∧A) ∨ (\neg A∧B) ∨ (\neg B∧A) ∨ (\neg B∧B)$	By distributivity
	$\equiv 0 ∨ (\neg A∧B) ∨ (\neg B∧A) ∨ 0$	
	$\equiv (\neg A∧B) ∨ (\neg B∧A)$	
	$\equiv (A∧\neg B) ∨ (\neg A∧B)$	

Essentially the tableau method is a direct attempt to expose inconsistencies in a set of logical formulae by uncovering conflicting pairs of expressions, A and ¬A. If all branches of a tableau are closed by virtue of having such inconsistent pairs then the original formulae at the root of the tableau are shown to be mutually inconsistent. If, at the end of tableau development, even one branch remains unclosed, that indicates a possible state of affairs whereby the original formulae can all be true together, and are therefore mutually consistent.

From an unclosed branch it is easy, by inspection, to assign truth values through which the formulae can all be made true. In other words, it is easy to construct a model. Consider, for example, the following tableau:

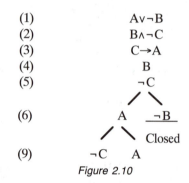

Figure 2.10

We obtain the model, v, as follows: assign the value T to each *atomic proposition* (i.e. proposition consisting of a propositional variable only or its negation, e.g. A or ¬A) in an unclosed branch. So, we get the model v(B) = T, v(¬C) = T, i.e. v(C) = F, and v(A) = T. It is easy to check that under these truth assignments, A∨¬B, B∧¬C and C→A are all true.

Exercise

2.1 Determine, using a tableau in each case, whether the following sets of expressions are mutually consistent:

(i)   A∧B, ¬A∧B

(ii)   A∧B, ¬A∨B

(iii)   A→B, A∨B, ¬B

(iv)   A→B, B→A

(v)   A→B, B→C, C→D, A→D

(vi)   A→B, B→C, C→D, A∧¬D

(vii) (A∧B) → C, ¬A→D, B∧¬C∧¬D

(viii) A∨B, A ∨ (B∧C), A→¬C

(ix) A→B, (A∧B) → C, B→¬A

(x)   ¬A∨B, B∧¬C, C→D, E∨¬D, A∧¬E

2.4 Problem-solving with Semantic Tableaux

Let us reconsider a problem we dealt with in Chapter 1 and see how we can use semantic tableaux to solve it.

Example 2.3

If the violinist plays the concerto, then crowds will come if the prices are not too high. If the violinist plays the concerto, the prices will not be too high. Therefore, if the violinist plays the concerto, crowds will come.

Is this argument valid? In other words, does the conclusion (the third statement) follow logically from the premises (the first two statements)? Again, in order to determine whether the argument is valid we use the strategy of seeing if the negation of the conclusion is inconsistent with the premises. As before we adopt the following notation:

Let   P stand for 'the violinist plays the concerto'
        C stand for 'crowds will come'
        H stand for 'prices are too high'

The argument is $P \rightarrow (\neg H \rightarrow C)$
                    $P \rightarrow \neg H$
                    $\therefore\ P \rightarrow C$

We negate $P \rightarrow C$ to get $\neg(P \rightarrow C)$ and set up our tableau as follows:

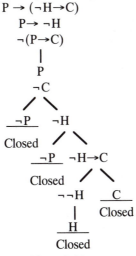

Figure 2.11

We have presented the complete tableau in one piece, but it should be fairly easy to follow at this stage. The first two closings occur because of the presence of P and $\neg P$ in the corresponding branches, the next closing occurs because of $\neg C$ and C, and the final one because of $\neg H$ and H.

The fact that the tableau is completely closed reveals that the root statements are mutually inconsistent. Since one of those was the negation of the conclusion of the argument, we deduce that, if the premises are true, then the negation of the conclusion cannot be true. Therefore the conclusion *is* true. Therefore the argument is valid.

Let us consider another example.

Example 2.4

John or Joyce or both will go to the party. If Joyce goes to the party then Clare will go unless Stephen goes. Stephen will go if John does not go. Therefore Clare will go to the party.

Is the argument valid?

Let   J stand for 'John will go to the party'

Y stand for 'Joyce will go to the party'

C stand for 'Clare will go to the party'

S stand for 'Stephen will go to the party'

We symbolise as follows:

$J \lor Y$ for 'John or Joyce (or both) will go to the party'

$Y \to (\neg S \to C)$ for 'If Joyce goes to the party then Clare will go unless Stephen goes'

$\neg J \to S$ for 'Stephen will go to the party if John does not go'

Expressing the argument formally we have:

$$J \lor Y$$
$$Y \to (\neg S \to C)$$
$$\neg J \to S$$
$$\therefore \quad C$$

To try to solve our problem we negate the conclusion, getting $\neg C$, and then see if $J \lor Y$, $Y \to (\neg S \to C)$, $\neg J \to S$ and $\neg C$ are mutually inconsistent.

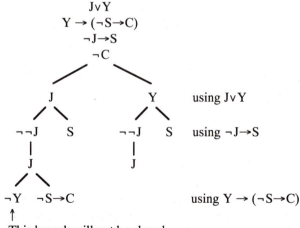

This branch will not be closed.

Figure 2.12

Although we have not completed the tableau we see that at least one branch is not going to be closed, and so we conclude that the originating expressions are not mutually inconsistent. Hence the conclusion 'Clare will go to the party' does not follow from the premises. In fact, we can see that model for the premises and the negation of the conclusion is provided by v(C) = F, v(J) = T, v(Y) = F and v(S) = F or T. It is easy to check that J∨Y, Y → (¬S→C), ¬J→S and ¬C are all true under this truth valuation.

2.4.1 Important Note

It is important to realise that the tableau method is essentially a search for invalidity. Thus, it is necessary to negate the conclusion of an argument and seek to close the tree. It would not do to leave the conclusion un-negated and see if every branch of the ensuing tableau remained open. For example, consider (A→A) ∨ (B∧¬B), which is clearly a tautology since the first term is always true. If we construct a tableau without negating the formula we get

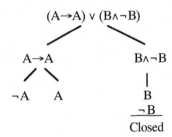

Figure 2.13

Not every branch remains open. But if we negate the formula we get

$$¬((A→A) ∨ (B∧¬B))$$
$$¬(A→A)$$
$$¬(B∧¬B)$$
$$A$$
$$\underline{¬A}$$
Closed

Figure 2.14

thereby indicating that the formula cannot be false.

Similarly, and trivially, the formula A would be classified as a tautology, since of course the tree with just A as a node would have all its branches open.

Exercise

2.2 In the above argument, would the conclusion follow if the conditions were changed in either of the following ways:

(a) Stephen goes to the party if John goes; otherwise conditions remain the same?

(b) John *and* Joyce go to the party; otherwise conditions remain the same? What changes to the conditions could you make to render the argument valid?

2.5 Summary

- In this chapter we have studied semantic tableaux. These provide a very direct mechanical method of determining the mutual consistency of statements and the validity of arguments.
- A tableau is a form of inverted tree structure. It is constructed by starting with the expressions whose consistency is to be evaluated and then using one of a number of rules at each step to extend an existing branch or to fork into two branches. A branch is closed if it contains a logical form and the negation of that form. If all branches are closed, the originating expressions are adjudged to be mutually inconsistent.
- The rules used in constructing semantic tableaux are based on various equivalences between logical formulae. They essentially facilitate reduction to simpler and simpler forms.
- A good rule of thumb in developing semantic tableaux is to apply non-branching rules before branching rules.

In this chapter we have

- briefly reviewed why truth tables are inadequate in practice.
- developed rules for checking the validity of arguments by means of semantic tableaux.
- explained why semantic tableaux rules are reasonable.
- studied the construction and use of semantic tableaux.
- applied semantic tableaux to the resolving of problems.

Semantic tableaux offer a semantic approach to questions of validity. In the next chapter we study a more syntactically based approach.

Miscellaneous Exercises

1. Determine the status (consistent or inconsistent) of each of the following sets of logical forms:
   (i) A∧B, ¬A, B
   (ii) A∧B, ¬A, ¬B
   (iii) A∨B, ¬A, B
   (iv) A∨B, ¬A, ¬B
   (v) A→B, A, ¬B
   (vi) A→B, C→B, (A∧C) → B
   (vii) A→B, C→B, (A∨C) → B
   (viii) A↔B, B↔C, ¬C, ¬A
   (ix) (A∨B) → B, A∨C → B, A, B
   (x) A→B, ¬C→¬B, C→¬D, A∧D

2. Are the following arguments valid?
   (i) If Paul lives in Dublin, he lives in Ireland. Paul lives in Dublin. Therefore Paul lives in Ireland.
   (ii) If Paul lives in Dublin, he lives in Ireland. Paul lives in Ireland. Therefore Paul lives in Dublin.
   (iii) If Paul lives in Dublin, he lives in Ireland. Paul lives in Dublin. Therefore Paul lives in Europe.
   (iv) If Paul lives in Dublin, he will be happy. If he is happy and likes his work, he will get on well at his job unless he falls in love. If he falls in love, he likes his work even more. Therefore, if he lives in Dublin, he will get on well at his job.
   (v) If Spain reached the World Cup finals, then either Ireland slipped up or Denmark played very well. Ireland did not slip up unless Spain reached the World Cup finals. Denmark did not play very well. Therefore, Spain reached the World Cup finals if and only if Ireland slipped up.
   (vi) Jo Ann will get her degree only if she enrols as a music student and attends a satisfactory number of lectures. She will not get a degree unless she passes all her examinations. If she attends a satisfactory number of lectures, she will pass all her examinations. She has enrolled. Therefore she will get a degree.
   (vii) Barbara and Jo Ann will both go to the party. If Jo Ann goes to the party then Clare will go unless Stephen does not go. Stephen will go if Jo Ann goes. Jo Ann will go if Clare goes. Therefore Clare will go to the party.

CHAPTER 3

Natural Deduction

Chapter Aims

(1) To become more fully acquainted with formal proofs.
(2) To learn and understand rules of natural deduction.
(3) To apply natural deduction methods to theorem proving.
(4) To learn and understand elements of the sequent calculus.

At the end of this chapter you should
(a) know the rules of a Gentzen system of natural deduction.
(b) know the rules of the sequent calculus.
(c) understand the reasoning behind all the rules.
(d) be able to apply the rules in proving theorems.

3.1 Introduction

So far in our treatment of logic we have emphasised the themes of consistency (understood as the mutual truth of a number of propositions) and the validity of arguments. We have based our development on the semantic notions of True and False. We turn now to a more formal or syntactic treatment and to a more explicit consideration of proof and deduction. Essentially we will be concerned with proving logical forms, or deriving logical forms from given hypothesised logical forms, using formal rules of deduction. As mentioned in the last chapter, we could view semantic tableaux in this manner (i.e. purely formally), but it is more helpful to consider them from a semantic point of view as trying to establish whether a set of formulae can all be true together.

The rules of deduction will be like the rules of a game, such as chess. They permit or license certain logical moves. They must be adhered to in order to play the formal game of logic. Whether they bear any relation to the real world or are somehow 'true' is not of immediate concern! But, of course, unlike the rules of chess, they are ultimately intended to capture mechanisms of correct reasoning in real life and to deliver true conclusions from true premises. So, formal though they be, we will sketch lines of justification for them in terms of their common-sense plausibility. Again, we remind ourselves that when we are concerned with form we are involved in syntactic considerations, whereas when we are concerned with true and false, or relationships with the real world, or meaning, we are involved in semantics.

3.1.1 Falsum

Before we introduce the formal rules of deduction, let us declare our intention to make use of an important logical constant. This constant has the value false. The symbol we shall use is $\bot$. It is often known by the Latin name *falsum*. Essentially, it is the same as **0** which we used in the first two chapters, but $\bot$ is the more traditional symbol for falsehood. We can think of $\bot$ as denoting an 'absurdity', such as A *and not* A. We want to make use of $\bot$ to express the operation of negating. Hence, we will define $\neg$A as A$\rightarrow\bot$.

If you look back at the truth table for $\rightarrow$ in Chapter 1 you will see that A$\rightarrow\bot$ is true when A is false, and false when A is true (remember that $\bot$ is always false), which is exactly what we want for $\neg$A. From now on we will use $\neg$A and A$\rightarrow\bot$ interchangeably as the occasion suits.

3.2 Rules of Natural Deduction

The rules of derivation we are going to use are intended to represent in a formal fashion the intuitive or 'natural' methods of reasoning used by humans – hence the name 'natural deduction'. They were developed by Gerhard Gentzen in the 1930s.

The rules are as follows (A, B, C stand for any logical forms):

Rule (1): $\wedge$I ($\wedge$–introduction)

$$\frac{A \qquad B}{A\wedge B}$$

What exactly does the rule say? It says that if (in a derivation) we have deduced or hypothesised both A and B, then we can further deduce A$\wedge$B. This seems perfectly reasonable, I think you will agree. If we know that 'The cat sat on the mat' and that 'The cat imbibed the whiskey', then it is not too difficult to conclude that 'The cat sat on the mat *and* imbibed the whiskey'.

In general, in the presentation of the rules, the formulae that appear above the line are the ones that have already been arrived at, and the formulae below the line are those that can be derived.

Rule (2): $\wedge$E ($\wedge$–elimination)

$$\frac{A\wedge B}{A}$$

Rule (3): $\wedge$E ($\wedge$–elimination)

$$\frac{A\wedge B}{B}$$

For obvious reasons Rules (2) and (3) are both called ∧–elimination rules, or ∧E for short. They assert that if A∧B has been derived, then we can further deduce A (or B). Again the reasoning is clear. If 'The cat sat on the mat and drank the brandy', then we can conclude, for example, that 'The cat drank the brandy'.

Rule (4): ∨I (∨–introduction)

$$\frac{A}{A \vee B}$$

Rule (5): ∨I (∨–introduction)

$$\frac{B}{A \vee B}$$

On reflection Rules (4) and (5) seem a little strange. For example, from the statement 'The dog barked', they license conclusions such as 'The dog barked or the cat got drunk', 'The dog barked or the cat drank more whiskey', 'The dog barked or the man shouted', 'The dog barked or the cat did not get drunk', 'The dog barked or the cow jumped over the Christmas tree', etc. In other words, from A we can deduce A *or* B, where B is any statement whatsoever. It is important to remember that we are using the inclusive sense of *or*, and that the conclusions are perfectly valid in a *logical sense*, even if the relevance, which is a hallmark of ordinary discourse, is suspect.

Rule (6): ∨E (∨–elimination)

$$
\begin{array}{ccc}
\not{A} & & \not{B} \\
\cdot & & \cdot \\
\cdot & & \cdot \\
A \vee B \quad C & & C \\
\hline
& C &
\end{array}
$$

What Rule (6) states is that if C is derived from A, and C is derived from B, then C may be derived from A∨B. The reason that A and B are crossed out is that they are no longer needed – A∨B takes their place. If A and B are assumptions, they are said to be discharged. Essentially this rule captures the notion of reasoning by cases: if something follows when case 1 holds, and the same thing follows when case 2 holds, then it follows when either case 1 or 2 holds.

Rule (7): →I (→–introduction)

$$
\begin{array}{c}
\not{A} \\
\cdot \\
\cdot \\
\underline{C} \\
A \rightarrow C
\end{array}
$$

The interpretation of Rule (7) is that if C can be derived from the assumption A, then we can drop, or discharge, the assumption, and conclude that A→C. This seems reasonable. Suppose, for example, we conclude that 'The cat drank the cream' from the assumption that 'The saucer is empty'. Then it is reasonable to make the assertion 'If the saucer is empty, the cat drank the cream'. And we do not need to hold on to the assumption 'The saucer is empty', since it is contained in the assertion.

Rule (8): →E (→–elimination)

$$\frac{A \quad A{\rightarrow}C}{C}$$

In other words, if A holds, and A implies C, then C holds. This is the famous *modus ponens* rule of reasoning, and it scarcely requires any comment, since it is so obviously sound.

Rule (9): ⊥

$$\frac{\bot}{C}$$

Simply called ⊥, Rule (9) states that, from *falsum*, any conclusion C can be drawn, i.e. from an absurdity or contradiction, anything follows. In a sense, this is an inverse way of saying that you can't have a contradiction, since clearly not everything is the case. If a contradiction is accepted 'all hell breaks loose' – anything can be the case.

Rule (10): RAA (Reductio Ad Absurdum)

Rule (10) formalises the famous *proof by contradiction* method of arguing. If assuming that A is not the case leads to a contradiction, then we can conclude that A *is* the case. We use a form of expression related to this in ordinary language to emphasise a point, e.g. 'If she doesn't pass her logic examination, I'm a monkey's uncle'.

We can use Rule (7) along with the definition of ¬A as A→⊥ to get a very useful complementary form of this rule:

It is established as follows:

$$
\begin{array}{ll}
A & \text{Assumption} \\
\cdot & \\
\cdot & \\
\cdot & \\
\underline{\perp} & \text{Deduction from assumption} \\
A \rightarrow \perp & \text{By } \rightarrow I \\
\text{i.e.} \quad \neg A &
\end{array}
$$

We will refer to this form of the rule as RAA also.
Finally we have the obvious rule

Rule (11): Id (identity)

$$\frac{A}{A}$$

Any formula can be deduced from itself.

Historical Notes

The method of natural deduction was introduced by the German/Polish mathematician Gerhard Gentzen in a paper *Investigations into Logical Deduction* published in 1935. At the beginning of the paper Gentzen set down clearly his justification for developing the method:

My starting point was this: The formalization of logical deduction, especially as it has been developed by Frege, Russell, and Hilbert, is rather far removed from the forms of deduction used in practice in mathematical proofs. Considerable formal advantages are achieved in return.

In contrast, I intend to set up a formal system which comes as close as possible to actual reasoning.

Gerhard Gentzen was born in Pomerania, which was then part of Germany but is now in Poland, on 24th November, 1909. He was deeply interested in Mathematics from an early age and when he went to University in Greifswald, Pomerania, was described as a 'particularly gifted student'. He gained a doctorate in Mathematics from the University of Göttingen at the age of twenty-three.

During the second world war Gentzen was conscripted into the German army, but within a short time became seriously ill and was freed from military duty after an extended period in hospital. When he had sufficiently recovered he returned to the University at Göttingen. In 1943 he became director of the Mathematical Institute of the German University at Prague. In 1945 the staff of the University were all taken into custody, and, tragically, Gentzen died of malnutrition in prison some months later.

3.2.1 *Natural* Deductions

Now that we have our rules of reasoning let us see how they are deployed in constructing proofs or making inferences.

When a conclusion C is derived from a set of assumptions $\{A_1, A_2, ..., A_n\}$ we write $\{A_1, A_2, ..., A_n\} \vdash C$.

If the set of assumptions is empty, i.e. there are no assumptions, we write $\vdash C$.

$\vdash$ is called the 'turnstile'.

Theorem 3.1

$$\{A \wedge B\} \vdash B \wedge A$$

Proof   The general strategy is to start with one or more assumptions and use the rules to make progress from there. In this case the obvious assumption is $A \wedge B$

$\dfrac{A \wedge B}{B}$	$\dfrac{A \wedge B}{A}$	Assumption
		by $\wedge E$
$B \wedge A$	by $\wedge I$	

(End)

Notice that we can use an assumption as often as we like or need to.

Theorem 3.2

$$\vdash A \wedge B \rightarrow B \wedge A$$

Proof   The proof follows the same lines as theorem 3.1, with one extra step to discharge the assumption.

$\dfrac{A \wedge B}{B}$	$\dfrac{A \wedge B}{A}$	Assumption
		by $\wedge E$
$\dfrac{B \wedge A}{}$		by $\wedge I$
$A \wedge B \rightarrow B \wedge A$		by $\rightarrow I$

(End)

Notice that discharging the assumption involves discharging all occurances of it as they are the same thing.

Exercises

3.1 Prove $\vdash A \rightarrow (B \rightarrow (A \wedge B))$.

3.2 Prove $A \vee B \vdash B \vee A$.

3.3 Prove $\vdash (A \vee B) \rightarrow (B \vee A)$.

Theorem 3.3

$$\{B\} \vdash A \rightarrow B$$

Proof		
	A̸	Assumption
	B	Assumption
	B	Id
	A→B	→I

(End)

Here we see an important technique at work.

Heuristic for natural deduction of the form A→B

If asked to deduce a formula of the form A→B, then it is very often useful to make A an assumption, with the idea of discharging it later using the →I rule.

The result of theorem 3.3 is also important. It says that if a result, say B, has been established, then a further result is A→B, where A is *any* logical form.

Theorem 3.4

$$\vdash B \rightarrow (A \rightarrow B)$$

Proof   The proof follows exactly the same lines as theorem 3.3, with just one more step, to discharge the second assumption.

A̸	Assumption
B̸	Assumption
B	Id
A→B	→I, from 1st line
B → (A→B)	→I, from 2nd line

(End)

Exercises

3.4 Prove $\{(A\rightarrow B), (B \wedge C)\} \vdash A \rightarrow C$.

3.5 Prove $\vdash ((A \rightarrow B) \wedge (B \rightarrow C)) \rightarrow (A \rightarrow C)$.

3.6 Prove $\vdash (A \rightarrow (B \rightarrow C)) \rightarrow ((A \rightarrow B) \rightarrow (A \rightarrow C))$.

Theorem 3.5

$$\{A, \neg A\} \vdash \bot$$

Proof Remember that ¬A is equivalent to A→⊥. With this the proof is quite easy.

A	A→⊥	Assumptions
	⊥	→E

(End)

Theorem 3.5 will prove to be extremely useful in practice.

Theorem 3.6

$$\{\neg A\} \vdash (A \to B)$$

Proof We make the extra assumption A along with the given ¬A and employ theorem 3.5. The result drops out fairly easily.

¬A	A	Assumptions
⊥		Theorem 3.5
B		⊥
A→B		→I, using A on line 1

(End)

Exercises

3.7 Prove ⊢ ¬A → (A→⊥).

3.8 Prove ⊢ A → (¬A→B).

Theorem 3.7

$$\vdash (\neg B \to \neg A) \to (A \to B)$$

Proof The general idea is to use ¬B → ¬A and A as assumptions, try to derive B, and then discharge the assumptions to get the result. Let's see what happens.

A	¬B→ ¬A	Assumptions

We can't make much progress from here. It would be better if we had ¬B as an assumption. But, is this just a shot in the dark, fired because we can use modus ponens on ¬B and ¬B→¬A?

Well, maybe yes to begin with! But a little reflection indicates that it might be worth assuming ¬B for another reason. If we can derive ⊥ from the use of ¬B, then we can use the RAA rule to cancel ¬B and deduce B. So,

¬B	¬B→ ¬A	Assumptions
	¬A	→E

Now let us use our assumption A to combine with ¬A to get a contradiction.

$$\begin{array}{ll} & \overset{(1)}{\neg B} \qquad \overset{(3)}{\neg B \to \neg A} & \text{Assumptions} \\ & \overset{(2)}{\neg A \qquad A} & \to E \text{ and assumption} \\ & \underline{\quad \bot \quad} & \text{Theorem 3.5} \\ & \underline{\quad B \quad} & \text{RAA, assumption (1) } \neg B \\ & \underline{\quad A \to B \quad} & \to I, \text{ using assumption (2) A} \\ & (\neg B \to \neg A) \to (A \to B) & \to I, \text{ using assumption (3) } \neg B \to \neg A \\ & & \textit{(End)} \end{array}$$

The numbers indicate the order in which the assumptions are cancelled or discharged. Wherever useful we will employ this notation to clarify the proof.

Theorem 3.8

$$\vdash \ (B \to A) \to (\neg A \to \neg B)$$

Proof   This result is very similar to the last result and yields to the same method of attack.

$$\begin{array}{ll} & \overset{(1)}{B} \qquad \overset{(3)}{B \to A} & \text{Assumptions} \\ & \overset{(2)}{A \qquad \neg A} & \to E \text{ and assumption} \\ & \underline{\quad \bot \quad} & \text{Theorem 3.5} \\ & \underline{\quad \neg B \quad} & \text{RAA, assumption (1) B} \\ & \underline{\quad \neg A \to \neg B \quad} & \to I, \text{ using assumption (2) } \neg A \\ & (B \to A) \to (\neg A \to \neg B) & \to I, \text{ using assumption (3) } B \to A \\ & & \textit{(End)} \end{array}$$

Exercises

3.9   Prove $\vdash (A \to \bot) \to \neg A$.

3.10 Prove $\vdash (\neg A \to B) \to (\neg B \to A)$.

3.11 Prove $\vdash (A \to \neg B) \to (B \to \neg A)$.

Theorem 3.9

$$\vdash \ \neg\neg A \to A$$

Proof   Again we will base our strategy on *proof by contradiction*.

$$\begin{array}{ll} & \overset{(1)}{\neg A} \qquad \overset{(2)}{\neg\neg A} & \text{Assumptions} \\ & \underline{\quad \bot \quad} & \text{Theorem 3.5} \\ & \underline{\quad A \quad} & \text{RAA, from assumption (1) } \neg A \\ & \neg\neg A \to A & \to I \text{ using assumption (2) } \neg\neg A \\ & & \textit{(End)} \end{array}$$

Exercise

3.12   Prove ⊢ A→ ¬¬A.

Theorem 3.10

$$\{A \lor B, \neg B\} \vdash A$$

Proof   The presence of A∨B as an assumption suggests that we should first try to deduce A from A and also from B (with the aid of the assumption ¬B). Then, we can use the ∨E rule, discharging the assumptions A and B, leaving us with only the given assumptions, A∨B and ¬B. Clearly it is easy to deduce A from A – simply use Id. But how can we deduce A from B? Well, we cannot deduce A from B on its own. But we have the assumption ¬B to work with. Aha! If we use B and ¬B, then we can get a contradiction, from which we can deduce anything, even A!

		B	¬B	Assumptions
		A	⊥	Assumption and theorem 3.5
A∨B	A	A		Assumption, Id and ⊥
	A			∨E

(End)

Discharging A in introducing A∨B seems fine, but you might wonder how we can choose to discharge B. After all we had to use both B and ¬B to get A. So why discharge B instead of ¬B? Would it be logically wrong to discharge ¬B?

No, it would not. It would have been *irrelevant* rather than wrong. If we had used ¬B instead of B we would have got a different result. We would have proved {A∨ ¬B, B} ⊢ A (which, of course, is another valid theorem!)

So, it pays to keep an eye on the *required* result as we work through a deduction.

Exercises

3.13   Prove {A∨B, ¬A} ⊢ B.

3.14   Prove {A∨B, B∧ ¬A} ⊢ B.

Theorem 3.11

$$\vdash \neg A \lor B \to (A \to B)$$

Proof   The presence of ¬A∨B as an assumption suggests that it might be worth trying to deduce A→B from ¬A and from B separately. If we look back over our theorems so far we see that we have effectively shown that these two tasks can be accomplished – see theorems 3.6 and 3.3.

$$\frac{\cancel{\neg A} \qquad \cancel{B}}{\underbrace{\neg A \vee B \quad A \rightarrow B \quad A \rightarrow B}_{\displaystyle \frac{A \rightarrow B}{\neg A \vee B \rightarrow (A \rightarrow B)}}}$$

Assumptions

Assumption, and theorems 3.6 and 3.3

∨E, using ¬A∨B

→I, discharging ¬A∨B

(End)

Theorem 3.12

$$\vdash \ (A \rightarrow B) \rightarrow (\neg A \vee B)$$

Proof This is a bit more difficult. Our first thought might be to try to prove either ¬A or B from A→B. Because, if we had either ¬A or B then we would immediately have ¬A∨B by the ∨I rule. But, unfortunately neither ¬A nor B follows from (A→B). So it is the whole expression or none at all!

Well, maybe we could use A→B and something else to advance the proof. But what? The only expression that suggests itself is A. So let's try.

$$\frac{\frac{A \qquad A \rightarrow B}{B}}{\underbrace{\frac{\neg A \vee B}{(A \rightarrow B) \rightarrow (\neg A \vee B)}}}$$

Assumptions

→E

∨I

→I, using assumption A→B

Aha!

But, our joy is short lived. We have not really proved our theorem, because we still have the undischarged assumption A.

Let's think again. Maybe we should fall back on proof by contradiction. Maybe we should assume ¬(¬A∨B) and try to derive a contradiction with the use of A→B.

$$\neg(\neg A \vee B) \quad A \rightarrow B \qquad\qquad \text{Assumptions}$$

But there is no obvious way to proceed. We need ¬A∨B to 'cancel' ¬(¬A∨B) as it were. But this is what we want to prove.

We need to be a bit more subtle. Another assumption, perhaps. Try ¬A. Why? Because this will give us ¬A∨B and maybe we can make some progress.

So, here goes.

$$\frac{\neg A}{\underbrace{\neg A \vee B \qquad \neg(\neg A \vee B)}_{\perp}}$$

Assumption

∨I, Assumption

⊥

Where to now?

Well, we can cancel ¬A using RAA to get A. And then use the assumption A→B to get B. And use this to get ¬A∨B. Maybe we are on the right track!?

$$\begin{array}{ll}
\dfrac{\qquad}{\neg A} \; {}^{(1)} & \text{Assumption} \\[4pt]
\dfrac{\neg A \lor B \qquad \neg(\neg A \lor B)}{} & \text{vI, Assumption} \\[4pt]
\dfrac{\perp}{} \quad {}^{(2)} & \perp \\[4pt]
\dfrac{A \qquad A{\to}B}{} & \text{RAA (using } \neg A), \text{ assumption} \\[4pt]
\dfrac{B}{} & {\to}E \\[4pt]
\dfrac{\neg A \lor B}{} & \text{vI} \\[4pt]
(A{\to}B) \to (\neg A \lor B) & {\to}I, \text{ using } A \to B
\end{array}$$

But, frustration again! We have not been able to cancel the assumption ¬(¬AvB), so we have not proved the result we wanted. The problem was we had to use ⊥ to cancel ¬A to give us A, and then we couldn't derive ⊥ again to allow us to cancel ¬(¬AvB).

Is there any way out of our impasse?

Is it worth sticking with ¬(¬AvB) and RAA as a strategy? Is there any way of deriving A, maybe using ¬(¬AvB) directly, without resorting to assuming ¬A? Is it the case that ¬(¬AvB) ⊢ A? Let us break off our proof to see if we can establish this result.

Theorem 3.13

$$\neg(\neg A \lor B) \vdash A$$

Proof If we examine this carefully we will see an easy way to prove the result. Rather than trying to prove ¬(¬AvB) ⊢ A directly, we will use ¬A to get (¬AvB) by vI, then introduce ¬(¬AvB), and use the resulting contradiction to get A.

$$\begin{array}{ll}
\dfrac{\qquad}{\neg A} & \text{Assumption} \\[4pt]
\dfrac{\neg A \lor B \qquad \neg(\neg A \lor B)}{} & \text{vI, Assumption} \\[4pt]
\dfrac{\perp}{} & \text{Theorem} \\[4pt]
A & \text{RAA, using } \neg A
\end{array}$$

(End)

Now back to our attempt at proving theorem 3.12.

$$\begin{array}{ll}
\dfrac{\qquad}{\neg(\neg A \lor B)} \; {}^{(1)} & \text{Assumption} \\[4pt]
\dfrac{A \qquad A{\to}B}{} \quad {}^{(2)} & \text{Theorem, assumption} \\[4pt]
\dfrac{B}{} \qquad {}^{(1)} & {\to}E \\[4pt]
\dfrac{\neg A \lor B \qquad \neg(\neg A \lor B)}{} & \text{vI, assumption ((1) repeated)} \\[4pt]
\dfrac{\perp}{} & \perp \\[4pt]
\dfrac{\neg A \lor B}{} & \text{RAA, using assumption (1) } \neg(\neg A \lor B) \\[4pt]
(A{\to}B) \to (\neg A \lor B) & {\to}I, \text{ using assumption (2) } A{\to}B
\end{array}$$

(End)

At last, at last!! The proof turned out to be quite short in the end, but it was hard to find.

Exercise

3.15   Prove each of the following using the rules of natural deduction:

(i) $\vdash$ A→A

(ii)   {A∧B} $\vdash$ A∨B

(iii) $\vdash$ (A→B) → ((B→C) → ((C→D) → (A→D)))

(iv) $\vdash$ ⊥ → (¬A∧A)

(v) $\vdash$ (¬A∧A) → ⊥

(vi) $\vdash$ ¬(¬A∧A)

3.3 The Sequent Calculus

In addition to presenting natural deduction along the lines of the rules outlined above, Gentzen also presented it in the form of a so-called *sequent calculus*, and to this we now briefly turn. Although not part of Gentzen's motivation for developing the approach, the sequent calculus is seen to have an advantage in being easy to automate. It is also considered to have the advantages of offering 'natural' means of developing proofs (as with the rules above) and of being based on the commendable strategy of attempting to find a falsifying valuation for a set of propositions (as with semantic tableaux).

Definition   A *sequent* is defined to be a pair of proposition sequences, (L,R), i.e. L = <P_1, P_2, ..., P_m>, R = <Q_1, Q_2, ..., Q_n>, where P_i and Q_i are propositions. L and R are finite, possibly empty. L is called the *antecedent* of the sequent; R is called the *succedent*.

A sequent (L,R) is usually written L ⇒ R.

Within proof theory, sequents are purely formal constructions which are subject to the rules to be laid out below. Nevertheless, in order to make sense of them and see that they are reasonable, it is useful to consider them from a semantic (or meaning) point of view. Thus, L ⇒ R may be taken as symbolising that if all of the propositions in L are true under a truth valuation v (i.e an assignment of true or false) then at least one of the propositions in R is true under v. Equivalently, we may think of it as stating that at least one of the members of L is false or at least one element of R is true. For ease of reading, and without doing a disservice to the intended interpretation, we may read L ⇒ R as 'R follows from L'.

3.3.1 Sequent Schemata

For clarity in stating the rules for manipulating sequents we will use upper case Greek letters for sequences of propositions, and the usual upper case roman letters for individual formulae. The rules are written

$$\frac{S_1}{S_2}$$

the idea being that if formulae matching the schema S_1 are present in a derivation, they may be replaced by formulae matching the schema S_2. Essentially S_1 gives the premises of a deduction (step) and S_2 the conclusion. Each rule is such that the conclusion is true for a valuation if and only if all the premises are true under that valuation. Equivalently (and more importantly in practice) we may view a rule as stating that a valuation will falsify a conclusion if and only if it falsifies at least one of the premises.

Rule (1): R∧

$$\frac{\Gamma_1 \Rightarrow A, \Delta_1 \qquad\qquad \Gamma_2 \Rightarrow B, \Delta_2}{\Gamma_1, \Gamma_2 \Rightarrow A \wedge B, \Delta_1, \Delta_2}$$

Effectively this says that if the sequence A, Δ_1 follows from Γ_1, and if B, Δ_2 follows from Γ_2, then $A \wedge B, \Delta_1, \Delta_2$ follows from Γ_1, Γ_2. In terms of a valuation, v, we note that v falsifies $\Gamma_1, \Gamma_2 \Rightarrow A \wedge B, \Delta_1, \Delta_2$ if and only if it satisfies all the members of Γ_1 and Γ_2 and falsifies $A \wedge B$ and all the members of Δ_1 and Δ_2. To falsify $A \wedge B$ it must falsify one of A or B (or both) and so, if the other conditions mentioned hold, v will falsify $\Gamma_1 \Rightarrow A, \Delta_1$ or $\Gamma_2 \Rightarrow B, \Delta_2$ (or both).

Note the similarity to the first of our earlier list of rules of natural deduction – ∧I. For convenience we may refer to the rule as R∧, because of the way $A \wedge B$ appears on the right-hand side.

Rule (2): L∧

$$\frac{\Gamma, A \Rightarrow \Delta}{\Gamma, A \wedge B \Rightarrow \Delta}$$

Rule (3): L∧

$$\frac{\Gamma, B \Rightarrow \Delta}{\Gamma, A \wedge B \Rightarrow \Delta}$$

Rules (2) and (3) (which are very much the same) state that if Δ follows from Γ, A (or Γ, B), then Δ follows from Γ, $A \wedge B$. They remind us of ∧E above.

Rule (4): R∨

$$\frac{\Gamma \Rightarrow A, \Delta}{\Gamma \Rightarrow A \vee B, \Delta}$$

Rule (5): R∨

$$\frac{\Gamma \Rightarrow B, \Delta}{\Gamma \Rightarrow A \vee B, \Delta}$$

If A, Δ follows from Γ, or if B, Δ follows from Γ, then A$\lor$B, Δ follows from Γ. This is similar to $\lor$I above.

Rule (6): L$\lor$

$$\frac{\Gamma_1, A \Rightarrow \Delta_1 \qquad \Gamma_2, B \Rightarrow \Delta_2}{\Gamma_1, \Gamma_2, A \lor B \Rightarrow \Delta_1, \Delta_2}$$

If Δ_1 follows from Γ_1, A, and if Δ_2 follows from Γ_2, B, then Δ_1, Δ_2 follows from $\Gamma_1, \Gamma_2, A \lor B$. This is similar to $\lor$E above.

Rule (7): R$\rightarrow$

$$\frac{\Gamma, A \Rightarrow B, \Delta}{\Gamma \Rightarrow A \rightarrow B, \Delta}$$

which is similar to $\rightarrow$I above.

Rule (8): L$\rightarrow$

$$\frac{\Gamma_1 \Rightarrow A, \Delta_1 \qquad \Gamma_2, B \Rightarrow \Delta_2}{\Gamma_1, \Gamma_2, A \rightarrow B \Rightarrow \Delta_1, \Delta_2}$$

which is similar to $\rightarrow$E, and thus to modus ponens. The idea is that if A can be derived, then from A$\rightarrow$B, B can be derived and thence whatever can be derived from B. This is seen most simply if Γ_2 and Δ_1 are empty.

$$\frac{\Gamma_1 \Rightarrow A \qquad B \Rightarrow \Delta_2}{\Gamma_1, A \rightarrow B \Rightarrow \Delta_1, \Delta_2}$$

Rule (9): R$\neg$

$$\frac{\Gamma, A \Rightarrow \Delta}{\Gamma \Rightarrow \neg A, \Delta}$$

Rule (10): L$\neg$

$$\frac{\Gamma \Rightarrow A, \Delta}{\Gamma, \neg A \Rightarrow \Delta}$$

Rules (9) and (10) have no direct counterpart above. Note the change in sign as A is 'brought across' the sequent symbol.

These ten rules may be called introduction rules in that a logical connective is introduced below the line in each case. There are also some rules which are referred to as structural rules.

Rule (11): RT

$$\frac{\Gamma \Rightarrow \Delta}{\Gamma \Rightarrow A, \Delta}$$

Rule (12): LT

$$\frac{\Gamma \Rightarrow \Delta}{\Gamma, A \Rightarrow \Delta}$$

These are called thinning or weakening rules. They allow us to include an extra formula on either the right or left of the sequents below the line. You might ask if this is justified.

Well, think about RT. If at least one of the members of Γ is false above the line, clearly this still holds good below the line. On the other hand, if at least one of the members of Δ is true above the line, then at least one of the members of A and Δ is true below the line. You should convince yourself that LT is similarly justified.

Rule (13): RC

$$\frac{\Gamma \Rightarrow A, A, \Delta}{\Gamma \Rightarrow A, \Delta}$$

Rule (14): LC

$$\frac{\Gamma, A, A \Rightarrow \Delta}{\Gamma, A \Rightarrow \Delta}$$

These are called contraction rules for an obvious reason.

Rule (15): RR

$$\frac{\Gamma \Rightarrow A, B, \Delta}{\Gamma \Rightarrow B, A, \Delta}$$

Rule (16): LR

$$\frac{\Gamma, A, B \Rightarrow \Delta}{\Gamma, B, A \Rightarrow \Delta}$$

These are called reordering rules. We will often make use of these rules implicitly to place formulae in the order that suits us.

Rule (17): Cut

$$\frac{\Gamma_1 \Rightarrow A, \Delta_1 \quad \Gamma_2, A \Rightarrow \Delta_2}{\Gamma_1, \Gamma_2 \Rightarrow \Delta_1, \Delta_2}$$

Much of Gentzen's original paper is devoted to showing that this rule can be done without, i.e. that any theorem which can be proved by making use of the cut rule can also be proved without using it. The use of the rule resembles the use of an already-proved theorem to prove another theorem, rather than going back to first principles.

Finally we have the starting rule.

Rule (18): Id

$$A \Rightarrow A$$

for any formula A. Clearly this sequent cannot be falsified.

3.3.2 Proofs Using Sequents

To get a taste of the flavour of the sequent calculus let us work through just a few proofs.

Prove $\quad \Rightarrow A \to (B \to A)$

Proof

A ⇒ A	Id
A, B ⇒ A	LT
A ⇒ B→A	R→
⇒ A → (B→A)	R→

(End)

This is relatively straightforward.

The rules being used to advance the proof are named to the right of each line.

Prove   ⇒ ¬A → (A→B)

Proof

A ⇒ A	Id
¬A, A ⇒	L¬
¬A, A ⇒ B	RT
¬A ⇒ A→B	R→
⇒ ¬A → (A→B)	R→

(End)

Again, this is relatively straightforward.

Prove   ⇒ (¬A→ ¬B) → (B→A)

Proof

A ⇒ A	B ⇒ B	Id, Id
⇒ ¬A, A	¬B, B ⇒	L¬, R¬
¬A→¬B, B ⇒ A		L→
¬A→ ¬B ⇒ B→A		R→
⇒ (¬A→¬B) → (B→A)		R→

(End)

This is just a little more complicated, and perhaps it is worth enquiring if there is a strategy whereby proofs involving sequents can be constructed, rather than apparently 'by pulling them out of the air'. In fact there is! We said above that the sequent calculus makes use of the idea of proof by falsification. Let us see how we can use this to construct the above proof. In the process we will develop some more useful heuristics.

Heuristic for first step of a proof in sequent calculus

We start with the formula to be proved – at the bottom, as it were – and ask how it could be falsified.

So, given (¬A→¬B) → (B→A)

This is false if ¬A→¬B is true and B→A is false. We place ¬A→ ¬B to the left of the ⇒ sign and B→A to the right.

Heuristic for proofs in sequent calculus

In general, we place the formulae we require to be true to the left of $\Rightarrow$, and those required to be false to the right.

We now have

$$\neg A \rightarrow \neg B \Rightarrow B \rightarrow A$$
$$\Rightarrow (\neg A \rightarrow \neg B) \rightarrow (B \rightarrow A)$$

the last two lines of the above proof.

To make $B \rightarrow A$ false we require B to be true and A to be false. Hence we place B along with $\neg A \rightarrow \neg B$ to the left of $\Rightarrow$ and A to the right to get

$$\neg A \rightarrow \neg B, B \Rightarrow A$$
$$\neg A \rightarrow \neg B \Rightarrow B \rightarrow A$$
$$\Rightarrow (\neg A \rightarrow \neg B) \rightarrow (B \rightarrow A)$$

Our next requirement is to make $\neg A \rightarrow \neg B$ true. This can be done by making $\neg A$ false or $\neg B$ true. In order to effect this we split our development into two sequents

$$\Rightarrow \neg A \qquad \neg B \Rightarrow$$

Combining these with the development so far we have

$$\Rightarrow \neg A, A \qquad \neg B, B \Rightarrow$$
$$\neg A \rightarrow \neg B, B \Rightarrow A$$
$$\neg A \rightarrow \neg B \Rightarrow B \rightarrow A$$
$$\Rightarrow (\neg A \rightarrow \neg B) \rightarrow (B \rightarrow A)$$

Making $\neg A$ (or $\neg B$) false is equivalent to making A (or B) true and so we finish off with $A \Rightarrow A$ and $B \Rightarrow B$ which, inserted into our tree, gives the complete development:

$$A \Rightarrow A \qquad B \Rightarrow B$$
$$\Rightarrow \neg A, A \qquad \neg B, B \Rightarrow$$
$$\neg A \rightarrow \neg B, B \Rightarrow A$$
$$\neg A \rightarrow \neg B \Rightarrow B \rightarrow A$$
$$\Rightarrow (\neg A \rightarrow \neg B) \rightarrow (B \rightarrow A)$$

Since we end up with the sequents $A \Rightarrow A$ and $B \Rightarrow B$, which are impossible to falsify, we deduce that the conclusion is impossible to falsify and is therefore valid.

Prove $\Rightarrow (A \rightarrow (B \rightarrow C)) \rightarrow ((A \rightarrow B) \rightarrow (A \rightarrow C))$

Proof

$C \Rightarrow C$	Id
$B \Rightarrow B \qquad B, C \Rightarrow C$	Id, LW
$B, B, B \rightarrow C \Rightarrow C$	L$\rightarrow$
$A \Rightarrow A \qquad B, B \rightarrow C \Rightarrow C$	Id, LC
$A \Rightarrow A \qquad A, B, A \rightarrow (B \rightarrow C) \Rightarrow C$	Id, L$\rightarrow$
$A, A, A \rightarrow B, A \rightarrow (B \rightarrow C) \Rightarrow C$	L$\rightarrow$
$A, A \rightarrow B, A \rightarrow (B \rightarrow C) \Rightarrow C$	LC
$A \rightarrow B, A \rightarrow (B \rightarrow C) \Rightarrow A \rightarrow C$	R$\rightarrow$
$A \rightarrow (B \rightarrow C) \Rightarrow (A \rightarrow B) \rightarrow (A \rightarrow C)$	R$\rightarrow$
$\Rightarrow (A \rightarrow (B \rightarrow C)) \rightarrow ((A \rightarrow B) \rightarrow (A \rightarrow C))$	R$\rightarrow$

(End)

Again let us employ the falsification strategy to see if we can make this rather complicated proof more perspicuous.

We want to falsify $(A \rightarrow (B \rightarrow C)) \rightarrow ((A \rightarrow B) \rightarrow (A \rightarrow C))$.

Trying to make $A \rightarrow (B \rightarrow C)$ true and $(A \rightarrow B) \rightarrow (A \rightarrow C)$ false we get

$$A \rightarrow (B \rightarrow C) \Rightarrow (A \rightarrow B) \rightarrow (A \rightarrow C)$$
$$\Rightarrow (A \rightarrow (B \rightarrow C)) \rightarrow ((A \rightarrow B) \rightarrow (A \rightarrow C))$$

Trying to make $(A \rightarrow B) \rightarrow (A \rightarrow C)$ false we get

$$A \rightarrow B, A \rightarrow (B \rightarrow C) \Rightarrow A \rightarrow C$$
$$A \rightarrow (B \rightarrow C) \Rightarrow (A \rightarrow B) \rightarrow (A \rightarrow C)$$
$$\Rightarrow (A \rightarrow (B \rightarrow C)) \rightarrow ((A \rightarrow B) \rightarrow (A \rightarrow C))$$

Trying to make $A \rightarrow C$ false we get

$$A, A \rightarrow B, A \rightarrow (B \rightarrow C) \Rightarrow C$$
$$A \rightarrow B, A \rightarrow (B \rightarrow C) \Rightarrow A \rightarrow C$$
$$A \rightarrow (B \rightarrow C) \Rightarrow (A \rightarrow B) \rightarrow (A \rightarrow C)$$
$$\Rightarrow (A \rightarrow (B \rightarrow C)) \rightarrow ((A \rightarrow B) \rightarrow (A \rightarrow C))$$

Trying to make $A \rightarrow B$ true we get

$$A, A \rightarrow (B \rightarrow C) \Rightarrow C, A \qquad A, B, A \rightarrow (B \rightarrow C) \Rightarrow C$$
$$A, A \rightarrow B, A \rightarrow (B \rightarrow C) \Rightarrow C$$
$$A \rightarrow B, A \rightarrow (B \rightarrow C) \Rightarrow A \rightarrow C$$
$$A \rightarrow (B \rightarrow C) \Rightarrow (A \rightarrow B) \rightarrow (A \rightarrow C)$$
$$\Rightarrow (A \rightarrow (B \rightarrow C)) \rightarrow ((A \rightarrow B) \rightarrow (A \rightarrow C))$$

This new line is not one of the lines of our original proof. However, the first sequent can be simplified to A ⇒ A on the basis that the truth or falsity of the other formulae does not affect the truth of the sequent. Hence we get the replacement line

$$A \Rightarrow A \qquad A, B, A \rightarrow (B{\rightarrow}C) \Rightarrow C$$

which gives, as our new development,

$$\underline{A \Rightarrow A \qquad A, B, A \rightarrow (B{\rightarrow}C) \Rightarrow C}$$
$$\underline{A, A{\rightarrow}B, A \rightarrow (B{\rightarrow}C) \Rightarrow C}$$
$$\underline{A{\rightarrow}B, A \rightarrow (B{\rightarrow}C) \Rightarrow A{\rightarrow}C}$$
$$\underline{A \rightarrow (B{\rightarrow}C) \Rightarrow (A{\rightarrow}B) \rightarrow (A{\rightarrow}C)}$$
$$\Rightarrow (A \rightarrow (B{\rightarrow}C)) \rightarrow ((A{\rightarrow}B) \rightarrow (A{\rightarrow}C))$$

which, allowing for the line

$$A, A, A{\rightarrow}B, A \rightarrow (B{\rightarrow}C) \Rightarrow C$$

which can easily be accommodated, accords with the proof above.

Returning to our development we want to make A → (B→C) true. This can be done by having A false or B→C true. Hence we get the new line

$$A \Rightarrow A, C \qquad B, B{\rightarrow}C \Rightarrow C$$

which can be reduced to

$$A \Rightarrow A \qquad B, B{\rightarrow}C \Rightarrow C$$

from which we get the tree

$$\underline{A \Rightarrow A \qquad B, B{\rightarrow}C \Rightarrow C}$$
$$\underline{A \Rightarrow A \qquad A, B, A \rightarrow (B{\rightarrow}C) \Rightarrow C}$$
$$\underline{A, A{\rightarrow}B, A \rightarrow (B{\rightarrow}C) \Rightarrow C}$$
$$\underline{A{\rightarrow}B, A \rightarrow (B{\rightarrow}C) \Rightarrow A{\rightarrow}C}$$
$$\underline{A \rightarrow (B{\rightarrow}C) \Rightarrow (A{\rightarrow}B) \rightarrow (A{\rightarrow}C)}$$
$$\Rightarrow (A \rightarrow (B{\rightarrow}C)) \rightarrow ((A{\rightarrow}B) \rightarrow (A{\rightarrow}C))$$

Now we need B false or C true. Hence the line

$$B \Rightarrow B, C \qquad B, C \Rightarrow C$$

from which we easily get

$$B \Rightarrow B \qquad B, C \Rightarrow C$$

and then

$$\frac{C \Rightarrow C}{B \Rightarrow B \qquad B, C \Rightarrow C}$$

to give us our final tree

$$\frac{C \Rightarrow C}{\frac{B \Rightarrow B \qquad B, C \Rightarrow C}{\frac{A \Rightarrow A \qquad B, B \rightarrow C \Rightarrow C}{\frac{A \Rightarrow A \qquad A, B, A \rightarrow (B \rightarrow C) \Rightarrow C}{\frac{A, A \rightarrow B, A \rightarrow (B \rightarrow C) \Rightarrow C}{\frac{A \rightarrow B, A \rightarrow (B \rightarrow C) \Rightarrow A \rightarrow C}{\frac{A \rightarrow (B \rightarrow C) \Rightarrow (A \rightarrow B) \rightarrow (A \rightarrow C)}{\Rightarrow (A \rightarrow (B \rightarrow C)) \rightarrow ((A \rightarrow B) \rightarrow (A \rightarrow C))}}}}}}}$$

Apart from minor differences this is the tree which represented our original proof.

Exercises

3.16 Apply the above strategy to develop the proofs of A → (B→A) and ¬A → (A→B) shown above.

3.17 Prove each of the following sequents:
(i)   ⇒ C → (A → (B→C))
(ii) ¬¬A ⇒ A
(iii) ⇒ A→¬¬A

3.4 Summary

- ⊥ (falsum) has the constant value false.
- ¬A is defined as A → ⊥.
- Natural deduction was presented as an abstract system of propositional logic based on rules of derivation which are intended to capture certain aspects of ordinary human reasoning. Eleven rules in all were presented, including a formalisation of proof by contradiction or *reductio ad absurdum*.
- The rules of deduction were:

(1) ∧I $\dfrac{A \qquad B}{A \wedge B}$

(2) ∧E $\dfrac{A \wedge B}{A}$ (3) ∧E $\dfrac{A \wedge B}{B}$

(4) ∨I $\dfrac{A}{A \vee B}$ (5) ∨I $\dfrac{B}{A \vee B}$

(6) ∨E   A   B   (7) →I   A

           .   .   .

$$\dfrac{A \lor B \quad C \quad C}{C} \qquad \dfrac{\dfrac{C}{\;}}{A \to C}$$

(8) →E $\dfrac{A \quad A \to C}{C}$ (9) ⊥ $\dfrac{\bot}{C}$

(10) RAA   ¬A   (11)Id $\dfrac{A}{A}$

               .

$$\dfrac{\bot}{A}$$

- Most proofs involve the making and cancelling of assumptions.
- A sequent L ⇒ R is defined to be a pair of proposition sequences, L = <P_1, P_2, ..., P_m>, R = <Q_1, Q_2, ..., Q_n>, where P_i, Q_i are propositions.
- L and R are finite, possibly empty. L is called the antecedent of the sequent; R is called the succedent.
- L ⇒ R is satisfied if at least one of the members of L is false or at least one element of R is true.
- The rules for manipulating sequents are:

(1) R∧ $\dfrac{\Gamma_1 \Rightarrow A, \Delta_1 \qquad \Gamma_2 \Rightarrow B, \Delta_2}{\Gamma_1, \Gamma_2 \Rightarrow A \land B, \Delta_1, \Delta_2}$

(2) L∧ $\dfrac{\Gamma, A \Rightarrow \Delta}{\Gamma, A \land B \Rightarrow \Delta}$ (3) L∧ $\dfrac{\Gamma, B \Rightarrow \Delta}{\Gamma, A \land B \Rightarrow \Delta}$

(4) R∨ $\dfrac{\Gamma \Rightarrow A, \Delta}{\Gamma \Rightarrow A \lor B, \Delta}$ (5) R∨ $\dfrac{\Gamma \Rightarrow B, \Delta}{\Gamma \Rightarrow A \lor B, \Delta}$

(6) L∨ $\dfrac{\Gamma_1, A \Rightarrow \Delta_1 \qquad \Gamma_2, B \Rightarrow \Delta_2}{\Gamma_1, \Gamma_2, A \lor B \Rightarrow \Delta_1, \Delta_2}$

(7) R→ $\dfrac{\Gamma, A \Rightarrow B, \Delta}{\Gamma \Rightarrow A \to B, \Delta}$

(8) L→ $\dfrac{\Gamma_1 \Rightarrow A, \Delta_1 \qquad \Gamma_2, B \Rightarrow \Delta_2}{\Gamma_1, \Gamma_2, A \to B \Rightarrow \Delta_1, \Delta_2}$

(9) R¬ $\dfrac{\Gamma, A \Rightarrow \Delta}{\Gamma \Rightarrow \neg A, \Delta}$ (10) L¬ $\dfrac{\Gamma \Rightarrow A, \Delta}{\Gamma, \neg A \Rightarrow \Delta}$

(11) RT $\dfrac{\Gamma \Rightarrow \Delta}{\Gamma \Rightarrow A, \Delta}$ (12) LT $\dfrac{\Gamma \Rightarrow \Delta}{\Gamma, A \Rightarrow \Delta}$

(13) RC $\dfrac{\Gamma \Rightarrow A, A, \Delta}{\Gamma \Rightarrow A, \Delta}$ (14) LC $\dfrac{\Gamma, A, A \Rightarrow \Delta}{\Gamma, A \Rightarrow \Delta}$

(15) RR $\dfrac{\Gamma \Rightarrow A, B, \Delta}{\Gamma \Rightarrow B, A, \Delta}$ (16) LR $\dfrac{\Gamma, A, B \Rightarrow \Delta}{\Gamma, B, A \Rightarrow \Delta}$

(17) Cut $\dfrac{\Gamma_1 \Rightarrow A, \Delta_1 \qquad \Gamma_2, A \Rightarrow \Delta_2}{\Gamma_1, \Gamma_2 \Rightarrow \Delta_1, \Delta_2}$

(18) Id   A ⇒ A

In this chapter we have

(1)   studied formal rules of deduction in two forms, called here
      (a)   natural deduction
      (b)   sequent calculus.
(2)   justified the rules.
(3)   applied natural deduction methods to theorem proving.
(4)   applied rules of the sequent calculus to the proving of results.

    So far, we have explored systems for determining the validity or otherwise of a set of logical arguments. We next turn to a system which permits us to construct only valid arguments.

Miscellaneous Exercises

1.   Prove each of the following using
      (a) natural deduction rules
      (b) sequent calculus

    (i) $\vdash$ $(A{\rightarrow}B) \rightarrow ((B{\rightarrow}C) \rightarrow (\neg C{\rightarrow} \neg A))$

    (ii) $\{(A{\rightarrow}C), (B{\rightarrow}C)\} \vdash$ $(A{\wedge}B) \rightarrow C$

    (iii) $\vdash$ $(\neg A{\rightarrow}A) \rightarrow A$

    (iv) $\vdash$ $\neg(A{\wedge}B) \rightarrow (\neg A{\vee}\neg B)$

    (v) $\vdash$ $\neg(\neg A{\wedge}\neg B) \rightarrow (A{\vee}B)$

    (vi) $\vdash$ $\neg(\neg A{\vee}\neg B) \rightarrow (A{\wedge}B)$

    (vii) $\vdash$ $(\neg A{\rightarrow}B) \rightarrow ((\neg A{\rightarrow}\neg B) \rightarrow A))$

    (vii) $\vdash$ $(\neg A{\rightarrow}B) \rightarrow ((A{\rightarrow}B) \rightarrow B))$

    (ix) $\vdash$ $\neg((\neg A{\rightarrow}A) \wedge (A{\rightarrow}\neg A))$

    (x) $\vdash$ $\neg A{\vee}A$

2.   Comparing the proofs using natural deduction with those using sequent calculus what do you conclude?

CHAPTER 4

Axiomatic Propositional Logic

Chapter Aims

(1) To understand the idea of an axiomatic system.
(2) To study an axiomatic system for propositional logic.
(3) To develop insights into proving theorems.
(4) To develop a technical understanding of consistency.
(5) To distinguish between the key ideas of soundness and completeness of a system of logic.
(6) To prove the soundness and completeness of the axiomatic system of propositional logic.
(7) To establish that the system is decidable.

When you have completed your study of this chapter you should
(a) have a clear understanding of the structure of formal axiomatic systems.
(b) be familiar with a formal axiomatic system, AL, for propositional logic.
(c) be able to construct formal proofs of theorems.
(d) have a clear understanding of the syntactic notion of consistency.
(e) have a clear understanding of the concepts of soundness and completeness in formal systems.
(f) be able to prove soundness and completeness of the formal system AL.

4.1 Introduction

We turn now to the classic presentation of propositional logic – the axiomatic presentation. Building on a base of a few axioms and one rule of deduction we show how all the theorems of propositional logic can be proved. Again, our approach will be strictly formal and we will leave aside notions of truth and falsehood to begin with.

Axiomatic systems are probably the systems most favoured by mathematicians and computer scientists because of their elegance, solidity and because of their classical lineage. The presentation of a mathematical or scientific theory as an axiomatic system has often been seen as an ideal towards which all theories should be aimed.

Axiomatic structures can facilitate the establishment of properties of logical systems – so-called meta-theoretical results. However, proofs of theorems within such systems, even when short, are often subtle and demanding. Unlike tableau systems for example, there is no known mechanical procedure for progressing towards a conclusion. However, in the examples we shall study, we will make an attempt to uncover and explain some reasonable strategies and methods of attack. Effort spent in appreciating the subtleties of some of the techniques of theorem proving and in developing technical competence is well spent. It will help to deepen your grasp of logic and your understanding of the important meta-theoretical results.

4.2 Axiomatic Systems

In general, a formal axiomatic system has four types of ingredient:
(1) Σ: An *alphabet* of symbols, used to form strings or expressions in the system.
(2)   WF: The set of *well-formed formulae*, a subset of all the strings that can be formed using Σ, i.e. WF $\subseteq \Sigma^*$, where Σ^* is the set of all strings over the alphabet Σ.
(3)   Ax: The set of *axioms*, a subset of WF.
(4)   R: A set of *rules of deduction*.

4.2.1 An Axiomatic System for Propositional Logic

A suitable axiomatic system, AL, for propositional logic is the following:

$$\Sigma = \{\neg, \rightarrow, (,), p_1, p_2, \ldots, p_n, \ldots\}$$
$$WF = \{x \mid x = p_i, \text{ for } i = 1, 2, \ldots, n, \ldots$$
$$\text{or } x = (\neg A), \text{ where } A \in WF$$
$$\text{or } x = (A \rightarrow B), \text{ where } A \in WF, B \in WF\}$$

The p_i are often called *proposition letters*. They may be understood to stand for basic or so-called atomic propositions. Complex propositions (well-formed formulae) are then built up using the signs $\neg$ and $\rightarrow$, for example, $(p_{12} \rightarrow ((\neg(p_1 \rightarrow p_3)) \rightarrow (\neg(p_2) \rightarrow p_1)))$. Uppercase letters, A, B, C, etc. are used to stand for well-formed formulae in general, whether simple or complex. They are often called *proposition variables*.

Note carefully that the description of the set of well-formed formulae, WF, is *inductive*. A complex well-formed formula, e.g. A→B, is defined in terms of less complex well-formed formulae A and B. Whenever an entity is defined in terms of (simpler forms of) the entity itself we have an inductive definition.

Notice that we are being quite economical in our use of logical operators, confining ourselves to just two, $\neg$ and $\rightarrow$. This will reduce the amount of work we have to do in proving properties of our system. Also, although it is not really relevant at this stage, we know from Chapter 1 that ¬ and → are sufficient in the sense that the other operators can be expressed in terms of these two

$$(A \land B) \equiv \neg(A \rightarrow \neg B)$$
$$(A \lor B) \equiv (\neg A \rightarrow B)$$

In addition there is a certain elegance about a system which is constructed on a small base.

From now on we will use *wff* as shorthand for well-formed formula or well-formed formulae.

Exercise

4.1 Which of the following are wff and which are not?

(i) $(\neg(p1 \rightarrow p1))$

(ii) $(p1 \rightarrow (p2 \rightarrow p1))$

(iii) $(p2 \rightarrow ((\neg p4) \rightarrow p6))$

(iv) $\neg p1$

(v) $(((((\neg p3) \rightarrow p1) \rightarrow (((p5 \rightarrow p1) \rightarrow (\neg p9)) \rightarrow (p1 \rightarrow p1))) \rightarrow p1)$

(vi) $p1 \rightarrow p1$

(vii) $p1 \rightarrow (\neg p2)$

(ix) $(p1 \rightarrow \neg p2)$

(x) $\rightarrow (\neg p1)$

(xi) $\neg \rightarrow p10$

(xii) $(\neg (\rightarrow (p1 \rightarrow p2)))$

According to the definition, neither ¬A nor A→B is, strictly speaking, a wff because they are not enclosed in brackets. However, if we do fully bracket our sub-formulae they can become quite clumsy. We will take the liberty of dropping brackets wherever it makes no essential difference to the form of a wff. For example, we would write $(A \rightarrow ((\neg B) \rightarrow C))$ as $A \rightarrow (\neg B \rightarrow C)$, and $(((A \rightarrow (B \rightarrow C)) \rightarrow ((A \rightarrow B) \rightarrow (A \rightarrow C))))$ as $(A \rightarrow (B \rightarrow C)) \rightarrow ((A \rightarrow B) \rightarrow (A \rightarrow C))$. But, we cannot become too cavalier in our dropping of brackets. For example, it is necessary to use brackets in A→B→C to distinguish between $A \rightarrow (B \rightarrow C)$ and $(A \rightarrow B) \rightarrow C$. It is important also to note that ¬ takes precedence over →, so that ¬A→B is not the same as ¬(A→B).

Let us continue with our description of an axiomatic system for propositional logic. Our axioms will be:

Ax1 $A \rightarrow (B \rightarrow A)$

Ax2 $(A \rightarrow (B \rightarrow C)) \rightarrow ((A \rightarrow B) \rightarrow (A \rightarrow C))$

Ax3 $(\neg A \rightarrow \neg B) \rightarrow (B \rightarrow A)$

In fact, these are *axiom schemas* rather than axioms. They implicitly state that expressions of these *forms* are axioms where A, B and C stand for *any* wff. Thus they represent an infinite set of actual axioms. For example, $p_{17} \rightarrow (p_3 \rightarrow p_{17})$ is an instance of Ax1. $(\neg(\neg p_2 \rightarrow p_5) \rightarrow \neg p_1) \rightarrow (p_1 \rightarrow (\neg p_2 \rightarrow p_5))$ is an instance of Ax3, and so on.

The last ingredient in our axiomatic system is a set of rules of deduction. We shall use just one such rule – modus ponens (MP) – a form of which we saw in Chapter 3. Restated here:

From A and A→B, B can be derived, where A and B are any wff.

4.3 Deduction

The principal practical task in logic is to deduce wff from a *given* set of wff. The given set of wff may be called a set of hypotheses or assumptions.

A *deduction* in AL is a sequence of wff $F_1, F_2, ..., F_n$, such that for each i $(1 \leq i \leq n)$

    (a) F_i is an axiom

or (b) F_i is an hypothesis

or (c) F_i is derived, by modus ponens, from F_j, F_k, where j,k < i.

If H is the set of hypotheses involved in the deduction we say that F_n is a *deductive consequence* of H (or that F_n is deducible from H), and we write

$$H \vdash F_n$$

If the set of hypotheses H is empty we write $\vdash F_n$. In this case F_n is deduced from the axioms alone without the aid of hypotheses and we say that F_n is a theorem. The simplest theorems are instances of the axioms themselves. Thus, for example,

$$p_1 \rightarrow (p_3 \rightarrow p_1)$$

is a theorem, as is

$$(p_{10} \rightarrow (p_3 \rightarrow p_5)) \rightarrow ((p_{10} \rightarrow p_3) \rightarrow (p_{10} \rightarrow p_5))$$

For another simple example, let us consider a case where modus ponens is used.

$p_2 \rightarrow (p_3 \rightarrow p_2)$	Ax1
$(p_2 \rightarrow (p_3 \rightarrow p_2)) \rightarrow ((p_2 \rightarrow p_3) \rightarrow (p_2 \rightarrow p_2))$	Ax2
$((p_2 \rightarrow p_3) \rightarrow (p_2 \rightarrow p_2))$	MP on lines 1 and 2

Exercises

4.2 Prove the following theorems in AL.

(i)   ⊢ (¬p2→¬p1) → (p1→p2)

(ii)   ⊢ (¬p1→p3) → (¬p1→¬p1)

(iii)   ⊢ ((¬p2→¬p1) → p1) → ((¬p2→¬p1) → p2)

(iv)   ⊢ (¬¬p1→¬¬p2) → (p1→p2)

(v)   ⊢ p1→p1

(vi)   ⊢ p2→p2

(vii)   ⊢ p3→p3

4.3 Prove the following in AL.

(i)   {p1, (p1→p2), (p2→p3)} ⊢ p3

(ii)   {p1, (p2 → (p1→p3))} ⊢ p2→p3

(iii)   {p1 → (¬p2→¬p3)} ⊢ p1 → (p3→p2)

4.4 Meta-Theorems

Now that we have defined our axiomatic system of propositional logic, we will not devote all our time to constructing formal proofs *within* the system. We are more interested in establishing *general results about the system itself.* We would rather try to establish that, for example, ⊢ A→A for *any* wff A (as hinted at in parts (v), (vi) and (vii) of Exercise 4.2, or that {(A→B), (B→C)} ⊢ (A→C), for *any* wff A, B, C.

A result such as ⊢ A→A which holds for any and every wff A is a meta-theorem. From now on we shall concentrate on establishing such meta-theorems. In general they are not easy to prove, and we shall try to indicate plausible lines of attack wherever possible.

(Meta-)Theorem 4.1

$$⊢ A→A$$

Proof The first hurdle to surmount is the feeling of helplessness in the face of the apparent obviousness of the result. How can we get started on something so simple? Well, the only place we can start is with the axioms. Let's try the first one.

      1. A → (B→A)

This is not much use on its own. So let's try the second one. It seems reasonable to use a form of the second axiom that makes use of the first expression, namely A → (B→A).

      2. (A → (B→A)) → ((A→B) → (A→A))

Now we seem to be getting somewhere! The form we wish to prove appears at the end of this expression. If we could detach the rest of the wff we would have our result. Well, we can detach the first part anyway, by using modus ponens on lines 1 and 2. Hence,

3. $(A{\rightarrow}B) \rightarrow (A{\rightarrow}A)$ MP

But now we are stuck! We cannot detach the first part $(A{\rightarrow}B)$ to give us our result $(A{\rightarrow}A)$. We would need to establish it on its own and then use modus ponens. But there is no hope of this since $A{\rightarrow}B$ is not a (meta-) theorem by itself. What we would need is a (meta-)theorem. And what is the simplest form of (meta-)theorem? An axiom of course! If we had an axiom in place of $A{\rightarrow}B$ we might make further progress. Why not use the simplest axiom, $A \rightarrow (B{\rightarrow}A)$? We would like line 3 to read

$(A \rightarrow (B{\rightarrow}A)) \rightarrow (A{\rightarrow}A)$

Therefore we need line 2 to be

$(A \rightarrow ((B{\rightarrow}A) \rightarrow A)) \rightarrow ((A \rightarrow (B{\rightarrow}A)) \rightarrow (A{\rightarrow}A))$

And hence line 1 should be

$A \rightarrow ((B{\rightarrow}A) \rightarrow A)$

which is still clearly a form of Ax1.

Having thought our way through all this let us write out our proof from start to finish.

     $A \rightarrow ((B{\rightarrow}A) \rightarrow A)$ Ax1

     $(A \rightarrow ((B{\rightarrow}A) \rightarrow A)) \rightarrow ((A \rightarrow (B{\rightarrow}A)) \rightarrow (A{\rightarrow}A))$ Ax2

$\therefore$ $(A \rightarrow (B{\rightarrow}A)) \rightarrow (A{\rightarrow}A)$ MP

     $A \rightarrow (B{\rightarrow}A)$ Ax1

$\therefore$ $A{\rightarrow}A$ MP

(End)

We see then that (meta-)theorem proofs in axiomatic propositional logic can be tricky and hard to find. They usually require a shrewd mixture of bottom-up reasoning (seeing what you can do with the axioms or hypotheses you have) and top-down reasoning (seeing what might plausibly lead to the answer required). Let us try our hand at a few more results.

(Meta-)Theorem 4.2

$\vdash \neg A \rightarrow (A{\rightarrow}B)$

Proof To start with, it seems reasonable to have a look at the third axiom since that is the only one that uses the negation sign explicitly. So

$(\neg A{\rightarrow}\neg B) \rightarrow (B{\rightarrow}A)$

This statement of Ax3 has the last part the wrong way round. So, maybe we should use

$(\neg B{\rightarrow}\neg A) \rightarrow (A{\rightarrow}B)$

Now if only we had $\neg A$ instead of $\neg B \rightarrow \neg A$, we would have our result. So, we ask if there is any relationship between $\neg A$ and $\neg B{\rightarrow}\neg A$. And the answer is not too difficult to see:

$$\neg A \rightarrow (\neg B \rightarrow \neg A) \qquad\qquad \text{Ax1}$$

Remember that in our statement of the first axiom, namely A → (B→A), A and B could stand for any wff, including such things as ¬A and ¬B.

Let us combine our insights and see how far we can get.

$$\neg A \rightarrow (\neg B \rightarrow \neg A) \qquad\qquad \text{Ax1}$$
$$(\neg B \rightarrow \neg A) \rightarrow (A \rightarrow B) \qquad\qquad \text{Ax3}$$

But now we are stuck. What we want to do is to link the first and second expressions together, by eliminating ¬B→¬A. Later we will develop a rule to allow us to do things like this. But for the present we can't. So we need to exercise a little more ingenuity. We want to end up with ¬A → (A→B). If we had

$$(\neg A \rightarrow (\neg B \rightarrow \neg A)) \rightarrow (\neg A \rightarrow (A \rightarrow B))$$

then we could use modus ponens to detach the first part, which is an axiom, and get our result. If we look carefully at this last expression we see that it is related in form to the right-hand side of Ax2

$$(A \rightarrow (B \rightarrow C)) \rightarrow (\underline{(A \rightarrow B) \rightarrow (A \rightarrow C)})$$

where ¬A takes the role of A, ¬B→¬A takes the role of B, and A→B takes the role of C. So, we would need for our left-hand side (¬A → ((¬B→¬A) → (A→B))). The question is: could we establish this result? And the answer is: yes, relatively easily, as follows.

$$(\neg B \rightarrow \neg A) \rightarrow (A \rightarrow B)) \qquad\qquad \text{Ax3}$$
$$(\neg B \rightarrow \neg A) \rightarrow (A \rightarrow B)) \rightarrow (\neg A \rightarrow \underline{((\neg B \rightarrow \neg A) \rightarrow (A \rightarrow B))}) \qquad \text{Ax1}$$
$$\therefore \ (\neg A \rightarrow ((\neg B \rightarrow \neg A) \rightarrow (A \rightarrow B))) \qquad\qquad \text{MP}$$

Now that we have worked out the key stages of our proof let us put it all together in one smooth sequence.

1. $(\neg B \rightarrow \neg A) \rightarrow (A \rightarrow B)$ Ax3
2. $((\neg B \rightarrow \neg A) \rightarrow (A \rightarrow B)) \rightarrow (\neg A \rightarrow ((\neg B \rightarrow \neg A) \rightarrow (A \rightarrow B)))$ Ax1
3. $\therefore \ (\neg A \rightarrow ((\neg B \rightarrow \neg A) \rightarrow (A \rightarrow B)))$ MP on 1 and 2
4. $(\neg A \rightarrow ((\neg B \rightarrow \neg A) \rightarrow (A \rightarrow B))) \rightarrow (\neg A \rightarrow (\neg B \rightarrow \neg A)) \rightarrow (\neg A \rightarrow$
    $(A \rightarrow B))$ Ax2
5. $\therefore \ (\neg A \rightarrow (\neg B \rightarrow \neg A)) \rightarrow (\neg A \rightarrow (A \rightarrow B))$ MP on 3 and 4
6. $\neg A \rightarrow (\neg B \rightarrow \neg A)$ Ax1
7. $\therefore \ \neg A \rightarrow (A \rightarrow B)$ MP on 5 and 6

                                                                       (End)

It is worth returning briefly to the first three lines of the final text of the proof, because they illustrate an important strategic point to bear in mind.

Heuristic for Axiomatic Propositional Logic

Given any result, A, then you can also quickly get B→A, for any wffs A, B.

This is easily shown as follows:

$$A \qquad\qquad \text{Assumed already proved}$$
$$A \to (B{\to}A) \qquad \text{Ax1}$$
$$\therefore\ B{\to}A$$

For example, from any axiom Ax you have B→Ax.
Above, Ax was (¬B→¬A) → (A→B).
We needed ¬A → ((¬B→¬A) → (A→B)).

(Meta-)Theorem 4.3 (Transitivity of Implication)

$$\{A{\to}B,\ B{\to}C\} \vdash\ A \to C$$

Proof Here we have to deduce A→C from the hypotheses A→B and B→C. The hypotheses should make our task a little easier. Let us begin with the second one: B→C.

Taking our cue from the comments after the last theorem, we realise that we can immediately get A → (B→C), which looks as if it might be useful. In fact it is not too hard to see how the proof will proceed.

1.   B→C   Hypothesis
2.   (B→C) → (A → (B→C))   Ax1
3. ∴ A → (B→C)   MP on 1 and 2
4.   (A → (B→C)) → ((A→B) → (A→C))   Ax2
5. ∴ (A→B) → (A→C)   MP on 3 and 4
6.   A→B   Hypothesis
7. ∴ A→C   MP on 5 and 6

Hence, we conclude $\{A{\to}B, B{\to}C\} \vdash\ A{\to}C$

(End)

Essentially, this result shows that → is transitive. This is very useful in practice and can serve as another rule of deduction to complement the modus ponens rule. We will dignify it by the title transitivity of implication (TI).

Let us illustrate the usefulness of TI by displaying a much simpler proof of (Meta-)Theorem 4.2.

(Meta-)Theorem 4.2 (second version)

$$\vdash\ \neg A \to (A{\to}B)$$

Proof

1.   ¬A → (¬B→¬A)   Ax1
2.   (¬B→¬A) → (A→B)   Ax3
3. ∴ ¬A → (A→B)   TI from 1 and 2

(End)

Simple and elegant!

(Meta-)Theorem 4.4

$$\{B \to C\} \vdash (A \to B) \to (A \to C)$$

Proof The deduction here simply consists of the first 5 lines of the (Meta-)Theorem 4.3.

1.	$B \to C$	Hypothesis
2.	$(B \to C) \to (A \to (B \to C))$	Ax1
3. $\therefore$	$A \to (B \to C)$	MP on 1 and 2
4.	$(A \to (B \to C)) \to ((A \to B) \to (A \to C))$	Ax2
5. $\therefore$	$(A \to B) \to (A \to C)$	MP on 3 and 4

Therefore $\{B \to C\} \vdash (A \to B) \to (A \to C)$

(End)

(Meta-)Theorem 4.5

$$\vdash (B \to C) \to ((A \to B) \to (A \to C))$$

Proof Although this theorem continues the theme of the previous two results, it is a little harder to prove because we have no hypotheses to work with.

Nevertheless, we can make use of our strategic discovery of (Meta-) Theorem 4.2 – our heuristic – allied to the recognition that $(A \to B) \to (A \to C)$ is the right-hand side of Ax2, to advance our proof.

1.	$(A \to (B \to C)) \to ((A \to B) \to (A \to C))$	Ax2
2.	$(A \to (B \to C)) \to ((A \to B) \to (A \to C)) \to$	
	$\qquad ((B \to C) \to ((A \to (B \to C)) \to ((A \to B) \to (A \to C))))$	Ax1
3. $\therefore$	$(B \to C) \to ((A \to (B \to C)) \to ((A \to B) \to (A \to C)))$	MP on 1 and 2
4.	$(B \to C) \to ((A \to (B \to C)) \to ((A \to B) \to (A \to C))) \to$	
	$\qquad ((B \to C) \to (A \to (B \to C))) \to ((B \to C) \to ((A \to B) \to (A \to C)))$	Ax2
5. $\therefore$	$((B \to C) \to (A \to (B \to C))) \to ((B \to C) \to ((A \to B) \to (A \to C)))$	
		MP on 3 and 4
6.	$(B \to C) \to (A \to (B \to C))$	Ax1
7. $\therefore$	$(B \to C) \to ((A \to B) \to (A \to C))$	MP on 5 and 6

(End)

Taking advantage of the insights gained in the above proof and making use of (Meta-)Theorem 4.3, the proof of (Meta-)Theorem 4.5 can be simplified.

(Meta-)Theorem 4.5 (second version)

$$\vdash (B \to C) \to ((A \to B) \to (A \to C))$$

Proof

1.	$(B{\to}C) \to (A \to (B{\to}C))$	Ax1
2.	$(A \to (B{\to}C)) \to ((A{\to}B) \to (A{\to}C))$	Ax2
3. ∴	$(B{\to}C) \to ((A{\to}B) \to (A{\to}C))$	TI from 1 and 2

(End)

(Meta-)Theorems 4.3, 4.4 and 4.5 are clearly closely linked. The results

$$\{B{\to}C, A{\to}B\} \vdash A{\to}C$$
$$\{B{\to}C\} \vdash (A{\to}B) \to (A{\to}C)$$
$$\vdash (B{\to}C) \to ((A{\to}B) \to (A{\to}C))$$

seem to indicate that 'hypotheses' may be moved from the left to the right of the ⊢ sign to give valid results. And that *is* in fact the case. These three results are just examples of a general feature of our logic, which we will establish shortly. The importance of this general result is that it will enable us to prove some (meta-)theorems more easily (surely to be wished for!)

Exercise

4.4 Prove the following (meta-)theorems about AL.

(i) $\vdash (A{\to}\neg B) \to ((B{\to}\neg A) \to (A{\to}\neg B))$

(ii) $\vdash (\neg(A{\to}B) \to \neg\neg(B{\to}A)) \to (\neg(B{\to}A) \to (A{\to}B))$

(iii) $\vdash ((\neg A{\to}B) \to ((B{\to}\neg A) \to A)) \to$
$\qquad\qquad (((\neg A{\to}B) \to (B{\to}\neg A)) \to ((\neg A{\to}B) \to A))$

(iv) $\vdash \neg A{\to}\neg A$

(v) $\vdash (A{\to}B) \to (A \to (C{\to}B))$

(vi) $(\neg\neg A{\to}\neg\neg B) \vdash (A{\to}B)$

(vii) $\vdash (\neg\neg A{\to}\neg\neg B) \to (A{\to}B)$

(viii) $\neg\neg A \vdash A$

(ix) $\vdash \neg\neg A{\to}A$

(x) $\vdash A{\to}\neg\neg A$

(xi) $\vdash A \to (\neg B{\to}\neg\neg A)$

(xii) $\vdash A \to (\neg A{\to}B)$

Let us now turn our attention to establishing that important result we mentioned earlier: the meta-theorem which effectively licenses the moving of hypotheses across the ⊢ sign.

(Meta-)Theorem 4.6 (Deduction Theorem)

Let H be a set (possibly empty) of wff of AL, and let A and B be any wff of AL.

If $H \cup \{A\} \vdash B$ then $H \vdash (A{\to}B)$

Proof We recall that a deduction is a sequence of wff obeying certain conditions. To prove the deduction theorem we use *induction* on the number of wff in the deductive sequence. We begin with the base case, where the deduction of B from H ∪ {A} requires just one wff in the sequence, namely B itself.

Basis step: B must be an axiom or a member of the set of hypotheses, i.e. of H ∪ {A}.

(a) Suppose B is an axiom. Then we can construct the following deduction:

1.	B	Axiom
2.	B → (A→B)	Ax1
3.	∴ A→B	MP on lines 1 and 2
Hence	H ⊢ A→B	

This conclusion may appear a little odd at first. How can H ⊢ A→B follow from ⊢ A→B? Well, if you think about the definition of a deduction, you will see that it is perfectly legitimate. A deduction is a sequence of formulae each of which is either an axiom or a hypothesis or follows from previous members of the sequence by modus ponens. There is no mention of the requirement that all (or any) of the hypotheses be used or that those that are used are *relevant*. As long as one of the three conditions is met for each wff, the deduction is legitimate. So, if H is {H_1, H_2, ..., H_n} the above proof could be written as follows:

1.	H_1	
2.	H_2	
	.	
	.	
	.	
n.	H_n	
n+1.	B	Axiom
n+2.	B → (A→B)	Ax1
n+3.	∴ A→B	MP on lines n+1 and n+2
Hence	H ⊢ A→B	

Of course, in practice we try to identify and use only relevant formulae. But that is a matter of *psychology*, not a matter of logic.

(b) Now suppose B ∈ H ∪ {A}. The deduction, H ⊢ A→B follows similar lines to case a.

1.	B	Hypothesis
2.	B → (A→B)	Ax1
3.	∴ A→B	MP on lines 1 and 2
Hence	H ⊢ A→B	

Induction step: Let us first state our induction hypothesis which is

If H ∪ {A} ⊢ B in n steps or fewer then H ⊢ A→B

Now suppose B is deduced from $H \cup \{A\}$ in n+1 steps, n > 1.

If B is an axiom or an element of $H \cup \{A\}$ then $H \vdash A \rightarrow B$ follows as in the basis case. This, of course, is not likely in practice, because we would hardly prove in many steps what could be deduced in one. However, we include a statement about it for completeness.

Suppose then (more realistically) that B is deduced by modus ponens from two earlier formulae in the deduction sequence, say, B_j and $B_j \rightarrow B$. Clearly, the induction hypothesis applies to both B_j and $B_j \rightarrow B$, since they were deduced in n steps or less.

Hence, we have the following:

.
.
.

B_j [1]

.
.

$A \rightarrow B_j$ [2]   Induction hypothesis (using line [1])

.
.

$B_j \rightarrow B$ [3]

.
.

$A \rightarrow (B_j \rightarrow B)$ [4]   Induction hypothesis (on line [3])

$(A \rightarrow (B_j \rightarrow B)) \rightarrow ((A \rightarrow B_j) \rightarrow (A \rightarrow B))$ Ax2

$\therefore$ $(A \rightarrow B_j) \rightarrow (A \rightarrow B)$ MP (using line [4] and Ax2)

$\therefore$ $A \rightarrow B$ MP (using line [2])

Hence $H \vdash A \rightarrow B$

By the principle of mathematical induction we conclude then that in all cases

If $H \cup \{A\} \vdash B$ then $H \vdash (A \rightarrow B)$

(End)

We write this

$$H \cup \{A\} \vdash B \Rightarrow H \vdash (A \rightarrow B)$$

where we are using the meta-implication sign $\Rightarrow$ to stand for if ... then .... Be careful to distinguish between the signs $\rightarrow$ and $\Rightarrow$. The first is part of the *object* system AL, the second is part of the *meta-language*, i.e the language we use to talk *about* the system AL – in this case, of course, mostly English.

Note on Monotonicity

We remarked during the course of the above proof that a deduction $\vdash A \rightarrow B$ allows us to state that $H \vdash A \rightarrow B$, for any set of hypotheses H. This property of classical logic is the property of *monotonicity*.

Definition   A *monotonic* logic is one where a valid proof cannot be invalidated by the addition of extra premises or assumptions.

It does not matter what the extra assumptions are. One of the new assumptions could be the negation of the proved formula! It would not matter. We could even add contradictory assumptions! In fact, if contradictory assumptions are present, anything can be proved: a point to which we will return.

Since the property of monotonicity is not one that we feel comfortable with in our everyday reasoning, a number of attempts have been made to construct non-monotonic logics, especially when dealing with automated reasoning systems on computers. Among these may be mentioned Reiter's default reasoning and McCarthy's circumscription. A clear introduction to these topics is presented by Ramsay (1988) in his *Formal Methods in Artificial Intelligence*. Non-monotonic logic is especially important when reasoning about knowledge. We may have come to a valid conclusion on the basis of a number of reasonable assumptions. If we obtain some new information we may want to call into question our previous conclusions, e.g. when we find that a goal which was deemed to be valid was 'scored' by somebody who had handled the ball in the penalty area.

Let us immediately get a glimpse at how the deduction theorem can make deductions easier to construct.

Suppose we wish to prove the following:

$$\{A{\to}B\} \vdash A \to (C{\to}B)$$

Without using the deduction theorem a proof might run as follows (try it yourself first to experience the elusiveness of the first steps):

1.	$B \to (C{\to}B)$	Ax1
2.	$B \to (C{\to}B) \to (A \to (B \to (C{\to}B)))$	Ax1
3.	$\therefore (A \to (B \to (C{\to}B)))$	MP on 1 and 2
4.	$(A \to (B \to (C{\to}B))) \to ((A{\to}B) \to (A \to (C{\to}B)))$ Ax2	
5.	$\therefore (A{\to}B) \to (A \to (C{\to}B))$	MP on 3 and 4
6.	$A{\to}B$	Hypothesis
7.	$\therefore A \to (C{\to}B)$	MP on 5 and 6

Therefore $\qquad \{A{\to}B\} \vdash A \to (C{\to}B)$

Let us now look at a proof which makes use of the deduction theorem.

1.	A	Hypothesis (for the sake of the proof)
2.	$A \to B$	Hypothesis (given)
3.	$\therefore B$	MP
4.	$B \to (C \to B)$	Ax1
5.	$\therefore C \to B$	MP

So, we have $\qquad \{A{\to}B\} \cup \{A\} \vdash C{\to}B$

Hence $\qquad \{A{\to}B\} \vdash A \to (C{\to}B)$ $\quad$ by deduction theorem

You must admit that the second proof is intuitively simpler, and much easier to arrive at!

Note, by the way, that we could immediately derive another result, namely

$$\vdash (A{\rightarrow}B) \rightarrow (A \rightarrow (C{\rightarrow}B))$$

by making another use of the deduction theorem.

Heuristic based on Deduction Theorem

When a wff of the form C→D is to be established, it may be useful to include C among the hypotheses, derive D from the expanded set of hypotheses, and then conclude C→D from the original set.

If we think about this strategy we can see a *prima facie* reason for the usefulness of the deduction theorem. By including C among the hypotheses we have a *larger* set of hypotheses to work with, *and* we have a simpler formula to prove, namely D instead of C→D.

The converse of the deduction theorem also holds and we now set about proving this.

(Meta-)Theorem 4.7 (Converse of the Deduction Theorem)

Let H be a set (possibly empty) of wff, and let A and B be any wff.

$$H \vdash (A{\rightarrow}B) \Rightarrow H \cup \{A\} \vdash B$$

Proof The proof in this case is very straightforward.

1.	A→B	assumed deduced from H
2.	A	Hypothesis
3. ∴	B	MP on 1 and 2
Hence	$H \cup \{A\} \vdash B$	

(End)

The Deduction Theorem gives an alternative proof of (Meta-)Theorem 4.3.

(Meta-)Theorem 4.3 (Again)

$$\{(A{\rightarrow}B), (B{\rightarrow}C)\} \vdash (A{\rightarrow}C)$$

Proof The proof is again very straightforward.

1.	A	Hypothesis (for the sake of the proof)
2.	A→B	Hypothesis (given)
3. ∴	B	MP on 1 and 2
4.	B→C	Hypothesis (given)
5. ∴	C	MP on 4 and 5
So,	$\{(A{\rightarrow}B), (B{\rightarrow}C), A\} \vdash C$	
Hence	$\{(A{\rightarrow}B), (B{\rightarrow}C)\} \vdash A{\rightarrow}C$	by deduction theorem.

(End)

(Meta-)Theorem 4.8

$$\vdash \neg\neg A \to A$$

Proof Again we make use of TI

1.	$\neg\neg A \to (\neg\neg\neg\neg A \to \neg\neg A)$	Ax1
2.	$(\neg\neg\neg\neg A \to \neg\neg A) \to (\neg A \to \neg\neg\neg A)$	Ax3
3. $\therefore$	$\neg\neg A \to (\neg A \to \neg\neg\neg A)$	TI using 1 and 2
4.	$(\neg A \to \neg\neg\neg A) \to (\neg\neg A \to A)$	Ax3
5. $\therefore$	$\neg\neg A \to (\neg\neg A \to A)$	TI using 3 and 4
6.	$(\neg\neg A \to (\neg\neg A \to A)) \to ((\neg\neg A \to \neg\neg A) \to (\neg\neg A \to A))$	Ax2
7. $\therefore$	$(\neg\neg A \to \neg\neg A) \to (\neg\neg A \to A)$	MP on
8.	$\neg\neg A \to \neg\neg A$	Theorem of form A→A
9. $\therefore$	$\neg\neg A \to A$	MP

(End)

As you can see, although the deduction theorem does make proofs easier, it doesn't necessarily make them trivial. A little thought is required in order to come up with the first line of the above proof.

Another example of a bit of subtlety is the following proof of another important result.

(Meta-)Theorem 4.9

$$\vdash (\neg A \to A) \to A$$

Proof Reflecting on the deduction theorem it seems reasonable to take $\neg A \to A$ as a hypothesis and try to prove A from it. So, let us start with that and see if we can make any progress.

$\neg A \to A$ Hypothesis

Now we need something else: an axiom, say, or a theorem to advance our proof. Suppose we look at the axioms.

$(\neg A \to A) \to (A \to (\neg A \to A))$ Ax1

Here, $A \to (\neg A \to A)$ occurs the wrong way round, so maybe

$$A \to ((\neg A \to A) \to A)$$

The expression we want is tantalisingly there, but there does not appear to be much future in it, since we have no immediate way of detaching the A to get our result. So let's try the second axiom. We need something like

$$((\neg A \to A) \to (X \to A)) \to ((\neg A \to A) \to X) \to ((\neg A \to A) \to A)$$

where X would need to be such that we can prove $(\neg A \to A) \to (X \to A)$ and $(\neg A \to A) \to X$, so that we can detach both of these to get our result.

This seems a bit of a tall order, so we will leave it for the present and hope we don't have to come back to it. Let's try the third axiom.

$$(\neg(\neg A \to A) \to \neg A) \to (A \to (\neg A \to A))$$

This is the wrong way round again, so

$$(\neg A \to \neg(\neg A \to A)) \to ((\neg A \to A) \to A)$$

Again our result is tantalisingly close, but again there does not appear to be an immediate path to a proof. However, before we abandon this too hastily, let us consider that maybe, rather than trying to prove $(\neg A \to A) \to A$ directly, we should try to prove $\neg A \to \neg(\neg A \to A)$ instead. Then we would have our result next step. Our strategy then would be to try to prove $\neg(\neg A \to A)$ from $\neg A$.

Perhaps we should try

$$\neg A \to (X \to \neg(\neg A \to A))$$

and use the second axiom to make progress. But what can X be? Is there any X at all which will allow us to write down $\neg A \to (X \to \neg(\neg A \to A))$ immediately? Well, there is! Recall our theorem $\vdash \neg A \to (A \to B)$ where B is *any* wff. This theorem is extremely useful in practice and we will make use of it now.

$\neg A \to (A \to \neg(\neg A \to A))$	Theorem
$(\neg A \to (A \to \neg(\neg A \to A))) \to ((\neg A \to A) \to (\neg A \to \neg(\neg A \to A)))$ Ax2	
$\therefore (\neg A \to A) \to (\neg A \to \neg(\neg A \to A))$	MP

Well, we seem to be veering away from deducing $\neg A \to \neg(\neg A \to A)$ from $\neg A$. However, we are back to $\neg A \to A$, so maybe we should continue to see if something worthwhile turns up.

$(\neg A \to \neg(\neg A \to A)) \to ((\neg A \to A) \to A)$	Ax3
$\therefore (\neg A \to A) \to ((\neg A \to A) \to A)$	TI (previous two lines)
$\neg A \to A$	Hypothesis
$\therefore ((\neg A \to A) \to A)$	MP
$\therefore A$	MP (using hypothesis again)

We are in business! We have deduced A from the hypothesis $\neg A \to A$, and we can now use our deduction theorem to get our result. Thus

$$\{\neg A \to A\} \vdash A$$

Therefore $\vdash (\neg A \to A) \to A$ By deduction theorem

(End)

Exercise

4.5 Prove the following in AL.

(i) $\{B, A \rightarrow (B \rightarrow C)\} \vdash A \rightarrow C$

(ii) $\vdash (A \rightarrow (B \rightarrow C)) \rightarrow (B \rightarrow (A \rightarrow C))$

(iii) $\vdash (A \rightarrow B) \rightarrow (\neg B \rightarrow \neg A)$

(iv) $\vdash \neg(A \rightarrow B) \rightarrow \neg B$

(v) $\vdash \neg(A \rightarrow B) \rightarrow (\neg A \rightarrow \neg B)$

(vi) $\vdash \neg(A \rightarrow B) \rightarrow (C \rightarrow \neg B)$

(vii) $\vdash (A \rightarrow \neg A) \rightarrow \neg A$

(viii) $\vdash (\neg A \rightarrow B) \rightarrow ((\neg A \rightarrow \neg B) \rightarrow A)$

(ix) $\vdash (A \rightarrow B) \rightarrow ((\neg A \rightarrow B) \rightarrow B)$

Now we prove a (meta-)theorem which we will make use of later on.

(Meta-)Theorem 4.10

$$\vdash A \rightarrow (\neg B \rightarrow \neg(A \rightarrow B))$$

Proof The key to proving this theorem is a result from exercise 4.5 (iii) above. (I hope you have succeeded in proving it!) Look at

$$(\neg B \rightarrow \neg(A \rightarrow B))$$

and think of it the other way round

$$((A \rightarrow B) \rightarrow B)$$

Now look at (iii) above and notice that an instance of this result is

$$((A \rightarrow B) \rightarrow B) \rightarrow (\neg B \rightarrow \neg(A \rightarrow B))$$

So, if we could prove

$$A \rightarrow ((A \rightarrow B) \rightarrow B)$$

we could get the result we want immediately.

But, this is easy to prove – it is just a disguised form of modus ponens! We prove it as follows.

A	Hypothesis
A→B	Hypothesis
∴ B	MP

Hence $\{A, A \rightarrow B\} \vdash B$

Therefore $\vdash A \rightarrow ((A \rightarrow B) \rightarrow B)$ using deduction theorem twice

But $\vdash ((A \rightarrow B) \rightarrow B) \rightarrow (\neg B \rightarrow \neg(A \rightarrow B))$ Theorem (Exercise 4.5(iii))

Therefore $\vdash A \rightarrow (\neg B \rightarrow \neg(A \rightarrow B))$ TI

(End)

4.5 Important Properties of AL

Now that we have developed some practical expertise in the propositional logic system AL, it is time to consider how 'strong' a system it is: to determine whether it has some centrally important properties. We would like to know if the theorems we can prove in our system are all 'true', i.e. are all tautologies. We would like to make sure our system is consistent. And, it would be nice to find that our system is complete, i.e. that all the truths of propositional logic can actually be proved!

We turn our attention then to proving that AL has all three properties, i.e. that it is sound, consistent and complete.

4.5.1 Soundness

A propositional logic system in which all the theorems are tautologies is called *sound*. Up to this, of course, we have not considered the notions of truth and falsity in connection with AL. Our treatment has been purely formal. We have only been concerned with proofs and theorems, essentially with what wff followed from the formal axioms by the modus ponens rule of inference. It is time now to relate AL to the real world or, more particularly, the world of true and false.

To do this we define a truth valuation.

Definition A *truth valuation* is a function, v, from the set of well-formed formulae to the set {T,F} such that for any wff A and B:

(i) $v(\neg A) \neq v(A)$

(ii) $v(A \rightarrow B) = F$ if and only if $v(A) = T$ and $v(B) = F$

Thus, for example

$v(p_1) = T$ $v(p_2) = T$ $v(p_3) = F$ $v(p_4) = T$
$v(\neg p_1) = F$ $v(\neg p_3) = T$ $v(p_1 \rightarrow p_2) = T$ $v(p_1 \rightarrow p_3) = F$

is a possible part of a truth valuation, while

$v(p_1) = T$ $v(p_2) = T$ $v(p_3) = F$ $v(\neg p_1) = T$
$v(\neg p_3) = T$ $v(p_1 \rightarrow p_2) = F$ $v(p_1 \rightarrow p_3) = F$

is part of a mapping from the set of wff to {T,F} but it is *not* a truth valuation. Why?

Note that a truth valuation v is a *function*. So there is no question of a wff A having more than one value under a particular v. Hence v(A) cannot be both T and F at the same time.

You may like to check that this definition of truth values corresponding to ¬ and → accords with the truth table definitions in Chapter 1. Furthermore, although we have not made use of, or even referred to, the other logical connectives, ∧, ∨, ↔, in this chapter so far, we could define them in terms of ¬

and $\rightarrow$ and check that the value they acquire under the mapping v are also consistent with the truth tables of Chapter 1. Thus

$A \wedge B$ may be defined as $\neg(A \rightarrow \neg B)$

$A \vee B$ may be defined as $(\neg A \rightarrow B)$

$A \leftrightarrow B$ may be defined as $\neg((A \rightarrow B) \rightarrow \neg(B \rightarrow A))$

Then, for example,

$A \vee B$ is F

if and only if $(\neg A \rightarrow B)$ is F

i.e. if and only if $v(\neg A)$ is T and $v(B)$ is F

i.e. if and only if $v(A)$ is F and $v(B)$ is F.

This is exactly what our truth table would have told us.

Exercises

4.6 Show that the above definition of a truth valuation is in accordance with the truth table meanings of $\neg$ and $\rightarrow$.

4.7 Show that the truth values of $\wedge$ and $\leftrightarrow$ as defined above agree with the truth tables for these connectives.

Definition A wff A such that $v(A) = T$ for all truth valuations v is called a *tautology*. We write $\models A$

(Meta-)Theorem 4.11 (The Soundness Theorem)

Every (meta-)theorem in AL is a tautology
i.e. $\vdash A \Rightarrow \models A$

Proof We prove this (meta-)theorem by induction on the number of steps in the proof of a (meta-)theorem in AL. The simplest theorems are the axioms, which require just one step in each case, namely, simply writing down the axiom. As our basis for induction, then, we must show that each of the axioms is a tautology.

Basis step

Case 1

A has the form $B \rightarrow (C \rightarrow B)$.

Suppose $v(A) = F$ for some v.

Then $v(B) = T$ and $v(C \rightarrow B) = F$.

Hence $v(B) = F$ and $v(C) = T$.

But, as v is a function, we cannot have $v(B) = T$ and $v(B) = F$.

Therefore we conclude that there is no v such that $v(A) = F$.

Hence $\models A$.

Case 2

A has the form $(B \rightarrow (C \rightarrow D)) \rightarrow ((B \rightarrow C) \rightarrow (B \rightarrow D))$.

Suppose $v(A) = F$ for some v.

Then $v(B \rightarrow (C \rightarrow D)) = T$ and $v((B \rightarrow C) \rightarrow (B \rightarrow D)) = F$.

Hence, from the latter, $v(B \rightarrow C) = T$ and $v(B \rightarrow D) = F$.

And from the latter $v(B) = T$ and $v(D) = F$. *

Now, since $v(B) = T$ and $v(B \rightarrow C) = T$, we require $v(C) = T$,

and as $v(B) = T$ and $v(B \rightarrow (C \rightarrow D)) = T$ we require $v(C \rightarrow D) = T$.

Therefore, since $v(C)$ is required to be T we require $v(D) = T$.

But now we find that we need $v(D) = F$ (see * above) and $v(D) = T$!

Which, of course, we cannot have.

Therefore we conclude that there is no v such that $v(A) = F$.

Hence $\models$ A.

Case 3

A has the form $(\neg B \rightarrow \neg C) \rightarrow (C \rightarrow B)$.

Suppose $v(A) = F$ for some v.

Then $v(\neg B \rightarrow \neg C) = T$ and $v(C \rightarrow B) = F$.

Thence $v(C) = T$ and $v(B) = F$.

From $v(C) = T$ we have $v(\neg C) = F$.

But for $v(\neg B \rightarrow \neg C) = T$, we require $v(\neg B) = F$ and hence $v(B) = T$.

But we already need $v(B) = F$.

As these requirements are incompatible, we conclude that $v(A)$ cannot be F.

Hence $\models$ A.

Therefore if A is a theorem with a one-step proof it is a tautology.

Induction step

Suppose, if $\vdash$ A in n or fewer steps then $\models$ A (induction hypothesis).

And now suppose $\vdash$ A in n+1 steps.

If A is an axiom then $\models$ A as in basis case.

If A is not an axiom, it must follow by modus ponens from two earlier wff, say A_i, $A_i \rightarrow A$, in the proof. Since A_i, and $A_i \rightarrow A$ have been proved in n or fewer steps we can use the Induction Hypothesis to conclude that they are both tautologies.

But then A *must* be a tautology too, since if $v(A_i) = T$ (which it is because it is a tautology) and $v(A) = F$ then $v(A_i \rightarrow A) = F$, which would violate the induction hypothesis.

Therefore, by the principle of induction, if $\vdash$ A then $\models$ A.

(End)

Exercise

4.8   Show, using the definition of truth valuation given above, that each of the following is a tautology:

    (i) $A \rightarrow A$
    (ii) $\neg\neg A \rightarrow A$
    (iii) $\neg A \rightarrow (A \rightarrow B)$
    (iv) $(\neg A \rightarrow A) \rightarrow A$
    (v) $(\neg A \rightarrow B) \rightarrow ((A \rightarrow B) \rightarrow B)$

4.5.2 Consistency

We have already indicated that consistency is a central consideration in logic. Up to now we have relied on an intuitive appreciation of the concept. But what exactly do we mean by consistency? Can we give it a technical grounding?

For the present we shall use the word 'system' to refer to a system of propositional logic, i.e. a formal system which includes at least all the theorems of AL. We may speak about a system as being an *extension* of AL if it is constructed by modifying or enlarging the axiom system of AL so as to allow all the theorems of AL to be proved, and possibly more.

Definition   A system (such as AL itself) is *consistent* if it is not possible to prove both A and $\neg$A for any wff A
           i.e. not both $\vdash$ A and $\vdash$ $\neg$A.
           Hence if $\vdash$ A then $\nvdash$ $\neg$A, and if $\vdash$ $\neg$A then $\nvdash$ A.

We can now easily prove that AL is consistent.

(Meta-)Theorem 4.12

AL is consistent.

Proof   Suppose $\vdash$ A and $\vdash$ $\neg$A for some wff A.
        Then both A and $\neg$A are tautologies, by the soundness theorem.
        Therefore $v(A) = T$ and $v(\neg A) = T$ for every truth valuation v.
        Therefore $v(A) = v(\neg A)$.
        But this cannot be (by definition of v).
        Therefore not both $\vdash$ A and $\vdash$ $\neg$A, for any wff A.
        Therefore AL is consistent.

                                                 (End)

Consistency is a vitally important property for any system of logic to have; if a system is not consistent, all hell breaks loose and any and every wff can be proved! Let us explore a number of different ways of characterising consistency. First, let us prove the all hell breaks loose property.

We will be using a variation on the $\vdash$ symbol – essentially, we will use $\vdash_S$ to denote $\vdash$ in the system S.

(Meta-)Theorem 4.13

If a system S is inconsistent then $\vdash_S$ A for every wff A.

Proof   S is inconsistent.

∴ There is some wff B, say, such that $\vdash_S$ B and $\vdash_S$ ¬B

But ¬B → (B→A)   Theorem of AL, where A is any wff

∴ B→A   MP

∴ A   MP

(End)

Immediately we have another result.

(Meta-)Theorem 4.14

If a system S is inconsistent then $\vdash_S$ ⊥.

Proof Since $\vdash_S$ A for *any* wff A (by (meta-)theorem 4.13), then $\vdash_S$ ⊥.

(End)

(Meta-)Theorem 4.15

A system S is consistent if and only if there is at least one wff A such that $\nvdash_S$ A.

Proof

If: Suppose $\nvdash_S$ A . Assume S is inconsistent.

Then there is some wff B, say, such that $\vdash_S$ B and $\vdash_S$ ¬B

But ¬B → (B→A)   Theorem of AL

∴ B→A   MP

∴ A   MP

But this contradicts $\nvdash_S$ A

Hence S is consistent.

Only if: Suppose S is consistent.

Take any wff B.

If $\vdash_S$ B then $\nvdash_S$ ¬B.

Take A = ¬B

Otherwise take A = B

(End)

4.5.3 Completeness

At this stage we have established that AL has two important properties: it is sound and consistent. But there is one more property that we would like AL to have – completeness. What is completeness?

Definition   A system is *complete* if every tautology is a theorem

$$\text{i.e } \vDash A \Rightarrow \vdash A$$

It is a little more difficult to prove the completeness of AL than its soundness or consistency. First we prove a few preliminary theorems.

(Meta-)Theorem 4.16

Let A be any wff, and let $p_1, p_2, \ldots, p_n$ be the basic propositions of which A is formed. Let v be any truth valuation and let $q_1, q_2, \ldots, q_n$ be defined as follows:

$$q_i = p_i \text{ if } v(p_i) = T$$
$$q_i = \neg p_i \text{ if } v(p_i) = F$$

Also let A' = A if v(A) = T and A' = ¬A if v(A) = F. Then

$$\{q_1, q_2, \ldots, q_n\} \vdash A'$$

Proof By induction on the structure of A.

Basis step

The simplest form of A is $A = p_i$.

Then, if $v(p_i) = T$, $q_i = p_i$ and $A' = A = p_i$.

Hence to show that $\{q_i\} \vdash A'$ we need to show that $\{p_i\} \vdash p_i$ and this is patently true.

Similarly, if $v(p_i) = F$, $q_i = \neg p_i$ and $A' = \neg A = \neg p_i$.

Hence, $\{q_i\} \vdash A'$ since this is the same as $\{\neg p_i\} \vdash \neg p_i$, which is again clearly true.

Induction step

Case 1

A = ¬B

Suppose v(A) = T. Then v(B) = F and B' = ¬B

By induction hypothesis $\{q_1, q_2, \ldots, q_n\} \vdash B'$

i.e. $\{q_1, q_2, \ldots, q_n\} \vdash \neg B$

i.e. $\{q_1, q_2, \ldots, q_n\} \vdash A$

But A' = A, since v(A) = T

∴ $\{q_1, q_2, \ldots, q_n\} \vdash A'$

Now suppose v(A) = F. Then A' = ¬A.

And v(B) = T, B' = B.

By induction hypothesis $\{q_1, q_2, \ldots, q_n\} \vdash B'$

i.e. $\{q_1, q_2, \ldots, q_n\} \vdash B$

But $\vdash B \to \neg\neg B$

i.e. $\vdash B \to \neg A$ (since $A = \neg B$)

Hence $\{q_1, q_2, ..., q_n\} \vdash \neg A$

$\therefore \{q_1, q_2, ..., q_n\} \vdash A'$

Case 2

$A = B \to C$

Suppose $v(A) = F$. Then $A' = \neg A = \neg(B \to C)$.

And $v(B) = T$, $v(C) = F$.

Hence $B' = B$ and $C' = \neg C$.

By induction hypothesis

$\{q_1, q_2, ..., q_n\} \vdash B'$ and $\{q_1, q_2, ..., q_n\} \vdash C'$

i.e. $\{q_1, q_2, ..., q_n\} \vdash B$ and $\{q_1, q_2, ..., q_n\} \vdash \neg C$

But $\vdash B \to (\neg C \to \neg(B \to C))$ Theorem 4.11

$\therefore \{q_1, q_2, ..., q_n\} \vdash \neg(B \to C)$ Using MP twice

i.e. $\{q_1, q_2, ..., q_n\} \vdash A'$

If $v(A) = T$ there are essentially two cases to consider

(i) $v(B) = F$ (ii) $v(C) = T$

The reader is invited to establish the proof in these two cases for herself.

(End)

To see an illustration of the theorem consider the wff

$A = p_1 \to \neg(p_2 \to (\neg p_1 \to p_1))$

and suppose we have the truth valuation v such that $v(p_1) = T$, $v(p_2) = F$. Then we can determine without too much difficulty that $v(A) = F$.

Hence q_1 is p_1, q_2 is $\neg p_2$ and A' is $\neg A$.

The theorem says that $\{q_1, q_2\} \vdash A'$

i.e. $\{p_1, \neg p_2\} \vdash \neg A$

i.e. $\{p_1, \neg p_2\} \vdash \neg(p_1 \to \neg(p_2 \to (\neg p_1 \to p_1)))$

Exercises

4.9   Prove $\{p_1, \neg p_2\} \vdash \neg(p_1 \to \neg(p_2 \to (\neg p_1 \to p_1)))$ directly, i.e. using only the axioms, modus ponens and the deduction theorem.

4.10 Extract the appropriate theorems from the wff

$A = (p_2 \to \neg p_1) \to (\neg p_1 \to p_2))$

under the following truth valuations and prove them.

(i) $v(p_1) = T$, $v(p_2) = T$

(ii) $v(p_1) = T$, $v(p_2) = F$

(iii) $v(p_1) = F$, $v(p_2) = T$

(iv) $v(p_1) = F$, $v(p_2) = F$

(Meta-)Theorem 4.17

$\vdash (B \rightarrow A) \rightarrow ((\neg B \rightarrow A) \rightarrow A)$ **for any wff A, B.**

Proof Again we make use of the theorem $(B \rightarrow A) \rightarrow (\neg A \rightarrow \neg B)$ (see Exercise 4.5 (iii)). Using this, the proof is fairly straightforward.

1.	$B \rightarrow A$	Hypothesis
2.	$(B \rightarrow A) \rightarrow (\neg A \rightarrow \neg B)$	Theorem
3.	$\therefore \ \neg A \rightarrow \neg B$	MP on 1 and 2
4.	$\neg B \rightarrow A$	Hypothesis
5.	$\therefore \ \neg A \rightarrow A$	TI using 3 and 4
6.	$(\neg A \rightarrow A) \rightarrow A$	Theorem
7.	$\therefore \ A$	MP on 5 and 6

Hence $\{(B \rightarrow A), (\neg B \rightarrow A)\} \vdash A$.

Therefore $\{(B \rightarrow A)\} \vdash (\neg B \rightarrow A) \rightarrow A$ by the deduction theorem.

Therefore $\vdash (B \rightarrow A) \rightarrow ((\neg B \rightarrow A) \rightarrow A)$ by the deduction theorem.

(End)

(Meta-)Theorem 4.18

If $\{A_1, A_2, ..., A_{n-1}, A_n\} \vdash A$

and $\{A_1, A_2, ..., A_{n-1}, \neg A_n\} \vdash A$ **for any wff $A_1, ..., A_n, A$**

then $\{A_1, A_2, ..., A_{n-1}\} \vdash A$

Proof	$\{A_1, A_2, ..., A_{n-1}, A_n\} \vdash A$	Given
Therefore	$\{A_1, A_2, ..., A_{n-1}\} \vdash A_n \rightarrow A$	Deduction theorem
But	$\vdash (A_n \rightarrow A) \rightarrow ((\neg A_n \rightarrow A) \rightarrow A)$	Theorem 4.17
Therefore	$\{A_1, A_2, ..., A_{n-1}\} \vdash (\neg A_n \rightarrow A) \rightarrow A$	MP *
	$\{A_1, A_2, ..., A_{n-1}, \neg A_n\} \vdash A$	Given
Therefore	$\{A_1, A_2, ..., A_{n-1}\} \vdash \neg A_n \rightarrow A$	Deduction theorem *
Therefore	$\{A_1, A_2, ..., A_{n-1}\} \vdash A$	MP, using conclusions marked *

(End)

Now we are ready to prove the important completeness theorem.

(Meta-)Theorem 4.19 (The Completeness Theorem)

If A is a tautology then it is a theorem of AL

i.e. $\vDash A \Rightarrow \vdash A$

Proof We make direct use of (meta-)theorems 4.16 and 4.18.

If $p_1, p_2, ..., p_n$ are the basic propositions of which A is formed, and $q_1, q_2, ..., q_n$, A' are defined as in (meta-)theorem 4.16 then

$\{q_1, q_2, ..., q_n\} \vdash A'$

Now, since A is a tautology, A' is always = A and, therefore

$$\{q_1, q_2, ..., q_n\} \vdash A$$

Then if $v(p_n) = T$ then $q_n = p_n$, and, therefore, $\{q_1, q_2, ..., p_n\} \vdash A$.

While if $v(p_n) = F$ then $q_n = \neg p_n$, and, therefore, $\{q_1, q_2, ..., \neg p_n\} \vdash A$.

Hence, by (meta-)theorem 4.18, $\{q_1, q_2, ..., q_{n-1}\} \vdash A$.

But, again, because A is a tautology we would have

$$\{q_1, q_2, ..., p_{n-1}\} \vdash A$$

and $\{q_1, q_2, ..., \neg p_{n-1}\} \vdash A$

and hence $\{q_1, q_2, ..., q_{n-2}\} \vdash A$

Proceeding in this fashion, we eliminate all the q_i, and end up with $\vdash A$

(End)

Exercises

4.11 The wff $\neg(p_1 \to \neg p_2) \to p_2$ is a tautology. Prove $\vdash \neg(p_1 \to \neg p_2) \to p_2$ using the method employed in the completeness theorem.

4.12 Let $p_1, p_2, ..., p_n$ be the basic propositions occurring in a wff A, and let $A_1, A_2, ..., A_n$ be any wff. Let B be the wff which results from the substitution of A_i for all occurrences of p_i, $i = 1, ..., n$. Prove that B is a theorem of AL if A is.

4.6 Decidability

In these days of computer dominance it is often important to investigate whether problems will yield to a mechanical or algorithmic solution. We say that a question is *decidable* if there is an algorithm which will deliver its answer, say, yes or no. In the present context we are interested in whether AL is decidable, i.e. whether there is a mechanical procedure to reveal of any wff A whether or not it is a theorem of AL. In fact, given the completeness theorem, it is very easy to prove that AL is indeed decidable.

(Meta-)Theorem 4.20 (Decidability of AL)

AL is decidable

Proof Given any wff A, if A is a tautology then it is a theorem of AL
i.e. if $\models A$ then $\vdash A$

Consequently, to see if A is a theorem, first check to see if it is a tautology. But this can be done mechanically, say by means of a truth table.

Therefore AL is decidable.

(End)

The outcome of this (meta-)theorem is that it is very easy to decide if a wff is a theorem of AL or not; simply construct a truth table for the wff and see if it a tautology or not. Does this mean that the difficulties and subtleties of proving wff from the axioms and modus ponens (even with the aid of the deduction theorem) can all be forgotten about? To some extent, yes. But not completely; we had to prove the Soundness and Completeness Theorems before getting this far, and they required results which had to be established from first principles, as it were.

You may wonder whether our other approaches to propositional logic – tableau systems and natural deduction – are also sound and complete. Indeed they are! In our headlong rush to develop and sharpen our skills in deploying these systems we did not pause to prove that they have these properties, but no doubt the reader will now turn to that task herself.

4.7 Summary

- In this chapter we have studied the classic formulation of propositional logic – the axiomatic formulation. It is an elegant and economical system, built on a very lean base. But the very exiguity of the base meant that the resources for proving results were meagre and that deductions were often subtle, difficult and obscure. Nevertheless we were able to develop reasonably fruitful strategies for advancing proofs and we ended up with a number of interesting and important theorems.

- The formal axiomatic system of propositional logic, AL, has
  - (1) An alphabet of symbols $\Sigma = \{\neg, \rightarrow, (,), p_1, p_2, p_3, ..., p_n, ...\}$
  - (2) A set of well-formed formulae WF = $\{x \mid x = p_i,$ for i =1, 2, 3, ...

    or $x = (\neg A)$ where $A \in$ WF

    or $x = (A \rightarrow B)$, where $A \in$ WF, $B \in$ WF$\}$
  - (3) A set of axiom schemas

    Ax1 $A \rightarrow (B \rightarrow A)$

    Ax2 $(A \rightarrow (B \rightarrow C)) \rightarrow ((A \rightarrow B) \rightarrow (A \rightarrow C))$

    Ax3 $(\neg A \rightarrow \neg B) \rightarrow (B \rightarrow A)$
  - (4) A rule of deduction (modus ponens):

    From A and A→B, B can be derived, where A and B are any well-formed formulae.

  WF is given by an inductive definition.

  A deduction in AL is a sequence of wff $F_1, F_2, ..., F_n$, such that for each i $(1 \le i \le n)$,

           (a) F_i is an axiom

  or   (b) F_i is a hypothesis

  or   (c) F_i is derived by modus ponens from F_j, F_k, where j,k $\le$ i.

- A (meta-)theorem which plays an important role in facilitating the construction of proofs is the deduction theorem, namely, if $H \cup \{A\} \vdash B$ then $H \vdash (A \rightarrow B)$.

- The general strategy suggested by the deduction theorem is that whenever a wff of the form C→D is to be established it may be useful to include C among the hypotheses, derive D from the expanded set of hypotheses, and then conclude C→D from the original set.
- A truth valuation is a function, v, from the set of well-formed formulae to the set {T,F} such that for any wff A and B:
    - (i) $v(\neg A) \neq v(A)$
    - (ii) $v(A \rightarrow B) = F$ if and only if $v(A) = T$ and $v(B) = F$
- The soundness theorem states that every theorem in AL is a tautology,

    i.e. $\vdash A \Rightarrow \vDash A$
- A system is consistent if it is not possible to prove *both* A and ¬A for any wff A, i.e. not both $\vdash A$ and $\vdash \neg A$.
- The completeness theorem states that if A is a tautology then it is a theorem of AL

    i.e. $\vDash A \Rightarrow \vdash A$
- AL is decidable by means of truth tables.

In this chapter we have
(1)   defined the structure of a formal axiomatic system.
(2)   studied an axiomatic system for propositional logic, AL.
(3)   developed skill in proving (meta-)theorems.
(4)   understood the proof-theoretic notion of consistency.
(5)   distinguished between the ideas of soundness and completeness.
(6)   proved the soundness and completeness of AL.

In the next chapter we look at how we can develop a mechanical procedure for proving the validity of logical arguments.

Miscellaneous Exercises

1.   Which of the following are wff and which are not?
     (i) $(\neg(p_3 \rightarrow (\neg p_2)))$
     (ii) $(p_3 \rightarrow (\neg p_1 \rightarrow p_3))$
     (iii) $(p_3 \rightarrow ((\neg p_2)) \rightarrow p_1))$
     (iv) $\neg A$
     (v) $(((p_3) \rightarrow p_1) \rightarrow (((\neg p_4) \rightarrow p_2) \rightarrow (\neg p_3)) \rightarrow (p_2 \rightarrow p_1))) \rightarrow p_3$

2.   Prove the following in AL
     (i) $\{p_3\} \vdash p_2 \rightarrow p_3$
     (ii) $\{p_1, \neg p_1\} \vdash p_3$
     (iii) $\{p_1 \rightarrow (\neg p_2 \rightarrow p_3)\} \vdash p_1 \rightarrow (\neg p_3 \rightarrow \neg \neg p_2)$

3. Prove the following in AL:
   (i) $\{\neg B, A \rightarrow (\neg B \rightarrow C)\} \vdash A \rightarrow C$
   (ii) $\{\neg A, A \rightarrow (\neg B \rightarrow C)\} \vdash A \rightarrow C$
   (iii) $\vdash A \rightarrow (B \rightarrow (\neg B \rightarrow A))$
   (iv) $\vdash \neg(B \rightarrow C) \rightarrow (C \rightarrow B)$
   (v) $\vdash (\neg A \rightarrow B) \rightarrow (\neg B \rightarrow A)$
   (vi) $\vdash \neg(A \rightarrow \neg\neg B)) \rightarrow \neg(A \rightarrow B))$
   (vii) $\vdash (A \wedge B) \rightarrow A$
   (viii) $\vdash A \rightarrow (A \vee B)$
   (ix) $\{(A \rightarrow B), (A \rightarrow C)\} \vdash A \rightarrow (B \wedge C)$
   (x) $\vdash (A \wedge \neg A) \rightarrow B$
   (xi) $\vdash A \rightarrow (B \wedge C) \rightarrow (A \rightarrow (B \rightarrow C))$

4. Prove that $\vdash A \leftrightarrow B$ if and only if $\vdash A \rightarrow B$ and $\vdash B \rightarrow A$.

5. Extract the appropriate theorems from the wff
   $$A = (p_2 \rightarrow \neg(\neg p_1 \rightarrow p_3)) \rightarrow (\neg p_3 \rightarrow p_2)$$
   under the following truth valuations and prove them:
   (i) $v(p_1) = T, v(p_2) = T, v(p_3) = T$
   (ii) $v(p_1) = T, v(p_2) = F, v(p_3) = T$
   (iii) $v(p_1) = F, v(p_2) = T, v(p_3) = T$
   (iv) $v(p_1) = F, v(p_2) = F, v(p_3) = T$
   (v) $v(p_1) = F, v(p_2) = F, v(p_3) = F$

CHAPTER 5

Resolution in Propositional Logic

Chapter Aims

(1)   To justify a rule of deduction suitable for the automating of logic.
(2)   To introduce the idea of normal forms.
(3)   To understand the resolution rule as applied in propositional logic.
(4)   To apply resolution to problem solving.

After studying this chapter you should
(a)   understand the terms conjunctive normal forms, disjunctive normal forms, literal, clause, resolution.
(b)   be able to convert a wff to a normal form.
(c)   understand the resolution principle for propositional logic.
(d)   be able to construct resolution proofs and refutations.

5.1 Introduction

No doubt you will have been struck by the difference in difficulty between the problem solving strategies in Chapters 1 and 2 and those in Chapters 3 and 4. In the earlier chapters the approaches were mechanical and straightforward: even a dumb computer could be programmed to carry them out. But in the last two chapters considerable insight and ingenuity were often required to construct proofs and derivations. (All the more interesting and challenging, of course.)

In these days of computer dominance it is important to massage problems into a form suitable for solution by computer and to develop techniques which allow for mechanical implementation. This applies as much to computations in logic as in any other area (or even more). Hence, systems such as tableaux are of primary interest. However, there is an even more important and widely used mechanical method of dealing with problems in logic than tableaux systems, and it is to that method that we turn in this chapter.

The method in question is resolution. It was developed by J. A. Robinson in the 1960s and has undergone intensive investigation and implementation ever since. Like modus ponens in axiomatic logic, the resolution principle provides a single inference rule. The big difference is that the resolution rule is easily implemented on computers.

In order to make use of resolution, wff must be in a special so-called *normal form*. Before we examine the resolution principle, then, we must give consideration to normal (or canonical) forms.

5.2 Normal Forms

Our normal forms for propositional wff are based on the 'natural' connectives ∧, ∨ and ¬. Every wff can be transformed into an equivalent wff in normal form. To do this we make use of the equivalences established in Chapter 1, which we recall here.

$A \wedge 0 \equiv 0$	Zero of ∧
$A \wedge 1 \equiv A$	Identity of ∧
$A \vee 0 \equiv A$	Identity of ∨
$A \vee 1 \equiv 1$	Zero of ∨
$A \wedge A \equiv A$	Idempotence
$A \vee A \equiv A$	Idempotence
$A \wedge \neg A \equiv 0$	Contradiction
$A \vee \neg A \equiv 1$	Tatuology
$\neg \neg A \equiv A$	Law of double negation
$A \wedge B \equiv B \wedge A$	Commutativity
$A \vee B \equiv B \vee A$	Commutativity
$A \wedge (B \vee C) \equiv (A \wedge B) \vee (A \wedge C)$	Distributivity
$A \vee (B \wedge C) \equiv (A \vee B) \wedge (A \vee C)$	Distributivity
$A \wedge (A \vee B) \equiv A$	Absorption
$A \vee (A \wedge B) \equiv A$	Absorption
$A \vee (\neg A \wedge B) \equiv A \vee B$	Absorption
$A \wedge (\neg A \vee B) \equiv A \wedge B$	Absorption
$\neg(A \wedge B) \equiv \neg A \vee \neg B$	De Morgan's law
$\neg(A \vee B) \equiv \neg A \wedge \neg B$	De Morgan's law
$(A \wedge B) \vee (A \wedge \neg B) \equiv A$	
$A {\rightarrow} B \equiv \neg A \vee B$	
$A {\rightarrow} B \equiv \neg(A \wedge \neg B)$	

We recall that two wff, A and B, are equivalent if A has exactly the same truth value as B under all assignments of truth values to the basic propositions of which they are composed. Thus

$$(p_1 {\rightarrow} p_2) \rightarrow (\neg p_3 \vee p_1) \equiv \neg((p_1 {\rightarrow} p_2) \wedge \neg(\neg p_3 \vee p_1))$$

since $(p_1 {\rightarrow} p_2) \rightarrow (\neg p_3 \vee p_1)$ has the same truth value as $\neg((p_1 {\rightarrow} p_2) \wedge \neg(\neg p_3 \vee p_1))$ no matter what the values of p_1, p_2 or p_3.

In addition to the above we will also make use of the equivalence

$$A \leftrightarrow B \equiv (A \rightarrow B) \wedge (B \rightarrow A)$$

which, no doubt, the reader will verify for herself.

Our objective is to convert every wff into one containing only $\wedge$, $\vee$ and $\neg$.

The basic propositions of which wff are composed are called *atomic formulae* or *atoms*. In addition to atom we find the concept of literal useful.

Definition   A *literal* is simply an atom or the negation of an atom.

p_2 is a literal.

$\neg p_{12}$ is a literal.

A literal which consists of an atom is called a *positive literal*, e.g. p_1.

A literal which consists of the negation of an atom is called a *negative literal*, e.g. $\neg p_1$.

Definition   A wff is in *conjunctive normal form* (CNF) if it is a conjunction of disjunctions of literals, i.e. if it is in the form

$$A_1 \wedge A_2 \ldots \wedge A_i \ldots \wedge A_n$$

where each A_i is of the form

$$\lambda_1 \vee \lambda_2 \ldots \vee \lambda_j \ldots \vee \lambda_m$$

where each λ_j is a literal.

$(p_2 \vee p_5 \vee \neg p_3) \wedge (\neg p_2 \vee p_1 \vee p_3) \wedge (p_1 \vee p_2 \vee p_3 \vee p_7 \vee p_4)$ is in CNF

as is $(\neg p_1 \vee \neg p_3) \wedge (\neg p_2 \vee \neg p_1 \vee p_3)$

as is p_{10} (by default, as it were).

Definition   A wff is in *disjunctive normal form* (DNF) if it is a disjunction of conjunctions of literals, i.e. if it is in the form

$$A_1 \vee A_2 \ldots \vee A_i \ldots \vee A_n$$

where each A_i is of the form

$$\lambda_1 \wedge \lambda_2 \ldots \wedge \lambda_j \ldots \wedge \lambda_m$$

where each λ_j is a literal.

$(p_2 \wedge p_5 \wedge \neg p_3) \vee (\neg p_2 \wedge p_1 \wedge p_3) \vee (p_1 \wedge p_2 \wedge p_3 \wedge p_7 \wedge p_4)$ is in CNF

as is $(\neg p_1 \wedge \neg p_3) \vee (\neg p_2 \wedge \neg p_1 \wedge p_3)$

as is p_{10} (again, by default).

Exercise

5.1 Categorise each of the following as being in (a) CNF, (b) DNF or (c) neither:

(i) $(p_1 \wedge \neg p_3) \vee (p_2 \wedge \neg p_1)$

(ii) $p_1 \vee (p_2 \wedge \neg p_1)$

(iii) $(p_2 \vee \neg p_3) \vee (p_2 \wedge \neg p_1)$
(iv) $(p_3 \wedge \neg p_3) \vee (p_2 \wedge \neg p_2) \vee (p_1 \wedge \neg p_1)$
(v) $(p_1 \wedge \neg p_3) \vee \neg (p_2 \wedge \neg p_1)$
(vi) $(p_1 \wedge \neg p_3) \vee (p_2 \wedge p_1 \wedge \neg p_3) \vee (p_2 \wedge \neg p_1)$
(vii) $p_1 \wedge \neg p_3 \vee (p_2 \wedge \neg p_1)$
(viii) p_1
(ix) $\neg p_1$

From now on we will concentrate on conjunctive normal forms, i.e. expressions of the form

$$C_1 \wedge C_2 \dots \wedge C_i \dots \wedge C_n$$

where each C_i is a disjunction of literals, i.e it is of the form

$$\lambda_1 \vee \lambda_2 \dots \vee \lambda_j \dots \vee \lambda_m$$

and each λ_j is a literal.

C_i is called a *clause* – giving us the following definition.

Definition   a *clause* is a finite disjunction of literals. A clause may consist of just a single literal, e.g. p_1 or $\neg p_1$, in which case it is called a *unit clause*.

5.2.1 Converting to CNF

In order to work with conjunctive normal forms we need to be able to transform general wff to CNF. This may involve up to 5 stages.

Stage 1: Use the equivalence $A \leftrightarrow B \equiv (A \rightarrow B) \wedge (B \rightarrow A)$ to eliminate $\leftrightarrow$.

Stage 2: Use the equivalence $A \rightarrow B \equiv \neg A \vee B$ to eliminate $\rightarrow$.

Example 5.1

Eliminate $\leftrightarrow$ and $\rightarrow$ from the expression $(p_1 \wedge \neg p_3) \leftrightarrow (p_2 \rightarrow (p_1 \rightarrow \neg p_3))$.

$(p_1 \wedge \neg p_3) \leftrightarrow (p_2 \rightarrow (p_1 \rightarrow \neg p_3))$
$\equiv ((p_1 \wedge \neg p_3) \rightarrow (p_2 \rightarrow (p_1 \rightarrow \neg p_3))) \wedge ((p_2 \rightarrow (p_1 \rightarrow \neg p_3)) \rightarrow (p_1 \wedge \neg p_3))$
$\equiv (\neg (p_1 \wedge \neg p_3) \vee (p_2 \rightarrow (p_1 \rightarrow \neg p_3))) \wedge (\neg (p_2 \rightarrow (p_1 \rightarrow \neg p_3)) \vee (p_1 \wedge \neg p_3))$
$\equiv (\neg (p_1 \wedge \neg p_3) \vee (\neg p_2 \vee (p_1 \rightarrow \neg p_3))) \wedge (\neg (\neg p_2 \vee (p_1 \rightarrow \neg p_3)) \vee (p_1 \wedge \neg p_3))$
$\equiv (\neg (p_1 \wedge \neg p_3) \vee (\neg p_2 \vee (\neg p_1 \vee \neg p_3))) \wedge (\neg (\neg p_2 \vee (\neg p_1 \vee \neg p_3)) \vee (p_1 \wedge \neg p_3))$

Stage 3: Use De Morgan's laws $\neg (A \wedge B) \equiv \neg A \vee \neg B$ and $\neg (A \vee B) \equiv \neg A \wedge \neg B$ to push the negation sign $\neg$ immediately before atomic wff.

Stage 4: Use $\neg \neg A \equiv A$ to eliminate double negation signs.

Example 5.2

$\neg (p_1 \rightarrow \neg p_3) \wedge (\neg p_2 \rightarrow p_3)$ $\equiv \neg (\neg p_1 \vee \neg p_3) \wedge (\neg \neg p_2 \vee p_3)$
$\equiv (\neg \neg p_1 \wedge \neg \neg p_3) \wedge (p_2 \wedge p_3)$
$\equiv (p_1 \wedge p_3) \wedge (p_2 \wedge p_3)$

Of course, if double negation signs appear before the transformations in stage 3 are made there is no need to wait to apply stage 4 – the double negation signs can be dropped immediately.

Stage 5: Use the distributive law $A \lor (B \land C) \equiv (A \lor B) \land (A \lor C)$ to effect the conversion to CNF.

Example 5.3

Express the wff $(\neg p_1 \land (\neg p_2 \to p_3)) \leftrightarrow p_4$ in CNF

$(\neg p_1 \land (\neg p_2 \to p_3)) \leftrightarrow p_4$

$\equiv ((\neg p_1 \land (\neg p_2 \to p_3)) \to p_4) \land (p_4 \to (\neg p_1 \land (\neg p_2 \to p_3)))$	Stage 1
$\equiv ((\neg p_1 \land (\neg \neg p_2 \lor p_3)) \to p_4) \land (p_4 \to (\neg p_1 \land (\neg \neg p_2 \lor p_3)))$	Stage 2
$\equiv ((\neg p_1 \land (p_2 \lor p_3)) \to p_4) \land (p_4 \to (\neg p_1 \land (p_2 \lor p_3)))$	Stage 4
$\equiv (\neg(\neg p_1 \land (p_2 \lor p_3)) \lor p_4) \land (\neg p_4 \lor (\neg p_1 \land (p_2 \lor p_3)))$	Stage 2
$\equiv ((\neg \neg p_1 \lor \neg(p_2 \lor p_3)) \lor p_4) \land (\neg p_4 \lor (\neg p_1 \land (p_2 \lor p_3)))$	Stage 3
$\equiv ((p_1 \lor (\neg p_2 \land \neg p_3)) \lor p_4) \land (\neg p_4 \lor (\neg p_1 \land (p_2 \lor p_3)))$	Stage 3
$\equiv (((p_1 \lor \neg p_2) \land (p_1 \lor \neg p_3)) \lor p_4) \land ((\neg p_4 \lor \neg p_1) \land (\neg p_4 \lor (p_2 \lor p_3)))$	Stage 5
$\equiv (((p_1 \lor \neg p_2) \lor p_4) \land ((p_1 \lor \neg p_3) \lor p_4)) \land ((\neg p_4 \lor \neg p_1) \land (\neg p_4 \lor (p_2 \lor p_3)))$	Stage 5
$\equiv (p_1 \lor \neg p_2 \lor p_4) \land (p_1 \lor \neg p_3 \lor p_4) \land (\neg p_4 \lor \neg p_1) \land (\neg p_4 \lor p_2 \lor p_3)$	Stage 5

Note that redundant brackets have been removed in Example 5.3.

Exercise

5.2   Convert each of the following wff to conjunctive normal form:

(i) $p_1 \lor (p_2 \land p_3)$
(ii) $(p_1 \land p_3) \lor (p_2 \land p_3)$
(iii) $p_1 \to (p_2 \land p_3)$
(iv) $p_1 \leftrightarrow (p_2 \land p_3)$
(v) $(p_1 \lor p_2) \to p_2$
(vi) $\neg(p_1 \to p_2) \lor (p_1 \lor p_2)$
(vii) $\neg(p_1 \to p_2)$
(viii) $(p_1 \to p_2) \to p_3$
(ix) $(\neg p_1 \land (\neg p_2 \to p_3)) \to p_4$
(x) $(p_1 \land (\neg p_2 \leftrightarrow p_3)) \to p_3$

5.3 Resolving Arguments

We recall that logic is centrally concerned with deductions, proofs and the validity of arguments. Consider the following simple example of an argument.

If this apple is sweet then it is good to eat.
If it is good to eat then I will eat it.
Therefore, if this apple is sweet then I will eat it.

The argument is logically valid, even though (as Snow White found out to her cost), the real-world validity of the first premise is decidedly shaky. But, as emphasised right at the start of our studies, our interest is in logic rather than science. So let us examine the argument. Its essential form is

$$\{(A{\rightarrow}B), (B{\rightarrow}C)\} \models (A{\rightarrow}C)$$

where we are using A, B and C rather than the propositional variables p_1, p_2, etc., to represent basic statements.

We can look at this from a number of points of view.

We can see that, if A→B and B→C are both true, then A→C must be true. So A→C is a valid consequence of A→B and B→C.

We can also view it from a proof theoretical point of view as exemplifying the transitivity of implication (TI) in our axiomatic formal logic, i.e.

$$\{(A{\rightarrow}B), (B{\rightarrow}C)\} \vdash (A{\rightarrow}C)$$

We can also interpret it as showing that the negation of A→C is inconsistent with the assertion of both A→B and B→C, i.e. we cannot have

$$(A{\rightarrow}B) \wedge (B{\rightarrow}C) \wedge \neg(A{\rightarrow}C)$$

We will take this semantic (or model theoretic) point of view and express this incompatibility as

$$(A{\rightarrow}B) \wedge (B{\rightarrow}C) \wedge \neg(A{\rightarrow}C) \models \bot$$

which loosely (for the moment) states that from the premises we get falsum.

Suppose we convert the expression $(A{\rightarrow}B) \wedge (B{\rightarrow}C) \wedge \neg(A{\rightarrow}C)$ into conjunctive normal form. We get

$$
\begin{aligned}
(A{\rightarrow}B) \wedge (B{\rightarrow}C) \wedge \neg(A{\rightarrow}C) \ &\equiv (\neg A \vee B) \wedge (\neg B \vee C) \wedge \neg(\neg A \vee C) \\
&\equiv (\neg A \vee B) \wedge (\neg B \vee C) \wedge (\neg\neg A \wedge \neg C) \\
&\equiv (\neg A \vee B) \wedge (\neg B \vee C) \wedge A \wedge \neg C
\end{aligned}
$$

Consider now the pair of clauses $(\neg A \vee B)$ and $(\neg B \vee C)$. Notice that the first contains B while the second contains ¬B. We can argue about these two clauses as follows.

> If B is true then ¬B is false and the second clause depends on C for its truth value.
> If B is false then the first clause depends on ¬A for its truth value.
> Only one of B, ¬B can be true. So, if $(\neg A \vee B) \wedge (\neg B \vee C)$ is true, either ¬A or C *must* be true. We could argue then that if $(\neg A \vee B) \wedge (\neg B \vee C)$ is true, $(\neg A \vee C)$ must be true. If $(\neg A \vee C)$ is false, $(\neg A \vee B) \wedge (\neg B \vee C)$ cannot be true. In a sense then, the two clauses $(\neg A \vee B)$ and $(\neg B \vee C)$ can be *reduced* or *resolved* to the single clause $(\neg A \vee C)$. Essentially we cancel B and ¬B.

It is on this insight that the resolution principle is based. Before stating precisely what resolution is let us continue with this informal approach.

> We have resolved the clauses ($\neg$A$\lor$B) and ($\neg$B$\lor$C) into the 'resolvent' clause ($\neg$A$\lor$C). Now resolve clauses ($\neg$A$\lor$C) and A into the clause C.
> Finally, resolve C and $\neg$C into – what?
> An empty clause – cancelling C and $\neg$C – leaves us with nothing.
> How will we represent the empty clause? It seems reasonable to use $\bot$.
> Why? Well, we have been arguing that if the clauses that are being resolved are both true then the resolvent clause must be true. So, if both C and $\neg$C are true, their resolvent will be true. But C and $\neg$C can never be true together. So it seems reasonable to use an expression for their resolvent that can never be true, namely, $\bot$. Another way to look at this is that since a clause is a disjunction, one of the disjuncts must be true for the clause to be true. But if there is no disjunct there to render the clause true, the clause will be false. So, *the empty clause cannot be satisfied* – it is always false.

This use of $\bot$ also fits in with (A$\rightarrow$B) $\land$ (B$\rightarrow$C) $\land$ $\neg$(A$\rightarrow$C) $\vDash$ $\bot$ above.

Let us review what we have done, by representing the progression in the form of an inverted tree.

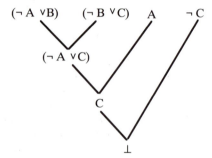

Figure 5.1

We started with the four clauses ($\neg$A$\lor$B), ($\neg$B$\lor$C), A and $\neg$C. We resolved ($\neg$A$\lor$B) with ($\neg$B$\lor$C) to get ($\neg$A$\lor$C). Then we resolved ($\neg$A$\lor$C) with A to get C. Finally, we resolved C with $\neg$C to get $\bot$.

When an argument is valid, we always get the empty clause by dealing with the situation in this fashion. The derivation of the empty clause signals that the clauses we started with were incompatible. It represents a way of constructing a standard refutation argument, i.e. negate the conclusion and show that it is inconsistent with the premises.

The beauty of this method is, once the argument is in conjunctive normal form, deriving the empty clause is purely mechanical and straightforward.

5.3.1 Sets of Clauses

It is usual to represent a wff in conjunctive normal form as a set. For example,

$$(\neg A \lor B) \land (\neg B \lor C) \land A \land \neg C$$

can be represented by

$$\{(\neg A \lor B), (\neg B \lor C), A, \neg C\}$$

where the $\land$'s have been suppressed. Since $\land$ is commutative ($A \land B \equiv B \land A$), the order of the clauses does not matter, and so we can use sets. In addition, since we know that we are dealing with CNF, we know that it is $\land$ that is involved rather than $\lor$.

But now, we do the same with $\lor$, i.e. represent the disjunctive clauses by sets. So

$$\{(\neg A \lor B), (\neg B \lor C), A, \neg C\}$$

is written

$$\{\{\neg A, B\}, \{\neg B, C\}, \neg A, C\}$$

Now that we use sets to represent both disjunctions and conjunctions, i.e. clauses and sets of clauses, we must be careful to interpret correctly in each case. Usually this is no problem, because the context makes the distinction clear. One situation where confusion might arise is the case of the empty set. But there is a radical difference between the interpretation of the empty set as a null conjunction and as a null disjunction. One case is always true, the other is always false!! Why is this?

Well, we have seen that the empty clause as an empty disjunction is always false, because there is no disjunct to make it true. But why is the empty set of clauses, i.e. the empty set as an empty conjunction, always true? Think about it. An expression such as $A_1 \land A_2 \ldots \land A_n$ will be false if one of the A_i is false. But if none of the A_i is false, then the whole conjunction will be true. It takes at least one component to be false to render the whole thing false. But if there is no component to be false, *because there is no component there at all,* the conjunction will be true, by default. So, the empty conjunction is always true.

If the reader does not find this reasoning satisfactory, she can simply accept that the empty conjunction is always true by *convention,* secure in the knowledge that this convention makes things turn out right.

5.3.2 Resolvents

We engaged in an informal introduction to the method of resolution above. Let us turn now to a more careful statement of what is is involved.

Literals p_i and $\neg p_i$ are called a *complementary pair.*

If two clauses contain a complementary pair of literals they may be *resolved* together to give a new clause called their *resolvent*. For example, the clauses {p1, p2, ¬p3} and {p3, p4} can be resolved to give {p1, p2, p4}.

Definition   In general, a *resolvent* of two clauses C_1 and C_2 containing the complementary literals λ and $\neg\lambda$ respectively, is defined as:
$$res(C_1, C_2) = C_1 - \{\lambda\} \cup C_2 - \{\neg\lambda\}$$

In the definition of resolvent the operator '−' is the set difference operator, the result of which is the set given by the first argument with the (sub-)set given by the second argument removed. For example, the result of {1, 2, 3, 4} − {2} is {1, 3, 4}.

Example 5.4
$$res(\{p_1, \neg p_2\}, \{p_2, \neg p_3\}) = \{p_1, \neg p_3\}$$

Example 5.5
$$res(\{p_1, \neg p_2, p_3, p_4\}, \{p_2, \neg p_3\}) = \{p_1, p_3, \neg p_3, p_4\}$$
$$\text{or } \{p_1, p_2, \neg p_2, p_4\}$$

A clause containing a complementary pair $p_i, \neg p_i$, will automatically be true. This is because a clause represents a disjunction, $p_i \vee \neg p_i$ is always true, and so is true*anything*. So, the clause in Example 5.5 resolves to true.

Notice that in example 5.5 there were two ways of resolving the clauses. Whenever there is more than one way of resolving, each resolvent is bound to have a complementary pair and is therefore bound to be true. Hence it would be a serious error to resolve, for example, {p1,¬p2} and {¬p1,p2} to ⊥, by resolving on both p1 and p2. Clearly the two clauses are mutually compatible, being satisfied by having p1 and p2 both true, for instance.

Exercise
5.3   Find all the resolvents of the following pairs of clauses:
  (i)   {p1,¬p2, p3}, {p1,¬p3}
  (ii)   {p1,¬p2, ¬p3, p4}, {p2,¬p3}
  (iii) {p1,¬p2, ¬p3, p4}, {¬p1,p2, ¬p3}
  (iv)   {p1,¬p2, ¬p3, p4}, {p2}
  (v)   {p1,¬p2, ¬p3, p4}, {¬p2}
  (vi)   {p3}, {¬p3}

Theorem 5.1 (The Resolution Principle)

A resolvent of two clauses, C_1, C_2, is a logical consequence of $C_1 \wedge C_2$
i.e. $C_1 \wedge C_2 \models res(C_1, C_2)$

Proof Let C_1 $= \{p_{11}, p_{12}, ..., p_{1m}, \lambda\}$

              C_2 $= \{p_{21}, p_{22}, ..., p_{2n}, \neg\lambda\}$

Then $res(C_1, C_2) = \{p_{11}, p_{12}, ..., p_{1m}, p_{21}, p_{22}, ..., p_{2n}\}$

Consider any truth valuation v, for which $v(C_1) = T$ and $v(C_2) = T$

If $v(\lambda) = F$ then $v(p_{1i}) = T$ for some p_{1i}, since $v(C_1) = T$

Hence $v(\{p_{11}, p_{12}, ..., p_{1m}, p_{21}, p_{22}, ..., p_{2n}\}) = T$

i.e. $v(res(C_1, C_2)) = T$

If $v(\lambda) = T$ then $v(\neg\lambda) = F$, and $v(p_{2i}) = T$ for some p_{2i}, as $v(C_2) = T$

Hence $v(\{p_{11}, p_{12}, ..., p_{1m}, p_{21}, p_{22}, ..., p_{2n}\}) = T$

i.e. $v(res(C_1, C_2)) = T$

Since $v(\lambda) = T$ or $v(\lambda) = F$, we conclude that if $v(C_1) = v(C_2) = T$, then $v(res(C_1, C_2)) = T$

i.e. $C_1 \wedge C_2 \vDash res(C_1, C_2)$

(End)

The basic idea behind resolution can be illustrated by examining the familiar modus ponens rule of deduction, namely $\{A, A \to B\} \vdash B$.

If we write A and $A \to B$ in clause form we get $\{\{A\}, \{\neg A, B\}\}$, because of theequivalence $A \to B \equiv \neg A \vee B$

If we resolve these two clauses we get $\{B\}$. So, essentially resolution is a disguised form of modus ponens!

5.4 Resolution

Our task, now, is to apply the above principle to deductions. We define a resolution deduction as follows:

Definition   A *resolution deduction* of a clause C from a set S of clauses is a finite sequence of clauses $C_1, C_2, ..., C_n = C$, such that each C_i is either a member of S or is a resolvent of two clauses taken from S or earlier members of the sequence.

From the resolution principle we deduce that, if S is true under some truth valuation v, then $v(C_i) = T$ for all C_i, and in particular $v(C) = T$.

Example 5.6

Prove $(p_1 \vee p_2 \vee p_3) \wedge (\neg p_2 \vee p_4) \wedge (\neg p_1 \vee p_4) \wedge (\neg p_3 \vee p_4) \vDash p_4$.

For convenience we express the clauses in set notation and number them:

       (1) $\{p_1, p_2, p_3\}$
       (2) $\{\neg p_2, p_4\}$
       (3) $\{\neg p_1, p_4\}$
       (4) $\{\neg p_3, p_4\}$

We proceed by carrying out the following resolutions:

(5) {p1, p3, p4} from (1) and (2)
(6) {p3, p4} from (3) and (5)
(7) {p4} from (4) and (6)

We conclude that

$$(p1 \lor p2 \lor p3) \land (\neg p2 \lor p4) \land (\neg p1 \lor p4) \land (\neg p3 \lor p4) \vDash p4$$

The derivation may be more perspicuously presented by means of a *resolution tree*.

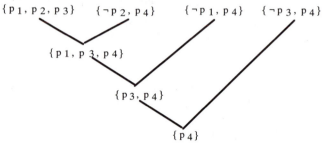

Figure 5.2

Example 5.7

Prove $\{(p_i \rightarrow p_j), (\neg(p_j \rightarrow p_k) \rightarrow \neg p_i)\} \vDash (p_i \rightarrow p_k)$.
First convert to clausal form.

$$(p_i \rightarrow p_j) \equiv (\neg p_i \lor p_j)$$
$$(\neg(p_j \rightarrow p_k) \rightarrow \neg p_i) \equiv (\neg\neg(p_j \rightarrow p_k) \lor \neg p_i)$$
$$\equiv ((p_j \rightarrow p_k) \lor \neg p_i)$$
$$\equiv (\neg p_j \lor p_k \lor \neg p_i)$$
$$(p_i \rightarrow p_k) \equiv (\neg p_i \lor p_k)$$

So, we must show that $\{\neg p_i, p_k\}$ follows from $\{\{\neg p_i, p_j\}, \{\neg p_j, p_k, \neg p_i\}\}$.
This is very easy, as one resolution does the job.

$$\{\neg p_i, p_j\} \qquad \{\neg p_j, p_k, \neg p_i\}$$

$$\{\neg p_i, p_k\}$$

Figure 5.3

Another, and more usual, method of establishing the result for example 5.7 is to negate the conclusion, $(p_i \rightarrow p_k)$, and then show that $\neg(p_i \rightarrow p_k)$ is incompatible with the premises, $(p_i \rightarrow p_j)$ and $(\neg(p_j \rightarrow p_k) \rightarrow \neg p_i)$.

$$\neg(p_i \rightarrow p_k) \equiv \neg(\neg p_i \lor p_k)$$
$$\equiv (\neg\neg p_i \land \neg p_k)$$
$$\equiv (p_i \land \neg p_k)$$

So the problem boils down to showing that the set of clauses S = {{¬pᵢ, pⱼ}, {¬pⱼ, pₖ, ¬pᵢ}, {pᵢ}, {¬pₖ}} is inconsistent, which in turn means showing that the empty clause can be deduced from S.

Definition A resolution deduction of ⊥ from a set of clauses S is called a *resolution refutation* of S

Clearly, a deduction of ⊥ from S shows that S is inconsistent, since, from what we have shown above, if all the clauses of S were true, then so would any clause deduced from S be true. In this case that would mean that ⊥ is true. But ⊥ cannot be true. Hence, neither can all the members of S be true at the same time.

To return to our problem in Example 5.7, we display a resolution refutation of {{¬pᵢ, pⱼ}, {¬pⱼ, pₖ, ¬pᵢ}, {pᵢ}, {¬pₖ}}

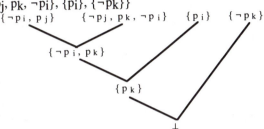

Figure 5.4

Exercises

5.4 Which of the following sets of clauses are inconsistent?
   (i)   {{p1, p2, p3}, {p1, ¬p3}, {¬p1, ¬p2}}
   (ii) {{p1, ¬p2, p3}, {p1, ¬p3}, {¬p1, p2}}
   (iii) {{¬p1, ¬p2, p3}, {p1, ¬p3}, {¬p1, p2}}
   (iv) {{p1, ¬p2, p3, ¬p4}, {p1, ¬p3}, {¬p1, p2, ¬p4}, {p4}}
   (v)   {{p1, ¬p2, p3}, {p1, ¬p3}, {p1, p2}}
   (vi) {{p1, ¬p2, p3}, {p1, p3}, {¬p1, p2, ¬p1}}

5.5 Use resolution to determine if the abstract arguments are valid.

   (i)   ¬A→B   (ii)   A→B
             ¬A∨C∨D   ¬B∨C
             ¬C ∨ (E∧F)   ¬C ∨ (C→A)
             (F∧¬D) → ¬E   ¬C
        ∴   ¬D→B   ∴   ¬A

5.5 Problem Solving

Let us put the method of resolution to work in solving logical problems.

Example 5.8

Consider again a problem that we solved in Chapter 1. Is the following argument valid?

If the violinist plays the concerto, then crowds will come if the prices are not too high.

If the violinist plays the concerto, the prices will not be too high.

Therefore, if the violinist plays the concerto, crowds will come.

We symbolised the argument as follows:

$$P \rightarrow (\neg H \rightarrow C)$$
$$P \rightarrow \neg H$$
$$\therefore P \rightarrow C$$

where P, H and C stood for 'the violinist plays the concerto', 'the prices are too high', and 'crowds will come', respectively. These are atomic statements, but we will continue to use the letters P, H and C, rather than p_i, p_j, etc. Following the familiar strategy of negating the conclusion, our job is to find out if the empty clause can be derived from $P \rightarrow (\neg H \rightarrow C)$, $P \rightarrow \neg H$ and $\neg(P \rightarrow C)$. We first convert to clausal form.

$$P \rightarrow (\neg H \rightarrow C) \equiv \neg P \vee (\neg \neg H \vee C) \equiv \neg P \vee H \vee C$$
$$P \rightarrow \neg H \equiv \neg P \vee \neg H$$
$$\neg(P \rightarrow C) \equiv \neg(\neg P \vee C) \equiv \neg \neg P \wedge \neg C \equiv P \wedge \neg C$$

Now, we try to show $\{\{\neg P, H, C\}, \{\neg P, \neg H\}, \{P\}, \{\neg C\}\} \models \bot$.

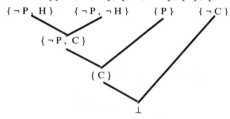

Figure 5.5

Example 5.9

For our final example in this chapter consider the following problem:

If the President broke the law, then the people were not alert or the cabinet was compliant.

If the cabinet was not compliant, then the people were alert.

The cabinet was compliant. But the President did not break the law.

Is the argument valid?

Let B stand for 'the President broke the law'.

Let A stand for 'the people were alert'.

Let C stand for 'the cabinet was compliant'.

The argument may be symbolised as follows:

$$B \rightarrow (\neg A \vee C) \wedge (\neg C \rightarrow A) \wedge C \models \neg B$$

As usual, we negate the conclusion and try to prove inconsistency of

$$B \rightarrow (\neg A \vee C) \wedge (\neg C \rightarrow A) \wedge C \wedge B$$

We now convert to clause form.

$$B \rightarrow (\neg A \vee C) \equiv \neg B \vee \neg A \vee C$$
$$\neg C \rightarrow A \equiv \neg \neg C \vee A \equiv C \vee A$$

We try to derive the empty clause from $\{\{\neg B, \neg A, C\}, \{C, A\}, \{C\}, \{B\}\}$

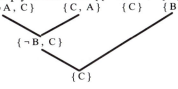

Figure 5.6

It is clear that we are not going to be able to derive the empty clause; there is no way we can cancel C. Hence, we conclude that the argument is *not* valid.

The reader may care to check that there is indeed a truth valuation which will satisy the premises and the negation of the conclusion, e.g. $v(A) = v(B) = v(C) = T$.

5.6 Combinatorial Search Problems

Combinatorial search problems arise throughout computer science and mathematics in such diverse areas as code generation and optimisation in compilers, scheduling, network design, database storage and retrieval, cryptography and graph theory. We may illustrate the nature of a combinatorial search problem using the idea of a jigsaw puzzle: here we have a large collection of parts that must be arranged to make a picture. The enjoyment (or perhaps frustration) involved in playing is that there are many possible ways to arrange the pieces but only one arrangement that works. Combinatorial search problems have a puzzle-like nature: a collection of objects that must be arranged in some way that satisfies given constraints. In our jigsaw puzzle example, the constraints are physically mainfest in that only certain pieces will fit together. Non-trivial problems typically have very large sets of possible solutions which means that finding an appropriate solution is like searching for a needle in a haystack. Unfortunately, it is this very characteristic that makes some combinatorial search problems very difficult to solve in a reasonable amount of time. In many cases we give up the goal of seeking an optimal (that is, perfect) solution and concentrate on choosing just a reasonable solution.

A combinatorial search problem may be rephrased as a *decision problem* – a problem whose solution is the answer 'yes' or 'no'.

Here are some examples.

1. A *graph* G = (V,E) is a collection of points (or *vertices*) V, some of which may be joined together by *edges* E. Vertices joined by an edge are said to be *adjacent*. Figure 5.7 depicts a graph.

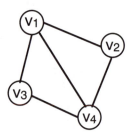

Figure 5.7

One decision problem on graphs is the *3-colouring problem*: given a graph G, is there a 3-colouring of G? That is, is there an assignment, c, of the three colours {RED, GREEN, BLUE} to the vertices such that no two adjacent vertices have the same colour? It turns out that, for this graph, the answer is 'yes' – a 3-colouring of the graph above is $c(v_1)$ = RED, $c(v_2)$ = GREEN, $c(v_3)$ = GREEN, $c(v_4)$ = BLUE.

2. Given a set P of propositional variables and a CNF formula C over those variables, can C be satisfied? In other words, is there a truth assignment over the variables P that satisfies formula C? (Recall that a CNF formula is a conjunction of disjunctions.) For example, given P = {{p_1}, {p_2, p_3}}, a satisfying truth assignment, v, would be $v(p_1)$ = true, $v(p_2)$ = true, $v(p_3)$ = false. This is known as the *satisfiability problem*.

It turns out that the 3-colouring problem is very difficult to solve in general. By 'difficult' we mean it takes an inordinately long time to solve non-trivial instances of the problem in general. The study of such problems forms a branch of computer science known as computational complexity theory. In the so-called theory of NP-completeness, the inherent intractability of problems can be demonstrated by showing that instances of the problem are *reducible to*, or can be transformed into, instances of the satisfiability problem. Propositional logic can play a key role in this process. We do not have the space here to explore the theory of NP-completeness, but we'll show how the 3-colouring problem is related to the satisfiability problem.

Given a graph G=(V,E), we create a CNF formula that determines whether it is 3-colourable or not. To achieve this, we must be precise about what a 3-colouring is. In a 3-colouring, each vertex is assigned exactly one colour and no edge has the same colour at both ends.

We proceed as follows.

(a) For each vertex v_i, we have propositional variables r_i, g_i, b_i.

(b) For each vertex v_i, we have the following disjunctions:

$r_i \lor b_i \lor g_i$ coloured RED or GREEN or BLUE

$$\left.\begin{array}{l} \neg r_i \lor \neg b_i \\ \neg r_i \lor \neg g_i \\ \neg b_i \lor \neg g_i \end{array}\right\} \text{ exactly one colour}$$

(c) For each edge (i,j), we have

$$\left.\begin{array}{l} \neg r_i \lor \neg r_j \\ \neg b_i \lor \neg b_j \\ \neg g_i \lor \neg g_j \end{array}\right\} \text{ not same colour at both ends}$$

The clauses from parts (b) and (c) are *and*ed together to obtain one formula. This formula is only satisfiable if there is a 3-colouring of the graph.

So, for example, given the graph in Figure 5.7 we could transform it into the following formula.

$$\{\{r1,b1,g1\},\{\neg r1,\neg b1\},\{\neg r1,\neg g1\},\{\neg b1,\neg g1\},$$
$$\{r2,b2,g2\},\{\neg r2,\neg b2\},\{\neg r2,\neg g2\},\{\neg b2,\neg g2\},$$
$$\{r3,b3,g3\},\{\neg r3,\neg b3\},\{\neg r3,\neg g3\},\{\neg b3,\neg g3\},$$
$$\{r4,b4,g4\},\{\neg r4,\neg b4\},\{\neg r4,\neg g4\},\{\neg b4,\neg g4\},$$
$$\{\neg r1,\neg r2\},\{\neg b1,\neg b2\},\{\neg g1,\neg g2\},$$
$$\{\neg r1,\neg r3\},\{\neg b1,\neg b3\},\{\neg g1,\neg g3\},$$
$$\{\neg r1,\neg r4\},\{\neg b1,\neg b4\},\{\neg g1,\neg g4\},$$
$$\{\neg r2,\neg r4\},\{\neg b2,\neg b4\},\{\neg g2,\neg g4\},$$
$$\{\neg r3,\neg r4\},\{\neg b3,\neg b4\},\{\neg g3,\neg g4\}\}$$

Then, we could apply resolution to this formula to see if it could be satisfied.

Exercises

5.6 Apply resolution to the above formula.

As it turns out, propositional logic is expressive enough to formalise any combinatorial search problem. In other words, given a combinatorial search problem, like the 3-colouring problem, we can transform any inastancce of the problem into an instance of the satisfiability problem in propositional logic. Unfortunately, this does not guarantee that we will solve the problem. The satisfiability problem itself is in the class of NP-complete problems.

Our purpose here is not to study the theory of NP-completeness. However, we have seen that propositional logic plays a key role in this area. For an excellent introduction to the topic see *Computers and Intractability* by Garey & Johnson (1979).

5.7 Summary

- This chapter has been devoted to a study of a new single rule of deduction, namely, resolution. We have seen that resolution is a generalised form of modus ponens.
- A literal is an atom or the negation of an atom.
- Two literals, one of which is the negation of the other, are called complementary literals.
- A wff is in conjunctive normal form (CNF) if it is a conjunction of disjunctions of literals, i.e. if it is in the form
  $$A_1 \wedge A_2 \ldots \wedge A_i \ldots \wedge A_n$$
  where each A_i is of the form
  $$\lambda_1 \vee \lambda_2 \ldots \vee \lambda_j \ldots \vee \lambda_m$$
  where each λ_j is a literal.
- A wff is in disjunctive normal form (DNF) if it is a disjunction of conjunctions of literals, i.e. if it is in the form
  $$A_1 \vee A_2 \ldots \vee A_i \ldots \vee A_n$$
  where each A_i is of the form
  $$\lambda_1 \wedge \lambda_2 \ldots \wedge \lambda_j \ldots \wedge \lambda_m$$
  where each λ_j is a literal.
- A clause is a finite disjunction of literals.
- A unit clause is a clause containing one literal only.
- A wff may be converted to CNF in a number of stages:
  Stage 1: Use equivalence $A \leftrightarrow B \equiv (A \rightarrow B) \wedge (B \rightarrow A)$ to eliminate $\leftrightarrow$.
  Stage 2: Use equivalence $A \rightarrow B \equiv \neg A \vee B$ to eliminate $\rightarrow$.
  Stage 3: Use De Morgan's Laws $\neg(A \wedge B) \equiv \neg A \vee \neg B$ and $\neg(A \vee B) \equiv \neg A \wedge \neg B$ to push the negation sign $\neg$ immediately before atomic wff.
  Stage 4: Use $\neg\neg A \equiv A$ to eliminate double negation signs.
  Stage 5: Use the distributive law $A \vee (B \wedge C) \equiv (A \vee B) \wedge (A \vee C)$ to effect the conversion to CNF.
- The resolvent of clauses C_1 and C_2 containing complementary literals λ and $\neg\lambda$ respectively, is defined as: $\text{res}(C_1, C_2) = C_1 - \{\lambda\} \cup C_2 - \{\neg\lambda\}$.
- The resolution principle states that a resolvent of two clauses, C_1, C_2, is a logical consequence of $C_1 \wedge C_2$, i.e. $C_1 \wedge C_2 \vDash \text{res}(C_1, C_2)$.
- A resolution deduction of a clause C from a set S of clauses is a finite sequence of clauses C_1, C_2, C_3, ..., $C_n = C$, such that each C_i is either a member of S or is a resolvent of two clauses taken from S or earlier members of the sequence.
- A resolution deduction of $\bot$ from a set of clauses S is called a resolution refutation of S.

In this chapter we have
- learned about normal forms, literals, clauses.
- studied the resolution principle as applied in propositional logic.
- constructed resolution proofs and refutations.
- applied resolution to problem solving.

We have now completed a fairly thorough study of formal propositional logic. In the next chapter we go beyond propositional logic to tackle the problems associated with the inner structure of sentences.

Miscellaneous Exercises

1. Convert each of the following wff to (a) conjunctive normal form, (b) disjunctive normal form:
   (i) $(p_1 \vee \neg p_3) \vee (p_2 \wedge p_3)$
   (ii) $(p_1 \wedge \neg p_3 \vee p_2) \vee (p_2 \wedge p_3)$
   (iii) $p_1 \rightarrow (p_2 \vee p_3)$
   (iv) $\neg p_1 \leftrightarrow (p_2 \vee p_3)$
   (v) $(p_1 \wedge p_2) \rightarrow p_2$

2. Which of the following sets of clauses are inconsistent?
   (i) $\{\{p_1, p_2, p_3\}, \{p_1, p_3\}, \{\neg p_1, \neg p_2\}\}$
   (ii) $\{\{\neg p_1, \neg p_2, p_3\}, \{p_1, \neg p_3\}, \{\neg p_1, p_2\}\}$
   (iii) $\{\{\neg p_1, \neg p_2, \neg p_3\}, \{p_1, p_3\}, \{p_1, p_2\}\}$
   (iv) $\{\{p_1, \neg p_2, \neg p_3, \neg p_4\}, \{p_1, \neg p_3\}, \{\neg p_1, p_2, \neg p_4\}, \{\neg p_1, p_4\}\}$
   (v) $\{\{p_1, \neg p_2, p_3\}, \{p_1, \neg p_3\}, \{\neg p_1, p_2\}\}$

3. Use resolution to determine if the following abstract arguments are valid:

(i)	(ii)	(iii)
$A \rightarrow B$	$A \rightarrow B$	$\neg A \wedge (\neg B \vee C)$
$\neg A \vee C \vee D$	$B \rightarrow C$	$B \wedge C$
$\neg C \vee (D \wedge A)$	$D \rightarrow C$	$C \rightarrow D$
$(C \wedge \neg D) \rightarrow \neg E$	$C \vee D$	$D \vee \neg A$
$\therefore \ \neg D \rightarrow B$	$\therefore \ \neg A \vee C$	$\therefore \quad \neg(\neg D \wedge A)$

4. Is the following argument valid?
   If Paul has holidays and it is snowing he will go skiing. He will go to France or Florida. There is no skiing in Florida. There is skiing in France. Paul has holidays and he goes to Florida. Therefore it is not snowing.

CHAPTER 6

Introduction to Predicate Logic

Chapter Aims

(1) To see why propositional logic needs to be extended.
(2) To introduce terms and quantifiers.
(3) To develop the notion of first order logical system.
(4) To further distinguish between syntax and semantics and to appreciate the role of interpretations.
(5) To distinguish between satisfaction, truth and validity for first order expressions.
(6) Discuss briefly the differences between first and higher order logics.

Following a thorough study of this chapter you should
(a) have a good knowledge of various concepts associated with the notion of first order language.
(b) understand the role of interpretations of first order languages.
(c) be aware of the distinction between interpretation and valuation.
(d) be able to distinguish between satisfaction, truth and validity for first order expressions.
(e) know the meaning of the concept model of a set of wff.
(f) be able to construct suitable interpretations of first order formulae.
(g) understand the differences between first and higher order logics.

6.1 Introduction

Up to this point we have made a fairly exhaustive (and probably exhausting) study of the logic of propositions. Unfortunately, there are important issues in logic that lie outside the scope of propositional logic. Consider, for example, the following argument:

> Every person is precious.
> Clare is a person.
> Therefore Clare is precious.

This argument would surely be accepted as sound, yet it cannot be handled effectively using only the resources of propositional logic. Why not? Well, if we attempt to symbolise the argument as a sequence of propositions we get something like the following:

$$A$$
$$B$$
$$\therefore C$$

and clearly this does not indicate a valid argument in any of the formalisms we have studied so far. But surely, you say, you shouldn't use three separate unrelated propositional letters to represent the propositions: after all they are related to each other, the first two through the link person, and the second and third through the individual Clare. That is so, but unfortunately there is nothing we can do about it in propositional logic. Think about it. Although we can see the conceptual links between the three statements they are in fact three different statements and need three different letters to symbolise them.

The nearest we can come to representing the above argument using the logic of propositions is

$$P \rightarrow Q$$
$$P$$
$$\therefore Q$$

which would represent

> If Clare is a person then she is precious.
> Clare is a person.
> Therefore she is precious.

This does not really capture the logic of the original. Why not? Well, consider the following:

> If Clare is a person then she is precious.
> Jo Ann is a person.
> Therefore she is precious.

It doesn't work!

Clearly we would have to change the first statement to 'If Jo Ann is a person then she is precious'. And we would have to do the same for Barbara and Milly and Molly and Joe and John and all. The problem with propositional logic is that it treats simple propositions as unanalysed wholes. The internal structure of propositions is suppressed. Thus, 'Billy loves Milly in spite of her faults' and 'Everyone loves Milly' would both be represented simply by propositional letters, in spite of the manifest differences in structure.

Therefore we need something richer than simple propositional logic. To find that richer system we turn to first order predicate logic. At the very least within predicate logic we need to be able to refer to the *objects* that are treated by propositions. We want to be able to distinguish between 'Clare is a person' and 'Jo Ann is a person' in some way other than by crudely using different propositional symbols, p_1 and p_2, say.

In general when we make a claim about some object, e.g. copper conducts electricity, we want to be able to symbolise both the claim and the object about which the claim is made. We call the claim a *predicate* and say that we are *predicating some property* of the object. Thus, in our example, 'conducts electricity' is a predicate. Very often, we find it convenient not to distinguish between the predicate part of a statement and the full statement, and we refer to the complete statement as a predicate.

In addition to stating properties of objects, we also often need to talk about *relations* between objects. For example, 'Dublin is west of London, Paris, Bonn and Rome' states a relation between the five cities Bonn, Dublin, London, Paris and Rome. We have an example of a five-place relation. n fact, using the idea of relation, we can think of a property as a one-place relation, and of a proposition (when we are not concerned with its details) as a zero-place relation.

Besides giving us facilities to refer to objects and predicates there is one other requirement that we would like predicate logic to fulfil – we would like to be able to symbolise and manipulate *quantifiers*. For example, if we look back at the first premise of the first argument above – 'Every person is precious' – we see that we will probably need to symbolise the word 'every'. 'Every' is an example of a so-called *universal quantifier*. Similarly we will want to symbolise *existential quantifiers* such as 'some' as in 'someone has eaten my last chocolate'.

6.2 Objects, Predicates and Quantifiers

The best way to come to grips with the notation usually adopted in first order predicate logic is to have a look at some examples. Consider 'Clare is a person'. This may be symbolised by P(c), which we may read (rather oddly) as 'person Clare' (with apologies to Clare for using a small letter in the formal symbolism). Similarly, P(b) could symbolise 'Barbara is a person'.

The notation is a prefix 'functional' type of notation. Capital letters are usually used for predicates. Thus P stands for the predicate 'is a person'. Small letters are usually used to stand for objects; thus c stands for Clare, b for Barbara. The usual convention is that letters near the beginning of the alphabet are used as constants to stand for particular named objects, while letters towards the end of the alphabet are used as variables to stand for general or non-specific objects. For example, if we wanted to symbolise the statement 'Persons are mortal' we might do it as follows, using M to stand for 'is mortal':

$$P(x) \to M(x)$$

i.e. in general, if someone is a person then he is mortal.

However, in first order predicate logic this symbolism would be considered incomplete. Since the sentence 'Persons are mortal' is understood to mean 'every person is mortal' we would symbolise it more carefully by

$$(\forall x)(P(x) \rightarrow M(x))$$

i.e. *for all* x, if x is a person, then x is mortal, where the quantifier ∀ stands for 'for all' (or 'every'). ∀ is called the *universal quantifier*.

Similarly, 'all prime numbers are odd' may be symbolised by

$$(\forall x)(P(x) \rightarrow O(x))$$

where this time P is used to stand for 'is prime', and of course O stands for 'is odd'. Notice that this statement is not true (at least within the full set of natural numbers).

If we did want to tell the truth that there is an even prime number we could do it as follows:

$$(\exists x)(P(x) \wedge E(x))$$

i.e. there exists (∃) a number x which is such that it is both prime and even. (A more pedantic rendering might be 'there exists a thing x such that it has the properties symbolised by P and E'.) ∃ is called the *existential quantifier*.

In order to become familiar with the notation let us consider some further examples of translations of English sentences into first order symbolism. We will assume that it is easy to see what predicates and objects the letters stand for in each case, so we will not comment further.

Jo Ann is brilliant	B(j)
If Barbara practises she will win	P(b) → W(b)
All grass is green	(∀y)(G(y) → R(y))

The object variable need not always be x, of course. But it must not be changed half-way as it were. Thus (∀y)(G(y) → R(x)) would be wrong.

Every dog has his day	(∀x)(G(x) → D(x))
Some cat did this	(∃x)(C(x) ∧ D(x))
There is a winning combination	(∃z)(C(z) ∧ W(z))
Something is rotten in the state of Denmark	(∃x)(D(x) ∧ R(x))

There is one significant feature of the above translations which, I trust, will not have escaped your attention. Situations involving the universal quantifier, ∀, are represented by the implication connective →: If every ... then ... . Situations involving the existential quantifier, ∃, are represented by conjunction: Some ... are both ... and ... .

The examples above have all involved unary predicates (or one-place relations). Naturally we expect our symbolism to accommodate general n-ary predicates, i.e. relations among n objects in general. Let us look at some examples.

Everybody loves Paris	$(\forall y)L(y,p)$
Every even number is divisible by 2	$(\forall x)(E(x) \rightarrow D(x,2))$
There is a city west of Brussels, Copenhagen and Oslo	
	$(\exists x)(C(x) \wedge W(x,b,c,o))$
There is no prime number between 23 and 29	$\neg(\exists x)(P(x) \wedge B(x,23,29))$
Paul knows everything	$(\forall x)K(p,x)$
Paul knows everybody	$(\forall x)K(p,x)$

It seems a pity not to distinguish between these last two situations. We could, of course, use two different predicate letters, K_1, K_2, say, one for indicating knowledge of things, the other to represent knowledge of people. But, that is a bit clumsy. In any event there is another issue that we have been avoiding up to now and it is time to face up to it. This is the issue of the *domain* of objects that we are making statements about. Consider, for example, $(\forall y)L(y,p)$, which we used above to represent 'Everybody loves Paris'. Clearly, y is intended to range over the set of all people, not the set of all things. It would not make much sense to say that 'every y loves Paris' where y might stand for rats or cats or cabbages or sticks or anything whatsoever.

As another example consider $(\forall x)(E(x) \rightarrow D(x,2))$, which we used above to represent 'Every even number is divisible by 2'. Here, the intended domain is clearly the set of natural numbers. It would not make (much) sense to speak of an even cloud, for example.

We could fix things up by allowing our quantified variables to range over the set of everything(?) and introduce extra predicates to pick the relevant objects out. For example, in the case of 'Everybody loves Paris' we could symbolise it as

$$(\forall y)(P(y) \rightarrow L(y,p))$$

This may be read 'For every y, if y is a person then y loves Paris', or, more pedantically, 'For every y, if y has the property P then y bears the relation L to p'.

Very often we will adopt this approach of using a general domain and picking out a relevant subset. This would be the case when the domain contains different kinds of entities and we wish to pick out a particular subset. For example, we might want the domain to be the set of all real numbers, but we might be interested in an assertion about the natural numbers.

In simple cases, however, we will assume a suitable underlying domain of interpretation, such as people, or natural numbers, or real numbers, etc.

Up to now our statements have involved the use of just one quantifier. Let us look at some situations where a number of quantifiers are required.

Everyone is loved by someone	$(\forall x)(\exists y)L(y,x)$

i.e. For every x there exists a y such that y L[oves] x.

If we were to assume that the domain of interpretation is not restricted to people we might use

$$(\forall x)(P(x) \rightarrow (\exists y)(P(y) \wedge L(y,x)))$$

i.e. For every x, if x is a person then there exists a y such that y is a person and y loves x.

Note carefully the uses of $\rightarrow$ and $\wedge$.

Note too the difference between 'Everyone is loved by someone' and 'Someone is loved by everyone' which would be rendered by, for example, $(\exists x)(\forall y)L(y,x)$. This indicates to us that *the order of the universal and existential quantifiers is significant*.

Any two numbers can be added together $\qquad (\forall x)(\forall y)(\exists z)(x+y = z)$

i.e. For every x and every y there exists a z which is the sum of x and y.

There is a prime number less than 10 which divides every even number between 100 and 1000

$$(\exists x)(P(x) \wedge L(x,10) \wedge (\forall y)((E(y) \wedge L(100,y) \wedge L(y,1000)) \rightarrow D(x,y)))$$

Exercise

6.1 Represent each of the following in symbolic form, assuming a suitable domain of interpretation in each case:

(i)   Stephen is a computer scientist.
(ii)   Clare, Jo-Ann and Barbara are musicians.
(iii)   If John wants work he must go to New York.
(iv)   Everybody likes Paul.
(v)   Everybody likes somebody.
(vi)   Everybody who likes Stephen likes Paul.
(vii)   Every natural number is either even or odd.
(viii) No integer is both even and odd.
(ix)   If everybody behaves rationally then no-one will commit a crime.
(x)   If two given sets S1 and S2 have the same members they are equal.
(xi)   John likes anybody who does not like himself.
(xii)   Nobody loves anyone who loves himself.
(xiii) Anyone who is torn between music, logic and computer science will not choose to study any subject.
(xiv)   If 5 numbers are arranged in descending order then the first number is at least as big as any of the others.

6.2.1 $\forall$ and $\wedge$, $\exists$ and $\vee$

Consider the finite set {2, 3, 5, 7, 11, 13}, each element of which is a prime number. We could express this set by $(\forall x)P(x)$, where P stands for the property 'prime'. We could also write $P(2) \wedge P(3) \wedge P(5) \wedge P(7) \wedge P(11) \wedge P(13)$. In this case

$$(\forall x)P(x) \equiv P(2) \wedge P(3) \wedge P(5) \wedge P(7) \wedge P(11) \wedge P(13)$$

Both expressions are making the same statement.

$(\forall x)P(x)$ is effectively stating that

> the first element has the property P
> *and* the second element has the property P
> *and* the third element has the property P
>
> .
> .
>
> *and* the last element has the property P.

It is clear that in general, for finite sets, a universally quantified statement is equivalent to an extended conjunction, i.e.

$$(\forall x)P(x) \quad \equiv \quad \wedge_{i=1}^{n}P(x_i)$$

For infinite sets, the quantifier would correspond to an infinite conjunction.

In the same manner, the existential quantifier corresponds to disjunction. For instance, in the above example we might want to state that the set contains one even element. We could express this as $(\exists x)E(x)$ or $E(2) \vee E(3) \vee E(5) \vee E(7) \vee E(11) \vee E(13)$.

In general

$$(\exists x)P(x) \quad \equiv \quad \vee_{i=1}^{n}P(x_i)$$

Again, for infinite sets we would need an infinite disjunction.

6.2.2 The Relationship between ∀ and ∃

Consider the assertion 'everybody isn't rich'. It is actually ambiguous, but let us take it to mean that while some persons may be rich, not everybody is: in other words, it is not the case that for all persons being a person implies being rich. We can then symbolise it as

$$\neg(\forall x)(P(x) \rightarrow R(x))$$

Since A→B is logically equivalent to $\neg(A \wedge \neg B)$, we could rewrite this as

$$\neg(\forall x)\neg(P(x) \wedge \neg R(x))$$

The presence of ∧ reminds us of the situation which usually accompanies the existential quantifier, ∃. If we replace $\neg(\forall x)\neg$ by $(\exists x)$ we get the formula

$$(\exists x)(P(x) \wedge \neg R(x))$$

which could be read as 'there is some person who is not rich', and this seems a reasonable rendering of the original 'everybody isn't rich'. So it would seem reasonable to take $\exists x$ as equivalent to $\neg(\forall x)\neg$.

$$\text{i.e. } \exists x \equiv \neg(\forall x)\neg$$

Exercises

6.2 Using a suitable example argue that it is reasonable to take $\forall x$ as equivalent to $\neg(\exists x)\neg$.

6.3 Using a suitable example argue that it is reasonable to take $\neg(\forall x)$ as equivalent to $(\exists x)\neg$.

6.4 Using a suitable example argue that it is reasonable to take $\neg(\exists x)$ as equivalent to $(\forall x)\neg$.

6.3 Functions

We have seen that one of our goals in developing predicate logic is to be able to refer to objects. So far we have used constants and variables to stand for objects. Thus we might symbolise 'Barbara is a musician' by M(b) where b stands for the 'object' Barbara, and we might represent 'houses costing more than £100,000 are dear' by $(\forall x)(C(x, 100000) \rightarrow D(x))$ where x stands for the generic object house. There are occasions when we would like to be somewhat more specific and informative in our representations of objects than we can be by using simple constants and variables.

Consider the assertion 'Jo Ann's father likes music'. We might try to symbolise this by

$$(\exists x)(F(x,j) \wedge L(x,m))$$

but this could be read as 'Jo Ann has at least one father and he likes music', which is a bit odd to say the least. What we would like is a way to specify that Jo Ann has just one father and to refer specifically to that unique and lucky individual. This we can do by making use of the idea of a *function*. So, we would render 'Jo Ann's father likes music' as L(f(j),m), where f is a function letter standing for 'father'. We could then represent Clare's father by f(c) and Clare's father's father, i.e. her paternal grandfather by f(f(c)).

The use of function symbols to refer to specific objects is extremely useful. The idea is, of course, exactly the same as that which you are familiar with from ordinary arithmetic, where functions for adding, multiplying, subtracting, etc. are extensively used. These are all binary functions (i.e. functions of two arguments), reminding us that functions can have more than one argument. We could represent the sum of 2 and 5 by s(2,5) where s stands for the 'sum' function. Similarly the product of 2 and 5 could be represented by p(2,5) where p stands for product. Or we could use the more familiar + and × signs and write +(2,5) and ×(2,5). These look a bit odd because they are in *prefix* functional notation instead of the more familiar *infix* forms 2+5 and 2×5. Usually we will use the more general prefix function notation, but occasionally, in the case of a familiar function, we will use the infix form. Thus, $f(a_1, a_2, \ldots, a_n)$ would represent a function of n arguments.

The function notation fits easily into the predicate logic symbolism we have developed so far. Let us look at a few examples.

Barbara's father loves her mother $\qquad$ L(f(b), m(b))
where f stands for the function 'father' and m stands for the function 'mother'.

Everyone loves Barbara's paternal grandmother $\qquad$ $(\forall x)L(x, m(f(b)))$

The square of an odd number is odd $\qquad$ $(\forall x)(O(x) \to O(s(x)))$

Anybody who visits the smallest of the cities New York, London, Moscow, Dublin and Sydney is charmed by its people

$$(\forall x)(V(x, s(y,l,m,d,n)) \to C(x, p(s(y,l,m,d,n))))$$

where s(y,l,m,d,n) stands for the smallest of the five cities and p(s(y,l,m,d,n)) stands for the function that picks out the people of the given city.

Exercise

6.5 Symbolise the following, using functions wherever suitable:
  (i) Billy loves Jilly's sister.
  (ii) Billy is afraid of Jilly's mother's sister's husband.
  (iii) Everybody loves the president who stopped the war.
  (iv) The greatest of the first one hundred primes is smaller than the greatest of the first ten factorials.
  (v) If the sum of two integers is greater than their product then one of the numbers must be zero.

6.4 First Order Languages

We have used the phrase 'first order predicate logic' a few times already and you may have wondered what 'first order' is all about. Well, now it is time to find out!

Let us begin by defining a general first order language. We have already identified the basic ingredients of such a language, namely

• constants, variables and function symbols to refer to objects
• predicate letters to refer to predicates
• logical connectives such as ∧ and → to build complex formulae.

Let us now put all this on a systematic basis. There are three aspects we need to explicate:

1. alphabet
2. terms
3. well-formed formulae

In general the alphabet of a first order language, L, will contain the following symbols:

(i)   constants $c_1, c_2, ..., c_n, ...$, which are sometimes called individual symbols
(ii)   variables $x_1, x_2, ..., x_n, ...$
(iii)   function letters f_i^n
(iv)   predicate letters P_i^n
(v)   logical connectives $\wedge, \vee, \neg, \rightarrow, \leftrightarrow$
(vi)   quantifiers $\forall, \exists$
(vii)   punctuation symbols (,) and ,

It is not necessary for the alphabet of a first order language to contain all of these symbols. It must contain variables, appropriate connectives, and at least one quantifier, but it need not contain all (or any) of the constants, function letters and predicate letters. Thus, different first order languages may be defined.

What does the notation f_i^n mean? The superscript n stands for the *arity* of the function, i.e. the number of arguments that the function takes. Thus, binary functions would have superscript 2, ternary functions have superscript 3, functions of 7 arguments have superscript 7, and so on.

The subscript is used simply to distinguish functions of the same arity. Thus, f_1^2, f_2^2, f_3^2 would name three (usually different) binary functions. We might intend, for example, f_1^2 to be interpreted as +, f_2^2 as −, and f_3^2 as ×. Then $f_1^2(c_1, x_3)$ would stand for $c_1 + x_3$.

The interpretation of the subscript, superscript notation is similar for the predicate letters. The predicate letters are used to symbolise relations among arguments. Thus, $P_1^2(c_1, c_5)$, $P_2^2(c_1, c_5)$, $P_3^2(c_1, c_5)$ would represent three (usually different) binary relations among the arguments c_1 and c_5. For example, we might take $P_1^2(c_1, c_5)$ to stand for $c_1 = c_5$, $P_2^2(c_1, c_5)$ to stand for $c_1 < c_5$, and $P_3^2(c_1, c_5)$ to stand for $c_1 \mid c_5$, i.e. c_1 divides c_5.

6.4.1 Terms and Well-formed Formulae

Terms are intended to stand for objects. Therefore, the simplest terms are the constants and variables.

Definition   We define *terms* recursively as follows:
        (i)   Every constant is a term.
        (ii)   Every variable is a term.
        (iii)   If $t_1, t_2, ..., t_n$ are terms then $f_i^n(t_1, t_2, ..., t_n)$ is a term.
        (iv)   Nothing else is a term.

So, constants, variables and functions are terms and are used to represent objects. First order predicate logic is concerned, among other issues, with relations between terms.

Just as in propositional logic, not every string of symbols from the alphabet of a first order language is considered to be properly formed for the purposes of logic. We must therefore give rules for the correct formation of formulae.

Definition   *Well-formed formulae* are defined recursively as follows:

(i) $P_i^n(t_1, t_2, ..., t_n)$ is a well-formed formula, where the t_i are terms.

(ii)   If A and B are well-formed formulae so are $(\neg A)$, $(A \wedge B)$, $(A \vee B)$, $(A \rightarrow B)$ and $(A \leftrightarrow B)$.

(iii)   If A is a well-formed formula so is $(\forall x_i)A$.

(iv)   If A is a well-formed formula so is $(\exists x_i)A$.

(v)   Nothing else is a well-formed formula.

As before we will abbreviate 'well-formed formula(e)' by wff.

Wff of type (i), i.e. $P_i^n(t_1, t_2, ..., t_n)$ are called *atomic* formulae. They symbolise relations among objects. For example, $P_2^5(t_1, t_2, t_3, t_4, t_5)$ might represent the predicate – t_1 is the largest of t_1, t_2, t_3, t_4, t_5.

Exercise

6.6   Categorise each of the following as (a) a term, (b) a well-formed formula or (c) ill formed:

(i) $\neg \forall AB \wedge C$

(ii) $(\neg(\forall x)((A \vee B) \wedge C))$

(iii) $(\neg(\forall x)((P_4^1(x) \vee P_3^1(x)) \wedge P_7^1(x)))$

(iv) $(\neg(\forall x_1)((P_4^1(x_1) \vee P_3^1(x_1)) \wedge P_7^1(x_1)))$

(v) $f(x, y, g(x,y), h(g(x,z), y))$

(vi) $f_1^4(x_1, x_2, f_1^2(x_2, x_4), f_5^2(f_1^2(x_3, x_1), c_3))$

(vii) $(\exists x_1)(\forall x_2)(P_2^2(f_1^3(x_1, x_2, f_5^2(f_1^2(x_3, x_1), c_3)), x_2) \rightarrow P_2^1(f_1^2(x_2, x_4)))$

Strictly speaking, an expression such as

$$(\forall x)(\exists y)(P(x, g(x)) \rightarrow Q(f(x), y, h(x,y,a)))$$

is not a wff of our first order langauge, because the letters x, y, z, f, g, h, P and Q are not in the alphabet. An acceptable expression would be something like

$$(\forall x_1)(\exists x_2)(P_1^2(x_1, f_2^1(x_1)) \rightarrow P_1^3(f_1^1(x_1), x_2, f_1^3(x_1, x_2, c_3))).$$

However, the notation of subscripts and superscripts is somewhat clumsy and we will use the simpler uncluttered form on the understanding that, if necessary, it could easily be replaced by a form in correct notation. In general then, we will use uppercase letters for predicates, lowercase letters from the beginning of the alphabet for constants, lowercase letters from the end of the alphabet for variables and lowercase letters from the middle or thereabouts of the alphabet for functions. We will also use uppercase letters to stand for wff in general. Thus B might stand for the previous wff

$$(\forall x_1)(\exists x_2)(P_1^2(x_1, f_2^1(x_1)) \rightarrow P_1^3(f_1^1(x_1), x_2, f_1^3(x_1, x_2, c_3))).$$

6.5 Quantifiers, Scope and Binding

In the wff $(\forall x_i)A$ and $(\exists x_i)A$, A is said to be the *scope* of the quantifier $(\forall x_i)$ or $(\exists x_i)$. This is best understood by means of examples.

Thus, in the wff $(\forall x_1)(P_1^2(x_1, x_2) \rightarrow P_1^1(x_1))$, the scope of $(\forall x_1)$ is $P_1^2(x_1, x_2) \rightarrow P_1^1(x_1)$ while in the wff $(\forall x_1)P_1^2(x_1, x_2) \rightarrow P_1^1(x_1)$ the scope is $P_1^2(x_1, x_2)$. Note carefully the positions of the brackets in each case.

In the wff $(\forall x_1)(P_1^2(x_1, x_2) \rightarrow (\exists x_1)P_1^1(x_1))$, the scope of $(\forall x_1)$ is $P_1^2(x_1, x_2) \rightarrow (\exists x_1)P_1^1(x_1)$ and the scope of $(\exists x_1)$ is $P_1^1(x_1)$.

In the wff $(\forall x_1)P_1^2(x_1, x_2)$ the occurrences of the variable x_1 are said to be *bound*. The occurrence of x_2 is said to be *free*.

When a variable x_i occurs within the scope of a quantifier $(\forall x_i)$ and $(\exists x_i)$ it is said to be bound. In addition the occurrence of x_i in $(\forall x_i)$ or $(\exists x_i)$ is also said to be bound. An occurrence that is not bound is free.

Note that occurrences of x_i within the scope of $(\forall x_i)$ or $(\exists x_i)$ are generally bound by this quantifier. However, if x_i is again quantified within the scope of the 'outer' quantifier, the binding is by the inner quantifier. For example, in $(\forall x_1)(P_1^2(x_1, x_2) \rightarrow (\exists x_1)P_1^1(x_1))$ the last two occurrences of x_1 are bound by\ $(\exists x_1)$.

Let us look at a few examples (using our looser notation without the subscripts and superscripts).

In $(\exists x)A(x,c)$, x occurs bound.
In $(\exists x)(A(x,c) \wedge B(y))$, x occurs bound and y occurs free.
In $(\exists x)(A(x,y) \wedge (\forall y)B(y))$, x occurs bound, but y occurs both free and bound – it is free in its first occurrence and bound in its next two occurrences.

Note carefully then that a variable may appear both bound and free in the same formula. Naturally, of course, in any single occurrence it must be either free or bound; it cannot be both.

A wff is said to be *closed* if it contains no free occurrences of any variable, for example, $P_1^2(c_1, f_1^1(c_2))$ is closed, as is $(\forall x_1)(\forall x_2)P_1^2(x_1, x_2)$.

Exercise

6.7 For each quantifier in the following examples state its scope.
For each variable state whether each occurrence is bound or free.
(i) $(\forall x)B(y,z)$

    (ii) $(\forall x)(\forall y)A(x,y,c)$

    (iii) $(\forall x)(\forall y)A(x,y,z)$

    (iv) $(\forall x)((\forall y)A(x,y,z) \rightarrow (\exists z)A(z,z,z))$

    (v) $(\forall x)((\forall y)A(x,y,z) \rightarrow (\exists x)A(x,z,z))$

    (vi) $(\forall x)(((\forall y)A(x,y,z) \wedge (\forall x)B(x)) \rightarrow (\exists z)A(z,z,z))$

6.6 Substitution

One defect of using the slightly more casual notation of uppercase letters to stand for predicates is that, without superscripts, it is not necessarily clear what the arity of the relation involved is. Again rather casually we have assumed that if we write $A(x, y)$ we are talking about a binary relation, and that $A(x_1, x_2, ..., x_n)$ refers to an n-ary relation.

However, as indicated above when we were introducing the idea of scope and free and bound variables, we want our uppercase letters to refer to wff in general, rather than be restricted to relations or atomic wff. In that case we adopt a rather loose convention with regard to the listing of variables following the name of the wff. The main objective is to list just the free variables to which we may wish to draw attention. In particular, we are interested in those variables for which we may wish to substitute terms.

Thus, $A(x)$ stands for a wff in which there may be free occurrences of x. It does not indicate that there definitely are free occurrences, nor that there are no free occurrences of other free variables. The idea is that we can write $A(t)$ for the wff which results from the substitution of t for *every* free occurrence of x in $A(x)$. Similarly, $A(x_1, t, x_3)$ would stand for the wff which results from the substitution of t for the free variable x_2, say.

In general we will use $A(x_1, x_2, ..., x_n)$ to indicate a wff in which the free variables, if there are any, are taken from the set $\{x_1, x_2, ..., x_n\}$. It does not preclude other free variables, but we will assume that there are no others.

Let us turn our attention now to the matter of substitution, because a certain amount of care is needed when substituting a term for a free variable. Consider, $(\forall x)A(y)$, for example (here we are using A to stand for a relation, in fact a one-place relation, or property). The wff symbolises the assertion that 'no matter what object x represents, the object that y stands for has the property represented by A'. Clearly, the intention of this interpretation would be preserved if we had used the wff $(\forall x)A(z)$, i.e. if we had used z instead of y. And similarly, if we had substituted w for y.

But, the interpretation would *not* be the same if we substituted x for y to get $(\forall x)A(x)$. Here the interpretation would be that the property A holds of every object in the domain of interpretation, and this is very different from saying that, regardless of what object x stands for, the object y (or z, or w) has the property A.

Of course, the wff $(\forall x)A(y)$ may strike you as a little odd: what is the point of $(\forall x)$ and what is the relevance of x to y's properties? The fact is that, in practice, we do expect strong inter-relevance between the different parts of a sentence (and even of a more extended discourse such as a paragraph, a chapter or even a book). We tend to depart from relevance only to make a (perhaps dramatic) point, e.g. 'I don't care what day of the week it is, I'm still a human being'. However, in first order predicate logic we are dealing with well-formed formulae in general, and we try to cover all kinds of possibilities. So, we will deal with 'odd' wff such as $(\forall x)A(y)$.

Let us get back to the question of substitution. We say that z is *free for* y in $(\forall x)A(y)$, but that x is not free for y. Similarly, $f(x)$ would not be free for y in $(\forall x)A(y)$, whereas $f(z)$, or even $f(y)$ would be. This makes sense when we consider a possible interpretation over the domain of human beings, where f might stand for 'mother'. Thus suppose A stands for 'is young'. It might be true to say that 'no matter who we talk about, Joe's mother is young', which might be the interpretation of $(\forall x)A(f(z))$ where z stands for Joe, but it is almost certainly false that 'everybody's mother is young', which would be the interpretation of $(\forall x)A(f(x))$.

The basic idea behind determining *free for* is that the term which is substituted for a free variable should not itself have a variable which becomes bound through the substitution.

Definition   In general, if A is any wff in a first order language L, a term t is *free for* x_i in A if no free occurrence of x_i falls within the scope of $(\forall x_k)$ or $(\exists x_k)$ where x_k occurs in the term t.

Example 6.1

Consider the wff $(\forall x_1)((\exists x_2)A_1^3(x_1, x_2, x_3) \wedge (\exists x_3)A_1^2(x_3, x_4))$.

x_5 is free for x_4.

x_4 is free for x_4.

$f_1^1(x_5)$ is free for x_4.

$f_1^1(x_2)$ is free for x_4, since x_4 does not lie within the scope of the quantifier $(\exists x_2)$.

$f_1^2(x_2, x_5)$ is free for x_4, since x_4 does not lie within the scope of the quantifier $(\exists x_2)$.

Any term not involving x_1 or x_3 is free for x_4.

x_5 is free for x_3, since there is a free occurrence of x_3 not within the scope of a quantifier involving x_5.

x_2 is not free for x_3, since the free occurrence of x_3 lies within the scope of a quantifier involving x_2.

$f_1^2(x_2, x_5)$ is not free for x_3.

x_3 is free for x_3.

$f_1^2(x_3, x_3)$ is free for x_3.

Any term is free for x_1! Why is this? Because there are no free occurrences of x_1 in the given wff, and therefore no substitution can take place. So, terms are free for x_1 by default, as it were.

There are a few observations about substitutions worth keeping in mind
1. A term containing only constants is free for any variable in any wff.
2. A variable is always free for itself, i.e. x_i is free for x_i.
3. Any term is free for any variable that has no free occurrences.
4. A term t is free for any variable in a wff A if none of the variables in t is bound in A.

Substitution of variables as terms for free variables is not to be confused with replacement of bound variables by other variables. For example, the wff

$$(\forall x_5)((\exists x_2)A_1^3(x_5, x_2, x_3) \land (\exists x_3)A_1^2(x_3, x_4))$$

is clearly equivalent to

$$(\forall x_1)((\exists x_2)A_1^3(x_1, x_2, x_3) \land (\exists x_3)A_1^2(x_3, x_4)).$$

(Now, of course, we must be wary of terms involving x_5 when contemplating substitutions.) Again care must be taken in choosing the new variable to avoid fresh binding. Thus

$$(\forall x_2)((\exists x_2)A_1^3(x_2, x_2, x_3) \land (\exists x_3)A_1^2(x_3, x_4))$$

would not do as a replacement for

$$(\forall x_1)((\exists x_2)A_1^3(x_1, x_2, x_3) \land (\exists x_3)A_1^2(x_3, x_4))$$

Exercise

6.8 For each of the terms x_1, x_2, $f_1^1(x_1)$, $f_1^2(x_2, x_5)$, decide whether or not it is free for x_2, in each of the following wff:

(i) $A_1^3(x_1, x_2, x_3)$

(ii) $(\forall x_1)A_1^3(x_1, x_2, x_3)$

(iii) $(\forall x_1)(A_1^3(x_1, x_2, x_3) \rightarrow (\exists x_3)A_1^2(x_2, x_4))$

(iv) $(\forall x_1)(A_1^3(x_1, x_2, x_3) \rightarrow (\exists x_3)A_1^2(f_1^2(x_2, x_5), x_4))$

(v) $(\forall x_1)(A_1^3(x_1, x_2, x_3) \rightarrow (\exists x_5)A_1^2(f_1^2(x_2, x_5), x_4)$

6.7 Interpretations

In our deliberations so far we have relied on the intuition that the well-formed formulae of a first order language could be related to some 'obvious' sensible or familiar domain of objects. Thus, we might think of $A_1^2(x_2, x_3)$ as 'meaning' x_2 is less than x_3 in the domain of natural numbers. It is time now to justify our intuitions and put the notion of interpretation on a firmer footing.

The paraphernalia of first order languages – alphabet, terms and well-formed formulae – give us the equipment to deal with the form or *syntax* of predicate logic. But, in order to deal with 'meaning' or semantics, with questions of truth and falsity, we need to look into the issue of interpretations. So, what is an interpretation of a first order language?

Essentially an interpretation of a first order language is an association of the terms of the language with objects in a structured domain, together with an association of atomic wff with relations over the domain.

There are two essential ingredients then:

      (1) a *non-empty* domain of 'objects' D_I

and   (2) an association function I which links constants, function symbols, and predicate letters to D_I.

In more detail, an interpretation, I, of a first order language, L, assigns

- a fixed (or distinguished) element c'_i of D_I to each constant c_i of $L - I(c_i)$ is c'_i
- an n-ary function $f^n_i: D^n_I \to D_I$ to each function letter f^n_i
- an n-ary relation $R^n_i \subseteq D^n_I$ to each predicate letter P^n_i.

Note, it is important that the domain of interpretation be not empty. If empty domains were allowed some important validities would not hold, e.g. $(\forall x)A(x) \to (\exists x)A(x)$ and $(\exists x)(x=x)$.

The essential features of an interpretation of a first order language are set out in the following table:

1st order language symbol	Interpretation over non-empty domain D
Name of constant	Element of D
N-ary function letter	Mapping of n-tuples of elements of D into elements of D
N-ary predicate letter	N-ary relations on D, i.e. sets of n-tuples of elements of D
Quantifiers	The set D

Table 6.1

Note that, in general, the 'meaning' assigned to a predicate is an *extensional* or denotative one, i.e. it is given in terms of the set (extension) of tuples satisfying the predicate. This contrasts with an *intensional* or connotative meaning given in terms of some property or characteristic common to the elements picked out by the predicate. The distinction between extensional and intensional may be made clear by considering an interpretation of the binary predicate P^2_1 as the relation 'less than' on the natural numbers, say. The extensional meaning is given by the set of couples $\{(0, 1), (0,$

2), (1, 2), (0, 3), (1, 3), (2, 3), ...}, while the intensional meaning is given by (the assumed understanding of) $<$. Intensional meaning may sometimes be given by a statement of necessary and sufficient conditions for membership of a set. Within computer science it may be given by a program to compute members of a set or to decide membership.

Effectively an interpretation provides a *concrete* realisation of the *abstract* structures expressible in a first order language.

Example 6.2

Consider, for example, a first order language which has just one constant c_1, one function symbol f_1^1 and two predicate letters P_1^2 and P_2^2. Let us take the set of natural numbers as the domain of interpretation and make the following interpretation assignments:

$I(c_1)$ is 0.
$I(f_1^1)$ is the successor function, i.e. $I(f_1^1(x))$ is $x+1$. (Here we are using notation a little loosely to make the point clearly.)
$I(P_1^2)$ is '=', i.e. $I(P_1^2(x,y))$ is $x=y$.
$I(P_2^2)$ is '<', i.e. $I(P_2^2(x,y))$ is $x<y$.

Then the wff $P_2^2(c_1, f_1^1(c_1))$ is interpreted as '0 is less than the successor of 0', i.e. $0<0+1$. It is instructive to work this out slowly

$$I(P_2^2(c_1, f_1^1(c_1))) \qquad \text{is} \quad I(c_1) < I(f_1^1(c_1))$$

since R_1^2 (i.e. $I(P_2^2)$) is $<$, and we are using the more usual infix notation. (Using prefix notation this would be $<(I(c_1), I(f_1^1(c_1)))$.)

$$
\begin{aligned}
&\text{is} \quad I(c_1) < I(f_1^1)(I(c_1)) \\
&\text{is} \quad I(c_1) < \text{successor } (I(c_1)) \\
&\text{is} \quad 0 < \text{successor } (0) \\
&\text{is} \quad 0 < 0+1 \\
&\text{is} \quad 0 < 1
\end{aligned}
$$

which is clearly the case. Similarly,

$$
\begin{aligned}
I(P_1^2(c_1, f_1^1(f_1^1(c_1)))) \qquad &\text{is} \quad I(c_1) = I(f_1^1(f_1^1(c_1))), \text{ since } I(P_1^2) \text{ is } = \\
&\text{is} \quad I(c_1) = I(f_1^1)I(f_1^1(c_1))) \\
&\text{is} \quad I(c_1) = \text{successor}(I(f_1^1)(c_1)) \\
&\text{is} \quad I(c_1) = \text{successor}(\text{successor}(I(c_1))) \\
&\text{is} \quad 0 = \text{successor}(\text{successor}(0)) \\
&\text{is} \quad 0 = \text{successor}(1) \\
&\text{is} \quad 0 = 2
\end{aligned}
$$

which is clearly not the case.

Example 6.2 indicates that it is through interpretations that we can deal with questions of truth and falsity. We shall come to that in more detail later.

Example 6.3

Let us consider the same first order language as in the last example, but interpret it differently. Our domain of interpretation will be the set of people {Lillian, John, Stephen, Paul, Clare, Jo Ann, Barbara}. We take the following interpretation:

$I(c_1)$ is Barbara.
$I(f_1^1)$ is mother, i.e. $I(f_1^1(x))$ is x's mother.
$I(P_1^2)$ is brother, i.e. $I(P_1^2(x,y))$ is x is y's brother.
$I(P_2^2)$ is sister.

In case you are wondering why we have chosen to use a function for 'mother' and predicates for 'brother' and 'sister', there is no special reason, except to emphasise that there is a choice in these matters. It also allows us to explore which is the more convenient representation.
This time,

$$I(P_2^2(c_1, f_1^1(c_1)))$$

is $sister(I(c_1), I(f_1^1(c_1)))$
is $sister(I(c_1), I(f_1^1)(I(c_1)))$
is $sister(I(c_1), mother(I(c_1)))$
is $sister(Barbara, mother(Barbara))$

which is clearly not true, since Barbara is not her mother's sister (in ordinary biological circumstances anyway).
What about $I(P_1^2(c_1, f_1^1(f_1^1(c_1))))$?

$$I(P_1^2(c_1, f_1^1(f_1^1(c_1))))$$

is $brother(I(c_1), I(f_1^1(f_1^1(c_1))))$
is $brother(I(c_1), I(f_1^1)(I(f_1^1(c_1))))$
is $brother(Barbara, mother(I(f_1^1(c_1))))$
is $brother(Barbara, mother(I(f_1^1)I(c_1)))$
is $brother(Barbara, mother(mother(Barbara)))$

which again is not true, since Barbara is nobody's brother, and certainly not her grandmother's!
Let us extend our first order language by including two new constants c_2 and c_3 and interpret them as Lillian and John respectively. Now suppose we want to express the fact that Lillian's mother is John's maternal grandmother's sister.
How would we do it?
We want to say 'sister(mother(Lillian), mother(mother(John)))'.
Try the following:
$$P_2^2(f_1^1(c_2), f_1^1(f_1^1(c_3)))$$

Exercises

6.9 Using the first order language described above symbolise each of the following statements:

(i) 0 is the successor of 0.

(ii) 0 has no successor.

(iii) 0 has no predecessor.

(iv) If two numbers have the same successor they are equal.

(v) The successor of the successor of any number is greater than the successor of that same number.

(vi) Barbara is somebody's sister.

(vii) Barbara is everybody's sister.

(viii) Barbara's sister's brother is Barbara's brother.

(ix) Anybody's sister's brother is that person's brother.

(x) If anybody is Barbara's mother then she is everybody's mother.

6.10 Using the first order language described above determine in each of the following whether it is satisfied by either or both of the suggested interpretations.

(i) $P_2^2(f_1^1(f_1^1(c_1)), f_1^1(c_1))$

(ii) $P_1^2(f_1^1(f_1^1(c_1)), c_1)$

(iii) $(\forall x_1)(P_2^2(x_1, f_1^1(x_1)))$

(iv) $(\forall x_1)(\exists x_2)(P_2^2(x_2, f_1^1(x_1)))$

At long last we are in a position to reflect on the meaning of the phrase 'first order'. Essentially it refers to the kinds of interpretation of the terms and predicates of a predicate language. The objects of the domain of interpretation which are the targets for the terms of a first order language are 'first order' or primary objects. In what sense? In the sense that the terms cannot be used to stand for parts of these objects, or sets of such objects or sets of sets of such objects, or sets of sets of sets … Likewise, predicates stand for relations among the primary objects, not for relations among sets of objects.

Thus, if the domain is people, then a term can be interpreted as a person, but not as a set of persons, such as a family or a team, or a set of sets, such as a club perhaps.

Of course it is perfectly possible for the objects of the domain to be sets of simpler 'objects'. But then these sets will not be treated as sets but as simple unanalysable objects. If the domain is a collection of teams, then we must refer to each team as a whole. We will not be able to identify individual members of a team (using our first order language).

Languages of higher order (second order, etc.) can be developed to deal with sets and sets of sets, but we will not concern ourselves with them in this text.

6.7.1 Valuations

Our discussion of interpretations so far has been notable for its omission of any consideration of the variables of a first order language. Essentially we have been concerned with interpretations as providing concrete structures with which to associate the constants, functions and predicates symbolised in a first order language. It is time now to deal with variables. We will define so-called *valuations* which will make assignments to all the terms of a first order language, including the variables.

Definition   A *valuation*, v, in an interpretation, I, of a first order language, L, is a function from the terms of L to the domain D_I, such that

(1) $v(c_i) = I(c_i)$, i.e. the same value as given by I itself

(2) $v(f_i^n(t_1, t_2, ..., t_n)) = f_i^n(v(t_1), v(t_2), ..., v(t_n))$

(3) $v(x_i) \in D_I$, i.e. each variable is mapped onto some element of D_I.

Note that part (2) of the definition is inductive. For an n-ary function f_i^n in L, the valuation v picks out the object in D_I got by applying the n-ary function over D_I associated with f_i^n through the interpretation I, to the n-tuple of objects in D_I given by the valuations of the terms t_i. The easiest way to visualise this is through an example.

Example 6.4

Consider a first order language with one constant c_1, a unary function letter f_1^1, and a binary function letter f_1^2. Consider an interpretation I

$$
\begin{array}{lll}
D_I & \text{is} & \text{N (the set of Natural Numbers)} \\
I(c_1) & \text{is} & 0 \\
I(f_1^1) & \text{is} & f_1^1 \text{ is successor} \\
I(f_1^2) & \text{is} & f_1^2 \text{ is sum, i.e. } f_1^2(x,y) \text{ is } x + y
\end{array}
$$

and valuation v where $v(x_i) = i-1$, i.e. $v(x_1) = 0$, $v(x_2) = 1$, etc.

Then $v(c_1) = I(c_1) = 0$

$v(x_5) = 4$

$v(f_1^1(x_5)) = f_1^1(v(x_5))$

$\qquad\qquad = \text{successor}(4) = 5$

$v(f_1^2(c_1, x_5)) = f_1^2(v(c_1), v(x_5))$

$\qquad\qquad = \text{sum}(0, 4) = 4$

$v(f_1^2(f_1^1(x_3), f_1^2(c_1, f_1^1(x_5)))) = f_1^2(v(f_1^1(x_3)), v(f_1^2(c_1, f_1^1(x_5))))$

$\qquad\qquad = \text{sum}(f_1^1(v(x_3)), f_1^2(v(c_1), v(f_1^1(x_5))))$

$\qquad\qquad = \text{sum}(f_1^1(2), f_1^2(0, f_1^1(v(x_5))))$

$\qquad\qquad = \text{sum}(f_1^1(2), f_1^2(0, f_1^1(4)))$

$$= \text{sum}(3, f_1^2(0, 5))$$
$$= \text{sum}(3, 5) = 8$$

Exercise

6.11 Using the first order language, the interpretation and the valuation described above evaluate each of the following:

    (i) $v(x_{50})$

    (ii) $v(f_1^1(x_{50}))$

    (iii) $v(f_1^1(f_1^1(x_{50})))$

    (iv) $v(f_1^2(f_1^1(x_{50}), x_{50}))$

    (v) $v(f_1^2(f_1^1(x_{50}), f_1^2(f_1^1(x_{50}), x_{50})))$

6.7.2 Satisfaction

Consider a first order language with a binary predicate P_1^2. Take an interpretation over the natural numbers where P_1^2 is interpreted as =. Then clearly $P_1^2(x_1, x_1)$ is *satisfied* by any valuation v, since $v(x_1) = v(x_1)$, no matter what $v(x_1)$ is. But, $P_1^2(x_1, x_2)$ may or may not be satisfied by a given valuation v. If $v(x_1) = 3$ and $v(x_2) = 3$, say, then clearly $P_1^2(x_1, x_2)$ is satisfied. But, if $v(x_1) = 3$ and $v(x_2) = 5$, say, then clearly $P_1^2(x_1, x_2)$ is not satisfied.

We must define the idea of satisfaction for all wff of a first order language.

Definition   Let I be an interpretation of a first order language L. Let v be a valuation in I and let A be any wff of L. Then

    (1)   If A is an atomic wff, $P_i^n(t_1, t_2, ..., t_n)$, v *satisfies* A iff the n-tuple $(v(t_1), v(t_2), ..., v(t_n))$ obeys the relation R_I^n, i.e. if $R_i^n(v(t_1), v(t_2), ..., v(t_n))$ holds over D_I.

    (2)   If A has the form $\neg B$, then v *satisfies* A iff v does not satisfy B.

    (3)   If A has the form $B \wedge C$, then v *satisfies* A iff v satisfies B and v satisfies C.

    (4)   If A has the form $B \vee C$, then v *satisfies* A iff v satisfies B or v satisfies C or v satisfies both B and C.

    (5)   If A has the form $B \rightarrow C$, then v *satisfies* A iff v does not satisfy B or v satisfies C, i.e v satisfies $\neg B$ or C.

    (6)   If A has the form $B \leftrightarrow C$, then v *satisfies* A iff v satisfies both B and C or v satisfies neither B nor C.

    (7)   If A has the form $(\forall x_i)B$, then v *satisfies* A iff v satisfies B for all elements of D_I, i.e. no matter what $v(x_i)$ is in D_I.

    (8)   If A has the form $(\exists x_i)B$, then v *satisfies* A iff v satisfies B for some element of D_I, i.e. there is some $v(x_i)$ for which B is satisfied.

Although we have defined a valuation, v, for terms only, we will extend its notational use to the extent of writing v(A) as a shorthand for the interpreted value of the wff A.

Example 6.5

Let us take a specific example. Consider a first order language with

> one constant c_1
> one unary function letter f_1^1
> two binary function letters f_1^2 and f_2^2
> two binary predicate letters P_1^2 and P_2^2

and take an interpretation I as

> D_I is the set of natural numbers.
> $I(c_1)$ is 0.
> $I(f_1^1)$ is successor.
> $I(f_1^2)$ is sum.
> $I(f_2^2)$ is product.
> $I(P_1^2)$ is '=', i.e. R_1^2 is '='.
> $I(P_2^2)$ is '<', i.e. R_2^2 is '<'.

Finally, let the valuation v be such that $v(x_i) = i$.

Consider the evaluation of $P_2^2(c_1, f_1^1(f_1^1(c_1)))$, i.e. $v(P_2^2(c_1, f_1^1(f_1^1(c_1))))$. v will satisfy this wff iff $R_2^2(v(c_1), v(f_1^1(f_1^1(c_1))))$, i.e if the pair $(v(c_1), v(f_1^1(f_1^1(c_1))))$, is in the relation < over D_I. In less stilted language, v will satisfy $P_2^2(c_1, f_1^1(f_1^1(c_1)))$ if $v(c_1)$ is less than $v(f_1^1(f_1^1(c_1)))$.

Clearly, this is the case, since

$$v(c_1) = 0$$

and

$$v(f_1^1(f_1^1(c_1))) = v(f_1^1)(v(f_1^1(c_1)))$$
$$= successor(v(f_1^1)(v(c_1)))$$
$$= successor(successor(0))$$
$$= 2$$

and $\quad 0 < 2$.

We can summarise this by saying that $v(P_2^2(c_1, f_1^1(f_1^1(c_1)))) = 0 < 2$ and that is the case in this interpretation.

Example 6.6

As another example, consider

$$P_2^2(c_1, f_1^1(c_1)) \rightarrow P_1^2(f_1^2(c_1, f_1^1(c_1)), f_2^2(c_1, f_1^1(c_1)))$$

With a little thought you will see that this states (in the given interpretation) that

$$(0<1) \rightarrow ((0+1) = (0\times1))$$
i.e. $\quad (0<1) \rightarrow (1=0)$

which is clearly not the case.

However let us work through the example more formally to see if we can come up with the same conclusion. The wff is in the form B→C, so we will possibly need to evaluate both B and C. If, of course, B is not satisfied we need not go on to evaluate C, since we know immediately from the definition that B→C will be satisfied. First let us evaluate B, i.e. $P_2^2(c_1, f_1^1(c_1))$.

$$
\begin{aligned}
v(P_2^2(c_1, f_1^1(c_1))) &= v(c_1) < v(f_1^1(c_1)) \\
&= 0 < v(f_1^1)(v(c_1)) \\
&= 0 < successor(0) \\
&= 0 < 1
\end{aligned}
$$

which, of course, is the case. So v satisfies B, i.e. $P_2^2(c_1, f_1^1(c_1))$. Too bad! We must now evaluate C, i.e. $P_1^2(f_1^2(c_1, f_1^1(c_1)), f_2^2(c_1, f_1^1(c_1)))$

$$
\begin{aligned}
v(P_1^2(f_1^2(c_1, f_1^1(c_1)), f_2^2(c_1, f_1^1(c_1)))) & \\
&= v(f_1^2(c_1, f_1^1(c_1))) = v(f_2^2(c_1, f_1^1(c_1))), \text{ since } I(P_1^2) \text{ is } =. \\
&= f_1^2(v(c_1), v(f_1^1(c_1))) = f_2^2(v(c_1), v(f_1^1(c_1))) \\
&= sum(v(c_1), v(f_1^1)(v(c_1))) = product(v(c_1), v(f_1^1)(v(c_1))) \\
&= sum(0, successor(0)) = product(0, successor(0)) \\
&= sum(0, 1) = product(0, 1) \\
&= 1=0
\end{aligned}
$$

which of course is not the case.

So, for this form, B→C, v satisfies B but does not satisfy C. Therefore v does not satisfy B→C, i.e. v does not satisfy

$$P_2^2(c_1, f_1^1(c_1)) \rightarrow P_1^2(f_1^2(c_1, f_1^1(c_1)), f_2^2(c_1, f_1^1(c_1)))$$

Example 6.7

Let us take another example, using the same interpretation and valuation as in example 6.6. Does v satisfy $(\forall x_1)P_2^2(x_1, f_1^1(x_1))$?

What would it mean to say that v satisfies $(\forall x_1)P_2^2(x_1, f_1^1(x_1))$?

It would mean that $P_2^2(x_1, f_1^1(x_1))$ is the case no matter what element of the domain x_1 is interpreted as, i.e. no matter what natural number x_1 stands for. Since P_2^2 is interpreted as <, and f_1^1 is interpreted as successor, that would mean in this case that, for every value of x_1, $x_1 <$ successor(x_1). Which, of course is the case. Therefore, v does indeed satisfy $(\forall x_1)P_2^2(x_1, f_1^1(x_1))$.

Example 6.8

Let us consider one final example. Does v satisfy the well-formed formula $(\forall x_1)(\exists x_2)P_1^2(x_2, f_2^2(x_2, x_1))$?

What are we looking for here? Putting it in fairly crude terms we want to see if, no matter what value x_1 has, there is some value for x_2, which makes the value of x_2 equal (P_1^2) to the product (f_2^2) of x_2 and x_1.

In other words is $x_2 = x_2 \times x_1$ for some x_2, no matter what x_1 is?

Clearly, the answer is yes, since, no matter what value x_1 has, if the value of x_2 is 0, then $x_2 = x_2 \times x_1$, i.e. $0 = 0 \times x_1$.

So, v does satisfy $(\forall x_1)(\exists x_2)P_1^2(x_2, f_2^2(x_2, x_1))$.

You may have a niggling worry about some of the discussion involving satisfaction when the quantifiers are involved. Take the last example for instance. You may think, 'Surely v has already given a value to x_2, namely 2'. How then can we give x_2 a different value, namely 0, and still talk about v satisfying the formula?

Well, essentially, the quantifiers behave differently from the other logical elements where valuations are concerned. In a sense they 'override' the specific values given to quantified variables. When we speak about a particular valuation, v, satisfying a wff of the form $(\forall x_i)A$ or $(\exists x_i)A$, we mean that, so long as we keep the values of terms not involving x_i the same, then the assertion which interprets A will hold. We mean that A is the case for all valuations which differ from v, if they differ at all, only in the value they give to x_i. It is convenient (following Hamilton, 1978) to call such valuations *i-equivalent valuations*.

Definition   Two valuations u and v are said to be *i-equivalent* if $u(x_j) = v(x_j)$ for every variable x_j, except *possibly* when $j = i$.

We may re-cast our definitions of satisfaction for quantified formulae in terms of i-equivalent valuations.

Re-definition   If A has the form $(\forall x_i)B$, then v *satisfies* A iff every valuation w which is i-equivalent to v satisfies A.

If A has the form $(\exists x_i)B$, then v *satisfies* A iff there is some valuation w which is i-equivalent to v which satisfies A.

What all this boils down to for the interpretation of the wff $(\forall x_1)(\exists x_2)P_1^2(x_2, f_2^2(x_2, x_1))$ is that it does not matter what values v gives to x_1 and x_2. We are simply concerned with whether there is any value of x_2 which, regardless of the value of x_1, allows the wff to be satisfied.

The essential point to grasp in dealing with the satisfaction of a wff is that it is the values given to the *free* variables which determine whether or not the wff is satisfied by a particular valuation or not. If there are no free occurrences of variables, then the actual valuation does not matter. The interpretation itself will determine whether or not the wff is satisfied. We will come back to this point later.

In the above formula the value of x_2 was the same regardless of the value of x_1, namely 0. But in general, in a situation involving $(\forall x_1)(\exists x_2)$ in that order, the value of x_2, if one exists, will depend on the value of x_1.

Take, for example, the wff $(\forall x_1)(\exists x_2)P_2^2(x_1, x_2)$. This asserts that for every x_1 there exists an x_2 bigger than x_1. This is clearly the case in the interpretation given above, but the value of x_2 is not indifferent to the value of x_1. If $v(x_1) = 79$, then there are many values that x_2 could take to bring about satisfaction of the wff, e.g. 80, 100, 133, etc. But those values must all be greater than 79. So, effectively, x_2 is a function of 79 or, in general, x_2 is a function of x_1.

Exercise

6.12 Using the first order language, interpretation and valuation given above, determine whether or not each of the following wff is satisfied.

(i) $P_1^2(f_1^1(c_1), f_1^1(c_1))$

(ii) $P_2^2(f_1^1(c_1), c_1)$

(iii) $(\exists x_1)P_1^2(f_1^1(c_1), x_1)$

(iv) $(\forall x_2)(\exists x_1)P_1^2(f_1^1(x_2), x_1)$

(v) $(\exists x_1)(\forall x_2)P_1^2(f_1^1(x_2), x_1)$

(vi) $(\forall x_1)(\forall x_2)(P_1^2(x_1, x_2) \rightarrow P_1^2(x_2, x_1))$

(vii) $P_2^2(c_1, f_1^1(c_1)) \wedge P_1^2(f_1^2(c_1, f_1^1(c_1)), f_2^2(c_1, f_1^1(c_1)))$

(viii) $P_2^2(c_1, f_1^1(c_1)) \vee P_1^2(f_1^2(c_1, f_1^1(c_1)), f_2^2(c_1, f_1^1(c_1)))$

(ix) $P_2^2(x_i, f_1^1(x_i))$

(x) $(\forall x_i)P_2^2(x_i, f_1^1(x_i))$

6.7.3 Truth

You may have noticed that in our discussions of satisfaction we have scrupulously eschewed all mention of truth. We have said things like 'it is the case' or 'it is always the case that', but never 'it is true', even for obvious truths like '0 < 2'. Well, we were being a bit pedantic, but basically we wanted to reserve the term 'true in an interpretation' for the technical meaning we are now about to give it.

Definition   A wff A is *true in an interpretation* I iff every valuation in I satisfies A.

A wff A is *false in an interpretation* I iff no valuation in I satisfies A.

For example, in the interpretation used in Exercise 6.12, the wff $(\forall x_1)P_2^2(x_1, f_1^1(x_1))$ is true, since it is interpreted as 'Every natural number is less than its successor'. So no matter what value is assigned to x_1, $x_1 < f_1^1(x_1)$. If we change the interpretation of f_1^1 to predecessor rather than successor, the wff will be false. This underlines the fact that *truth is relative to an interpretation*.

It is important to keep in mind that a wff may be neither true nor false in an interpretation. It may simply be satisfiable. Consider the wff $P_2^2(x_1, x_2)$ and our familiar interpretation over the natural numbers. Clearly this is neither true nor false, since it is satisfied by some valuations but not by others. It will be satisfied for all those valuations v such that $v(x_1) < v(x_2)$, but will not be satisfied by valuations for which $v(x_1) >= v(x_2)$.

If the wff A is true in I we express this by $I \vDash A$

Theorem 6.1

$$I \vDash A \text{ iff } I \vDash (\forall x_i)A$$

Proof

If Suppose $I \vDash A$ and take any valuation v in I. The question is, does v satisfy $(\forall x_i)A$?
For v to satisfy $(\forall x_i)A$, we require A to be satisfied no matter what value is given to x_i, i.e. we require every valuation i-equivalent to v to satisfy A. But this is the case since $I \vDash A$ and therefore every valuation (let alone the i-equivalent ones) satisfies A.

$\therefore$ v satisfies $(\forall x_i)A$

But v was arbitrary.

$\therefore$ Every valuation in I satisfies $(\forall x_i)A$

$\therefore$ $(\forall x_i)A$ is true in I, i.e. $I \vDash (\forall x_i)A$

Only if Suppose $I \vDash (\forall x_i)A$ and take any valuation v in I. The question is, does v satisfy A?
Since $I \vDash (\forall x_i)A$, v satisfies $(\forall x_i)A$.

$\therefore$ Every valuation i-equivalent to v satisfies A.

$\therefore$ v satisfies A, since v is i-equivalent to itself.

$\therefore$ Since v is arbitrary, every valuation in I satisfies A.

$\therefore$ $I \vDash A$

(End)

Exercises

6.13 Using the same conditions as in Exercise 6.12, determine which of the listed wff are true in the given interpretation.

6.14 If A is true in a given interpretation I, prove that ¬A is false.

6.15 Prove that A∧B is true in a given interpretation I iff both A and B are true in I.

6.16 Prove that A∨B is true in a given interpretation I iff either A or B or both are true in I.

6.17 Prove that A→B is false in a given interpretation I iff both A is true and B is false in I.

6.18 If x_1, x_2, ..., x_n are variables of L, possibly occurring in a wff A, prove that $I \vDash A$ iff $I \vDash (\forall x_1)(\forall x_2)...(\forall x_n)A$.

6.7.4 Validity

The notion of validity follows on from the notion of truth in an interpretation.

Definition   A wff, A, of a first order language, L, is *logically valid* if it is true in every interpretation of L. That means that for A to be valid it must be satisfied by every valuation in every interpretation.

Definition   A wff, A, of a first order language, L, is *contradictory* if it is false in every interpretation of L, in other words if it is not satisfiable in any interpretation.

In general then we see that a wff of a first order language may be characterised in one of the following ways:

1. It may be satisfied by some valuations and not satisfied by other valuations in a given interpretation. If it can be satisfied by some valuation it is said to be satisfiable.

2. It may be satisfied by every valuation in a given interpretation I, but not necessarily satisfied by every valuation in other interpretations. It is said to be true in I.

3. It may be satisfied by every valuation in every interpretation. It is said to be valid.

4. It may be satisfied by no valuation in any interpretation. It is said to be contradictory or inconsistent.

Exercises

6.19 Categorise each of the following wff as (a) satisfiable, (b) true in some interpretation, (c) valid, or (d) none of (a), (b), (c):

(i) $P_1^2(c_1, c_2)$

(ii) $P_1^2(x_1, x_2)$

(iii) $(\forall x_1)P_1^2(c_1, c_2)$

(iv) $(\forall x_1)P_1^2(x_1, x_2)$

(v) $(\forall x_1)(\forall x_2)P_1^2(x_1, x_2)$

(vi) $(\forall x_1)(\forall x_2)(P_1^2(x_1, x_2) \rightarrow P_1^2(x_1, x_2))$

(vii) $(\forall x_1)(\forall x_2)(P_1^2(x_1, x_2) \rightarrow P_1^2(x_2, x_1))$

(viii) $(\forall x_1)(\forall x_2)(P_1^2(x_1, x_2) \wedge P_1^2(x_2, x_1))$

(ix) $(\forall x_1)(\forall x_2)(P_1^2(x_1, x_2) \vee \neg P_1^2(x_1, x_2))$

(x) $(\forall x_1)(\forall x_2)(P_1^2(x_1, x_2) \rightarrow (\neg P_1^2(x_1, x_2) \rightarrow P_3^3(x_1, x_3, f_2^1(x_2))))$

6.20 Prove that if A and A→B are logically valid, then B is logically valid.

6.21 Prove that if A is logically valid, then $(\forall x_1)A$ is logically valid.

6.22 Prove that $(\forall x_1)A \rightarrow (\exists x_1)A$ is logically valid.

Historical Notes

Gottlob Frege (1848–1925)

Along with George Boole, Frege may be considered to be the founder of modern mathematical logic. Before them, logic had been virtually stagnant for two thousand years under the dominant influence of Aristotle's great work on the syllogistic forms of reasoning.

Frege's work was also deeply influential in the development of modern approaches to the philosophy of mathematics and the philosophy of language, and in laying the foundations of modern axiomatic approaches to mathematics and logic. His objective was to secure the validity of every step in a mathematical proof by making explicit the assumptions, axioms and rules of deduction being used and thus to eliminate intuition from mathematical arguments. He considered that arithmetic is basically a part of logic and could be expressed entirely using concepts and formalisms of logic.

Frege's main works were: *Begriffsshrift, eine der arithmetischen nachgebildete Formelsprache des reinen Denkens* (1879), *Die Grundlagen der Arithmetik* (1884) and *Grundgesetze der Arithmetik* (1893–1903).

His main interests were his family and his work. He was a subtle and profound thinker and a gifted and conscientious teacher, with a particular aptitude for explaining complex topics. He lived a quiet scholarly life which, unfortunately, was marred by tragedy on more than one occasion. His father died when he was just a boy, and later his children and his wife died young. In spite of his original thinking and profoundly seminal work, Frege received little public recognition during his lifetime. However, he is now one of the most studied of philosophers.

6.7.5 More on Satisfaction and Truth

Earlier we remarked that it is the free variables that determine whether a wff is satisfied by a particular valuation or not. This carries with it the implication that if a wff has no free variables then particular valuations can make no difference to whether it is satisfied or not. We want to prove this now. First we prove some important preliminary theorems.

Theorem 6.2

Let t be a term of a first order language which contains at least one occurrence of the variable x_i. Let s be another term, and let u and v be two i-equivalent valuations in an interpretation I such that $v(x_i) = u(s)$. Let t_s be the term obtained from t by substituting s for every occurrence of x_i in t. Then $v(t) = u(t_s)$.

Proof By induction on the structure of t.

Basis step t is just x_i.

Then $t_s = s$

and
$$v(t) = v(x_i) = u(s) \qquad \text{given}$$
$$= u(t_s) \qquad \text{since } s = t_s$$

Induction step Let $t = f_i^n(t_1, t_2, ..., t_n)$ and, as induction hypothesis, suppose $v(t_k) = u(t_{ks})$ where t_k is of lesser complexity than t, and t_{ks} results from substituting s for x_i in t_k.

Then $v(t) = f_i^n(v(t_1), v(t_2), ..., v(t_n))$

$\qquad\quad = f_i^n(u(t_{1s}), u(t_{2s}), u(t_{3s}), ..., u(t_{ns})) \qquad$ by induction hypothesis

$\qquad\quad = u(t_s), \quad$ since $t_s = f_i^n(t_{1s}, t_{2s}, ..., t_{ns})$

(End)

Theorem 6.3

Let $A(x_i)$ be a wff of a first order language which contains at least one free occurrence of the variable x_i. Let t be a term which is free for x_i, and let u and v be two i-equivalent valuations in an interpretation I such that $v(x_i) = u(t)$. Let A(t) be the wff obtained from $A(x_i)$ by substituting t for every occurrence of x_i in $A(x_i)$. Then u satisfies A(t) iff v satisfies $A(x_i)$.

Proof By induction on the structure of $A(x_i)$.

Basis step $A(x_i)$ is an atomic wff, say, $P_i^n(t_1, t_2, ..., t_n)$.

If v satisfies $A(x_i)$, then $(v(t_1), v(t_2), ..., v(t_n)) \in R_i^n$

But, $u(t_{it}) = v(t_i)$ from Theorem 6.2 where t_{it} is the term resulting from the substitution of t for x_i in t_i.

$\qquad$ Therefore $(u(t_{1t}), u(t_{2t}), ..., u(t_{nt})) = (v(t_1), v(t_2), ..., v(t_n))$

$\qquad$ Therefore $(u(t_{1t}), u(t_{2t}), ..., u(t_{nt})) \in R_i^n$

i.e. u satisfies A(t).

Induction step There are seven cases in all to consider, namely

$\qquad A(x_i) = \neg B(x_i)$

$\qquad A(x_i) = B(x_i) \wedge C(x_i)$

$\qquad A(x_i) = B(x_i) \vee C(x_i)$

$\qquad A(x_i) = B(x_i) \rightarrow C(x_i)$

$\qquad A(x_i) = B(x_i) \leftrightarrow C(x_i)$

$\qquad A(x_i) = (\forall x_k)B(x_i)$

$\qquad A(x_i) = (\exists x_k)B(x_i)$

The first five cases are straightforward and we will illustrate the technique through just one example: $A(x_i) = B(x_i) \rightarrow C(x_i)$.

If v does *not* satisfy $A(x_i)$, then v satisfies $B(x_i)$ and v does not satisfy $C(x_i)$. Hence, by induction hypothesis, u satisfies $B(t)$ and u does not satisfy $C(t)$.

∴ u does not satisfy $A(t)$

Conversely, if v does *not* satisfy $A(t)$, then v satisfies $B(t)$ and v does not satisfy $C(t)$. Hence, by induction hypothesis, u satisfies $B(x_i)$ and u does not satisfy $C(x_i)$.

∴ u does not satisfy $A(x_i)$

The last two cases are more interesting, but they are alike, so we will just deal with the universal quantifier case, $A(x_i) = (\forall x_k)B(x_i)$.

Suppose v does not satisfy $A(x_i)$. We want to show that u does not satisfy $A(t) = (\forall x_k)B(t)$.

This requires us to show that there is some valuation which is k-equivalent to u, which does not satisfy $B(t)$.

Now, since v does not satisfy $A(x_i)$, there is some valuation v' k-equivalent to v, which does not satisfy $B(x_i)$.

Let u' be i-equivalent to v' and be such that $u'(t) = v'(x_i)$, $u'(x_i) = u(x_i)$. (You may care to check that we can make this assignment and still have u' i-equivalent to v'.)

Then, by induction hypothesis, since v' does not satisy $B(x_i)$, u' does not satisfy $B(t)$.

But, u' is k-equivalent to u. This may be seen as follows:

$$u'(x_j) \quad = v'(x_j), j \neq i \quad \text{since u' is i-equivalent to v'}$$
$$= v(x_j), j \neq k \quad \text{since v' is k-equivalent to v}$$
$$= u(x_j), j \neq i \quad \text{since v and u are i-equivalent to each other}$$

∴ If $j \neq i$ and $j \neq k$, $u'(x_j) = u(x_j)$

Also, $u'(x_i) = u(x_i)$, by definition of u' above.

∴ u and u' differ at most on x_k, i.e. they are k-equivalent

∴ since u' does not satisfy $B(t)$, u does not satisfy $(\forall x_k)B(t) = A(t)$

Conversely suppose u does not satisfy $A(t) = (\forall x_k)B(t)$. We want to show that v does not satisfy $A(x_i) = (\forall x_k)B(x_i)$.

This requires us to show that there is some valuation which is k-equivalent to v and which does not satisfy $B(x_i)$.

Now, since u does not satisfy $A(t)$, there is some valuation u', k-equivalent to u, which does not satisfy $B(t)$.

Let v' be i-equivalent to u' and be such that $v'(x_i) = u'(t)$.

Then, by induction hypothesis, since u' does not satisy $B(t)$, v' does not satisfy $B(x_i)$.

But, v' is k-equivalent to v. This may be seen as follows:

$$v'(x_j) \quad = u'(x_j), j \neq i \quad \text{since v' is i-equivalent to u'}$$
$$= u(x_j), j \neq k \quad \text{since u' is k-equivalent to u}$$

$\quad\quad\quad\quad\quad = v(x_j), j \neq i \quad\quad$ since v and u are i-equivalent to each other

$\quad\quad\quad \therefore$ If $j \neq i$ and $j \neq k$, $v'(x_j) = v(x_j)$

$\quad$ Also, $v'(x_i) = u'(t)$

$\quad\quad\quad\quad\quad = u(t) \quad\quad$ since u and u' differ at most on x_k and t cannot contain x_k,

$\quad\quad\quad\quad\quad\quad\quad\quad\quad\quad$ otherwise it would not be free x_i for in $(\forall x_k)B(x_i)$.

$\quad\quad\quad\quad\quad = v(x_i)$

$\quad\quad\quad \therefore$ v' and v agree on all variables except possibly x_k

$\quad\quad\quad \therefore$ v' is k-equivalent to v, and v' does not satisfy $B(x_i)$

$\quad\quad\quad \therefore$ v does not satisfy $(\forall x_k)B(x_i) = A(x_i)$

$\quad\quad\quad\quad\quad\quad\quad\quad\quad\quad\quad\quad\quad\quad\quad\quad\quad\quad\quad\quad\quad\quad$ *(End)*

Exercise

6.23 Complete the proof of Theorem 6.3 by dealing with the other five cases in the induction step.

Theorem 6.4

Let A be a wff of a first order language. Let u and v be two i-equivalent valuations in an interpretation I such that $v(x_j) = u(x_j)$ for every free variable x_j of A.   Then u satisfies A iff v satisfies A.

Proof By induction on the structure of A.

Basis step A is an atomic wff, say, $P_i^n(t_1, t_2, ..., t_n)$.

Clearly $u(t_i) = v(t_i)$, since any variables that occur in t_i are free variables and u and v agree on those.

$\quad\quad\quad$ Therefore u satisfies A iff $R_i^n(u(t_1), u(t_2), ..., u(t_n))$

$\quad\quad\quad\quad\quad\quad\quad\quad\quad$ iff $R_i^n(v(t_1), v(t_2), ..., v(t_n))$

$\quad\quad\quad\quad\quad\quad\quad\quad\quad$ iff v satisfies A

Induction step Again there are seven cases to consider:

$\quad\quad A = \neg B$

$\quad\quad A = B \wedge C$

$\quad\quad A = B \vee C$

$\quad\quad A = B \rightarrow C$

$\quad\quad A = B \leftrightarrow C$

$\quad\quad A = (\forall x_i)B$

$\quad\quad A = (\exists x_i)B$

and again the first five cases are straightforward. We shall work through just one example: $A = B \wedge C$

u satisfies A $\quad$ iff u satisfies B and u satisfies C

$\quad\quad\quad\quad\quad\quad$ iff v satisfies B and v satisfies C, by induction hypothesis

$\quad\quad\quad\quad\quad\quad$ iff v satisfies A.

Suppose $A = (\forall x_i)B$, and suppose u satisfies A. Then, every valuation u' which is i-equivalent to u satisfies B. We want to show that every valuation v' which is i-equivalent to v also satisfies B. Take any such v' and let u' be such that $u'(x_k) = u(x_k)$, $k \neq i$ and $u'(x_i) = v'(x_i)$. Then u' is i-equivalent to u and therefore satisfies B.

Also $u'(x_j) = u(x_j)$ $(j \neq i)$, for every variable x_j free in B, since they agree on every variable except possibly x_i.

$\qquad = v(x_j)$, since u and v agree on all free variables of A and, so, B

$\qquad = v'(x_j)$

x_i may also be free in B, but $u'(x_i) = v'(x_i)$.

$\qquad \therefore$ u' and v' agree on all the free variables of B

$\qquad \therefore$ By induction hypothesis, since u' satisfies B, v' satisfies B

$\qquad \therefore$ v satisfies A

The converse, i.e. proving that, if v satisfies A then so does u, is proved in exactly the same way.

The proof in the case of $A = (\exists x_i)B$ is carried out in very similar fashion and is left to yourself.

(End)

Exercise

6.24 Complete the proof of Theorem 6.4 by dealing with the other five cases in the induction step.

At last we get to the result promised at the start of this sequence of theorems.

Theorem 6.5

Let A be a *closed* wff of a first order language L, and let I be an interpretation of L. Then I $\models$ A or I $\models$ ¬A

Proof Essentially we have to prove that either

$\qquad$ (1) Every valuation in I satisfies A.

$\qquad$ or (2) No valuation in I satisfies A, i.e. every valuation satisfies ¬A.

Suppose A is satisfied by some valuation u in I. Then A will be satisfied by every valuation v that agrees with u on the free variables (Theorem 6.4). Or, to put it another way, a valuation v must disagree with u on at least one free variable if it is to fail to satisfy A. But there are no free variables to disagree on, since there are no free variables in A at all (A is closed). Hence if one valuation u satisfies A, every valuation will satisfy A. Otherwise no valuation satisfies A, and hence every valuation satisfies ¬A.

(End)

6.8 Higher Order Logic

We have pointed out that the interpretation of a term of a first order language is a simple, or unstructured, object in a non-empty domain. The object itself may in fact have a structure when considered from different points of view, e.g. a car, but as the 'target' of a term of a first order language it is an integral unit. Forget about steering wheel, or distributor, or spark plug, or whatever.

Another aspect of first order languages which is important is that quantification takes place only over variables, and not over predicates and functions. Thus $(\forall x_i)P_1^1(x_i)$ is a well-formed formula, but $(\forall P_1^1)(\exists x_i)P_1^1(x_i)$ is not. The first wff states that every x_i has the property denoted by P_1^1, while the second says that for every property P_1^1 there is an x_i which has that property. This latter assertion is certainly meaningful, and it may even be true in some interpretations. However, it cannot be formalised in a first order language. Similarly the usual formalisation of the Peano 'induction' axiom for arithmetic is not a first order wff:

$$(\forall P)(P(0) \wedge (\forall x)(P(x) \rightarrow P(s(x))) \rightarrow (\forall y)P(y))$$

where s is the successor function, i.e. $s(x) = x+1$.

Second order logic allows quantification over first order predicates and functions and provides facilities for expressing properties of functions and predicates and representing predicates with predicates and functions as arguments. The above Peano axiom is a second order formula.

Third order logic (although this is a term that is rarely, if ever, used) allows quantification over predicates and functions of second order and so on up through a never ending hierarchy of higher order logics, each succeeding order allowing quantification over predicates of lower order. However, it must be admitted that logics of these individual orders are never singled out for individual treatment. In general, consideration of higher order expressions is often developed within a treatment of a *theory of types*, first enunciated by Bertrand Russell in 1908 in an attempt to deal with paradoxes such as membership of the set of all sets which do not contain themselves. Needless to say we will not torment ourselves here with these paradoxes, nor with the theory of types.

Incidentally, propositional logic is occasionally referred to as zeroth order logic.

6.9 Logic in Programming – Formalising Software

We saw, in the first chapter, an example of simple Boolean algebra applied to computer science – specifically, digital circuit design. As most modern computers are built from digital circuits, clearly the underlying mathematical description of their operation is in logic. However, when we program a computer to operate in some way we do not use instructions which are directly related to the digital circuitry (at least not any more). Modern programming languages are much closer to the natural languages with which we communicate than the language of the microchip. This does not mean, though, that modern programming languages are themselves not based on mathematical logic. Loosely speaking, we can use higher order logic when reasoning about the higher level programming languages in a similar way to how we use Boolean algebra when reasoning about digital circuitry.

Much effort has been spent in making programming a more mathematically sound activity. This effort has led to a number of areas in computer science which are generally grouped under the term formal methods. One of the fundamental aims of formal methods is to apply the underlying mathematics of computers – logic – to the *art* of developing software in such a way that tedious, and often laborious, testing is eliminated (or significantly reduced) because the behaviour of systems is *provably* correct. For mainstream imperative programming – generally, with third generation languages such as 'C', Pascal, Ada, etc. – first order predicate logic is most suitable.

To apply mathematical logic in developing and proving properties of code it is necessary first to describe the behaviour of each instruction of the language formally. In other words, the semantics of the programming language must be defined in terms of mathematical logic.

In so doing, we also require that the logical bases of the forms of data that are handled by computers are sound and consistent. For example, we must assume that a system of logic describing arithmetic on integer numbers can provide us with the results we need such as

$$\forall x \; \forall y \; ((x \geq y) \rightarrow (x+1 \geq y+1))$$

which may be more familiarly written as

$$\forall x \; \forall y \; (G(x, y) \rightarrow G(s(x), s(y)))$$

with an interpretation for x and y over the domain of integers, s as the 'successor' function and G as the 'greater than or equal to' relation.

So, we will assume that we have chosen appropriate domains of interpretation when defining the computer program. Those with programming experience will realise that there are certain limitations imposed by computers on our domains of interpretation. For example, the set of natural numbers that computers can represent is limited by some finite bounds (until quite recently -32,768 to 32,767). However, it should be obvious that even these limitations can be accounted for in a properly constructed system.

6.9.1 Semantics of Assignment Instructions

We will see how logic is used to describe the most fundamental instruction in imperative programming languages – the assignment instruction. We consider here a simple language similar to Pascal.

A program takes a computer from a so-called initial state to a final state. What does this mean?

Definition Given a program with n variables x_1, x_2, ..., x_n the *state* of the program is the n-tuple of values $(X_1, X_2, ..., X_n)$ where X_i is the value of the variable x_i.

The initial state describes the input data – the values of the input variables – as presented to the computer. The final state describes the output data that result when program execution terminates. We are most interested in ensuring that the program is written in such a way that its final state is one of what we consider to be a correct set of states when started in one of a set of possible initial states.

During execution of a program the computer is taken through a (usually large) sequence of states from the initial to the final state. We need to be able to describe or characterise only those states that are permitted during execution of the program.

Definition A *characteristic predicate* of a set of states is such that only those states that satisfy the predicate are members of the set, i.e. given S a set of states, P_S is a characteristic predicate of S if for every x an element of S $P_S(x)$ holds.

For example, the simple predicate $((X > 0) \wedge (X \leq 3) \wedge (Y = 10))$ characterises the set of states $\{(1,10), (2,10), (3,10)\}$ of (x,y).

The predicate $((X > 5) \wedge (Z = X+2))$ characterises the (infinite) set of states $\{(6,8), (7,9), (8,10), ... \}$

The assignment instruction can be seen as a function which transforms a state of the program into another state. For example, the set of states characterised by the first predicate above would be transformed by the tatement x := y–1 into the set of states characterised by the predicate $((X = 9) \wedge (Y = 10))$.

We want to distinguish the 'before' and 'after' characteristic predicates of a statement, to make it clear which is which, since both usually involve the same variables. To do this we place the before prdicate to the left of (or above) the statement and the after predicate to the right of (or below) the statement. Thus, we would write the above as

$$\{(X > 0) \wedge (X \leq 3) \wedge (Y = 10)\} \; x := y–1 \; \{(X = 9) \wedge (Y = 10)\}$$

or

$$\{(X > 0) \wedge (X \leq 3) \wedge (Y = 10)\}$$
$$x := y–1$$
$$\{(X = 9) \wedge (Y = 10)\}$$

Definition   An *inductive assertion* is a triple
    {P} *statement* {Q}
where P and Q are characteristic predicates such that the set of states characterised by P is transformed into the set of states characterised by Q on execution of the statement.

In an inductive assertion {P} s {Q}, P is usually termed the *precondition* and Q the *postcondition*.

It is important to note that a characteristic predicate need not completely define the state of the program – provided no state that would falsify the predicate can exist at the point of execution at which the predicate is used. Usually, it will mention the variables that are involved in the statement. For example, the inductive assertion given above may be in a program that also involves a variable z, the value of which could be anything without falsifying the preconditions and the postconditions.

In general we can define the semantics of the assignment instruction with the following inductive assertion:
    {P(X)[e\X]} x := e {P(X)}
where x is a variable and *e* is an expression in the appropriate domain of interpretation. The predicate P(X)[e\X] indicates a substitution of *e* for every occurrence of X in the predicate P(X).

If the precondition is true with the expression substituted for every occurrence of the variable, then the predicate without the substitution will be true after assignment. This is exactly what we would expect of an assignment statement – it changes the value of the variable to be equal to the result of the expression.

For example
    $\{((X > 20) \wedge (Y = 18))[y+4 \setminus X]\}$ x := y +4 $\{((X > 20) \wedge (Y = 18))\}$
is a valid inductive assertion as
    $((X > 20) \wedge (Y = 18))[Y+4 \setminus X]$
is the predicate
    $((Y+4 > 20) \wedge (Y = 18))$
which is
    $((Y > 16) \wedge (Y = 18))$
which is clearly true.

Often when programming one can describe the result that one wishes to obtain, so a useful strategy is to work backwards from the required postcondition. Using this general description of the semantics of the assignment instruction and given a specific assignment instruction and the postcondition we wish to establish, we can calculate the appropriate precondition.

The following are some examples

Given x := y×2 {(X = 8)}
we calculate {(X = 8)[Y×2 \ X]}
which is {(Y×2 = 8)} which is {(Y = 4)}
giving the inductive assertion
　　　{(Y = 4)} x := y×2 {(X = 8)}

Given x := 4 {(X = 20)}
we calculate {(X = 20)[4 \ X]}
which is {(4 = 8)} which is {false}.
Thus, there is no state in which assigning the value 4 to x will establish a
state in which X = 20.

Given x := 65 {(X = 65)}
we calculate {(X = 65)[65 \ X]}
which is {(65 = 65)} which is {true}.
Thus, it is possible to establish the state in which X = 65 from *any* state by
assigning the value 65 to x.

Given x := x×2 {(X = 20)}
we calculate {(X = 20)[X×2 \ X]}
which is {(X×2 = 20)} which is {(X = 10)}
giving the inductive assertion
　　　{(X = 4)} x := y×2 {(X = 8)}
Note that we must be careful about the distinction between the precondition
and postcondition variables – in an assignment in which the variable being
assigned to is used in the expression its value *before* execution of the
instruction is used for the expression.

Exercise

6.25 Calculate the preconditions of each of the following statement,
　　　postcondition pairs:
　　　(i)　　x := y+30 {(X > 30)}
　　　(ii)　　y := x+z–15 {(Y < 15)}
　　　(iii)　x := x×z {(X > 20) ∧ (Z = 3)}
　　　(iv)　z := z×z+z {(Z < 3)}

6.10 Summary

•　First order predicate logic provides us with means to deal with the internal
　　structure of simple statements by symbolising objects and quantifiers rather
　　than merely whole statements.
•　The quantifiers used are ∀ (for all) and ∃ (there exists).
•　The order of the quantifiers in an expression can be significant.

- $\exists x \equiv \neg (\forall x) \neg$
- In general the alphabet of a first order language, L, will contain the symbols:
  - (i)   constants $c_1, c_2, \ldots, c_n, \ldots$ (sometimes called individual symbols)
  - (ii)   variables $x_1, x_2, \ldots, x_n, \ldots$
  - (iii) function letters f_i^n
  - (iv)   predicate letters P_i^n
  - (v)   logical connectives $\wedge, \vee, \neg, \rightarrow, \leftrightarrow$
  - (vi)   quantifiers $\forall, \exists$
  - (vii) punctuation symbols $(,)$ and ,
- Terms stand for objects. They are defined recursively as follows:
  - (i)   Every constant is a term.
  - (ii)   Every variable is a term.
  - (iii) If $t_1, t_2, \ldots, t_n$ are terms then $f_i^n(t_1, t_2, \ldots, t_n)$ is a term.
- Well-formed formulae are defined recursively as follows:
  - (i) $P_i^n(t_1, t_2, \ldots, t_n)$ is a well-formed formula, where the t_i are terms.
  - (ii)   If A and B are well-formed formulae so are $(\neg A)$, $(A \wedge B)$, $(A \vee B)$, $(A \rightarrow B)$, and $(A \leftrightarrow B)$.
  - (iii) If A is a well-formed formula so is $(\forall x_i)A$.
  - (iv)   If A is a well-formed formula so is $(\exists x_i)A$.
- Wff of type $P_i^n(t_1, t_2, \ldots, t_n)$ are called atomic formulae.
- In the wff $(\forall x_i)A$ or $(\exists x_i)A$, A is said to be the scope of the quantifier $(\forall x_i)$.
- When a variable x_i occurs within the scope of a quantifier $(\forall x_i)$ or $(\exists x_i)$ it is said to be bound. The occurrence of x_i in $(\forall x_i)$ or $(\exists x_i)$ is also said to be bound. An occurrence that is not bound is free.
- A wff is said to be closed if it contains no free occurrences of any variable.
- A term t is free for x_i in a wff A if no free occurrence of x_i falls within the scope of $(\forall x_k)$ or $(\exists x_k)$ where x_k occurs in t.
- An interpretation, I, of a first order language, L, contains
       (1)   a *non-empty* domain of 'objects' D_I
  and (2)   an association function I which links constants, function symbols, and predicate letters to D_I

  I assigns a fixed (or distinguished) element c'_i of D_I to each constant c_i of L. Thus, $I(c_i) = c'_i$.

  I assigns an n-ary function $f_i^n: D_I^n \rightarrow D_I$ to each function letter f_i^n.

  I assigns an n-ary relation $R_I^n \subseteq D_I^n$ to each predicate letter P_i^n.
- A valuation, v, in an interpretation, I, of a first order language, L, is a function from the terms of L to the domain D_I, such that
  (1) $v(c_i) = I(c_i)$, i.e. the same value as given by I itself.
  (2) $v(f_i^n(t_1, t_2, \ldots, t_n)) = f_i^n(v(t_1), v(t_2), \ldots, v(t_n))$
  (3) $v(x_i) \in D_I$, i.e. each variable is mapped onto some element of D_I.

- Two valuations are said to be i-equivalent valuations if they differ at most in the value they give to x_i.
- A wff A is true in an interpretation I iff every valuation in I satisfies A.
- A wff A is false in an interpretation I iff no valuation in I satisfies A.
- A wff A of a first order language L is *logically valid* if it is true in every interpretation of L. This is symbolised by $\models$ A.
- Higher order logic involves quantification over predicates and functions of lower order, e.g. first order.

In this chapter we have
- seen the need to develop better means of dealing with propositions and arguments, which are sensitive to the inner structure of statements.
- introduced various concepts relating to first order languages – quantifier, term, well-formed formula, predicate letter, function letter, scope, bound variable, free variable, substitution, interpretation, valuation, satisfaction, truth relative to an interpretation, validity, closed wff, model.
- proved a number of theorems relating to validity and substitution.
- discussed briefly the differences between first and higher order logics.
- seen an example of the application of first order logic to computer software.

In the next chapter we develop a formal axiomatic approach to first order predicate logic.

Miscellaneous Exercises

1. Represent each of the following in symbolic form, assuming a suitable domain of interpretation in each case:
   - (i) Every natural number is the sum of two natural numbers.
   - (ii) Every natural number is not the product of two natural numbers.
   - (iii) If $x < y$ and $y < z$ then $x < z$.
   - (iv) Some natural numbers are prime.
   - (v) Anyone who does not study logic will be frustrated.
   - (vi) Some people either study logic or are frustrated.
   - (vii) You can fool all of the people some of the time, and you can fool some of the people all of the time, but you cannot fool all of the people all of the time.

   Categorise as (a) a term, (b) a well-formed formula or (c) ill formed:
   - (i) $\neg \forall AB \wedge C$
   - (ii) $(\neg(\forall x)((A \vee B) \wedge C))$
   - (iii) $(\neg(\forall x)((P_4^1(x) \vee P_3^1(x)) \wedge P_7^1(x)))$
   - (iv) $(\neg(\forall x_1)((P_4^1(x_1) \vee P_3^1(x_1)) \wedge P_7^1(x_1)))$

(v) $f(x, y, g(x,y), h(g(x,z), y))$

(vi) $f_1^4(x_1, x_2, f_1^2(x_2, x_4), f_5^2(f_1^3(x_3, x_1), c_3))$

(vii) $(\exists x_1)(\forall x_2)(P_2^2(f_1^4(x_1, x_2, f_5^2(f_1^3(x_3, x_1), c_3))), x_2) \rightarrow P_2^1(f_1^2(x_2, x_4)))$

2.   Categorise as (a) a term, (b) a well-formed formula or (c) ill formed within the resources of the defined first order language:

    (i) $\forall x_1(A \vee B)$

    (ii) $(\forall x)(A \vee B)$

    (iii) $(\forall x_1)(A(x_1) \vee B(x_1))$

    (iv) $f_1^2(x_2, (\exists x_1)P_1^1(x_1))$

    (v) $(\exists x_1)P_1^1(f_1^2(x_2, x_1))$

    (vi) $f_1^2(x_2, f_1^2(x_2, f_1^2(x_1, f_1^2(x_2, x_1))))$

    (vii) $(\neg(\forall x_1)((P_1^1(x_1) \vee P_3^2(x_1, x_2)) \wedge P_2^1(x_3)))$

3.   For each quantifier in the following examples state its scope.
    For each variable state whether each occurrence is bound or free.

    (i) $(\forall x_1)(\forall x_2)P_1^3(x_1, x_2, x_3)$

    (ii) $(\forall x_1)(\exists x_2)(P_1^3(x_1, x_2, x_3) \rightarrow (\exists x_1)P_1^2(x_1, x_2))$

    (iii) $(\forall x_1)(P_1^1(x_1) \rightarrow (\exists x_2)(P_1^2(x_1, x_2) \rightarrow (\exists x_1)(P_1^3(x_1, x_2, x_3))))$

4.   Let L be a first order language which has two constants c_1 and c_2, four function symbols f_1^1, f_2^1, f_3^1 and f_4^1, and four predicate letters P_1^2, P_2^2, P_3^2 and P_1^3.
    Let I be an interpretation with domain the set of all people, as follows:

    $I(c_1)$ is Lillian. $I(c_2)$ is John.

    $I(f_1^1)$ is mother. $I(f_2^1)$ is father. $I(f_3^1)$ is sister. $I(f_4^1)$ is brother.

    $I(P_1^2)$ is '=', i.e. $P_1^2(x,y)$ is interpreted as $x = y$.

    $I(P_2^2)$ is 'loves', i.e. $P_2^2(x,y)$ is interpreted as x loves y.

    $I(P_3^2)$ is 'admires', i.e. $P_3^2(x,y)$ is interpreted as x admires y.

    $I(P_1^3)$ is 'mediates between', i.e. $P_1^3(x,y,z)$ is interpreted as x mediates between
         y and z.

    Symbolise in L :

    (i)   Maternal grandfather.

    (ii)   Paternal grandmother.

    (iii)   Uncle.

    (iv)   John loves Lillian.

    (v)   Everyone loves his sibling.

    (vi)   John admires someone.

    (vii)   Lillian loves everyone she admires.

    (viii) If anyone does not love his sister John mediates between them.

    (ix)   If no one admires his mother someone will love her or someone will
           mediate between the two.

Categorise as (a) satisfiable, (b) true in the given interpretation, (c) valid, or (d) inconsistent:

(i) $P_1^2(c_1, c_2)$

(ii) $P_2^2(c_1, c_2)$

(iii) $(\forall x_1)P_1^2(c_1, c_1)$

(iv) $(\forall x_1)(\forall x_2)(P_2^2(x_1, x_2) \rightarrow P_2^2(x_1, x_2))$

(v) $(\forall x_1)(\forall x_2)(P_2^2(x_1, x_2) \rightarrow P_2^2(x_2, x_1))$

(vi) $(\forall x_1)(P_3^2(x_1, f_2^1(f_2^1(f_2^1(x_1)))$

(vii) $(\forall x_1)(\forall x_2)(\forall x_3)(P_1^3(x_1, x_2, x_3) \rightarrow \neg P_2^2(x_2, x_3))$

(viii) $(\forall x_1)(\forall x_2)(\forall x_3)((P_1^3(x_1, x_2, x_3) \rightarrow \neg P_2^2(x_2, x_3)) \wedge (P_2^2(x_2, x_3) \vee P_3^2(x_2, x_3)) \wedge (P_3^2(x_2, x_3) \rightarrow \neg P_1^3(x_1, x_2, x_3)))$

5.   Is $P_1^2(x_1, x_2)$ logically valid? Must a wff be closed in order to be valid? Use an example to argue your case.

CHAPTER 7

An Axiomatic Approach to Predicate Logic

Chapter Aims

(1) To consolidate the concept of axiomatic system.
(2) To establish an axiomatic system for first order logic.
(3) To develop skills in proving theorems in first order logic.
(4) To distinguish between logical and proper axioms.
(5) To see how proper axioms define special systems.

At the end of this chapter you should
(a) have a deeper knowledge of first order systems.
(b) be familiar with the first order axiomatic system FOPL.
(c) be able to prove theorems in FOPL.
(d) be aware that FOPL is sound and complete, but not decidable.
(e) know how proper axioms are used to define specific theories.
(f) have a basic knowledge of the first order theory of identity and of formal programming.

7.1 Introduction

In this chapter we turn to more formal aspects of predicate logic, in particular to the issue of formal proofs and deductions. Remember that, from a formal perspective, we are not concerned directly with such matters as truth and validity and reference to interpretations, but with the use of defined rules of inference to derive wff from axioms or other wff.

We will draw upon our acquaintance with formal procedures in propositional logic to facilitate the acquisition of skills in predicate logic. Predicate logic is somewhat more complicated than propositional logic, but the same basic strategies are employed, with the addition of some extra features to take account of the quantifiers.

Let us begin by reviewing the description of formal systems from Chapter 4.

We recall that a formal axiomatic system has four types of ingredient:

(1) Σ: An *alphabet* of symbols, used to form strings or expressions in the system.

(2) WF: The set of *well-formed formulae*, a subset of all the strings that can be formed using Σ, i.e. WF $\subseteq \Sigma^*$, where Σ^* is the set of all strings over the alphabet Σ.

(3) Ax: The set of *axioms*, a subset of WF.

(4) R: A set of *rules of deduction*.

7.2 An Axiomatic System for First Order Predicate Logic

Our system for first order predicate logic will be expressed in terms of a first order language, L, as described in the last chapter. We fix L first of all. We will make L slightly slimmer than in the last chapter (by dropping the existential quantifier $\exists$, and some of the logical connectives, as we did in our axiomatic presentation of propositional logic). Also, we include $\perp$ but will use either $\neg A$ or $A \rightarrow \perp$ where necessary.

So, it will have the following ingredients:

(i) constants $c_1, c_2, ..., c_n, ...$, sometimes called individual symbols

(ii) variables $x_1, x_2, ..., x_n, ...$

(iii) function letters f_i^n

(iv) predicate letters P_i^n, predicate constant $\perp$

(v) logical connectives $\neg, \rightarrow$

(vi) quantifier $\forall$

(vii) punctuation symbols $(,)$ and $,$

Similarly the (slimmer) set, WF, of wff is defined as follows:

(i) $P_i^n(t_1, t_2, ..., t_n)$ is a wff, where the t_i are terms. Also, $\perp$ is a wff. These are the atomic wff.

(ii) If A and B are wff so are $(\neg A)$ and $(A \rightarrow B)$.

(iii) If A is a wff so is $(\forall x_i)A$.

Now a suitable axiomatic system, FOPL, for first order predicate logic is the following (A, B and C are *any* wff except where stated):

(1) L.

(2) WF.

(3) Axiom schemas:

Ax1 $A \rightarrow (B \rightarrow A)$

Ax2 $(A \rightarrow (B \rightarrow C)) \rightarrow ((A \rightarrow B) \rightarrow (A \rightarrow C))$

Ax3 $(\neg A \rightarrow \neg B) \rightarrow (B \rightarrow A)$

Ax4 $(\forall x_i)A(x_i) \rightarrow A(t)$, where t is free for x_i in A

Ax5 $(\forall x_i)(A \rightarrow B) \rightarrow (A \rightarrow (\forall x_i)B)$, where A contains no free occurrences of x_i

(4) Rules of deduction:

(i) *modus ponens* – From A and A→B, can be derived B, where A and B are any wff.

(ii) *generalisation* – From A, $(\forall x_i)A$ can be derived, where A is any wff and x_i is any variable.

Note that an important instance of Ax4 is $(\forall x_i)A(x_i) \rightarrow A(x_i)$ (that is, $(\forall x_i)A \rightarrow A$, since x_i is free for x_i).

Why is there is a restriction on Ax5? Well, consider $(\forall x_i)(P_1^2(x_i, x_j) \rightarrow P_2^2(x_j, x_i))$, and interpret P_1^2 as < and P_2^2 as > over the domain of natural numbers. Then $(\forall x_i)(P_1^2(x_i, x_j) \rightarrow P_2^2(x_j, x_i))$ is interpreted as 'For every x, x<y → y>x', which is clearly the case. However, $P_1^2(x_i, x_j) \rightarrow (\forall x_i)P_2^2(x_j, x_i)$ would be interpreted as 'x<y → for every x, y>x', which is clearly not the case. Since we would like our axioms to be valid, we must not allow x_i to be free in A. It would be all right though to have $(\forall x_i)(A \rightarrow B) \rightarrow (A \rightarrow (\forall x_i)B)$ interpretable as 'For every x, z<y → y>z implies z<y → for every x, y>z'.

Although we have omitted the connectives ∧, ∨, ↔ and the quantifier ∃ for simplicity, they can always be re-admitted as 'shorthand' for expressions involving the allowed symbols. Thus

$$A \wedge B \equiv \neg(A \rightarrow \neg B)$$
$$A \vee B \equiv \neg A \rightarrow B$$
$$A \leftrightarrow B \equiv (A \rightarrow B) \wedge (B \rightarrow A)$$
$$(\exists x_i)A \equiv \neg(\forall x_i)\neg A$$

Notice also that the form of the first three axiom schemas is the same as in propositional logic. Since modus ponens is again used as a rule of deduction, many of the results attained in propositional logic will carry over intact to predicate logic. It must also be noted that, although the form of the axioms is the same, the 'content' in first order logic is richer. Thus, for example

$$(\forall x_i)P_1^1(x_i) \rightarrow ((\forall x_i)(\forall x_j)(P_2^1(x_i) \rightarrow \neg P_1^2(x_i, x_j)) \rightarrow (\forall x_i)P_1^1(x_i))$$

is an instance of Ax1 in predicate logic. But, the level of detail shown, involving variables and quantifiers, is not available in propositional logic.

It is also worth noting carefully that

$$(\forall x_i)(A \rightarrow (B \rightarrow A))$$

does *not* have the form of the first axiom, because of the presence of the leading quantifier. In propositional logic terms it simply has the form C (a single proposition).

7.2.1 Deduction

As always we are interested in deductions, i.e. the task of deriving well-formed formulae from a *given* set of well-formed formulae. The given set of wff may be called a set of hypotheses or assumptions.

A *deduction* in FOPL is a sequence of wff $F_1, F_2, ..., F_n$, such that for each i $(1 \le i \le n)$

    (a) F_i is an axiom

or (b) F_i is a hypothesis

or (c) F_i is derived by modus ponens from F_j, F_k, where $j, k < i$.

or (d) F_i is derived by generalisation from F_j, where $j < i$.

If H is the set of hypotheses involved in the deduction we say that F_n is a consequence of H or that F_n is deducible from H, and we write $H \vdash F_n$.

If the set of hypotheses H is empty we write $\vdash F_n$. In this case F_n is deduced from the axioms alone without the aid of hypotheses and we say that F_n is a theorem. Again the simplest theorems are instances of the axioms themselves. Thus, for example

$$(\forall x_i)A(x_i) \rightarrow ((\forall x_i)(\forall x_j)(B(x_i) \rightarrow \neg C(x_i, x_j)) \rightarrow (\forall x_i)A(x_i))$$

is a theorem, as it is an instance of an axiom.

Example 7.1

As a slightly harder example let us prove the following:

$$(\forall x_i)(\forall x_j)A \vdash (\forall x_j)(\forall x_i)A$$

Proof

1.	$(\forall x_i)(\forall x_j)A$	Hypothesis
2.	$(\forall x_i)(\forall x_j)A \rightarrow (\forall x_j)A$	Ax4
3. ∴	$(\forall x_j)A$	MP on 1 and 2
4.	$(\forall x_j)A \rightarrow A$	Ax4
5. ∴	A	MP on 3 and 4
6. ∴	$(\forall x_i)A$	Generalisation of 5
7. ∴	$(\forall x_j)(\forall x_i)A$	Generalisation of 6

                                                                                  (End)

To make any real progress in proving results in FOPL we need a version of the deduction theorem which we encountered in Chapter 4. Let us establish that now.

Theorem 7.1 (Deduction Theorem for Predicate Logic)

Let H be a set (possibly empty) of wff of FOPL, and let A and B be any wff of FOPL. If $H \cup \{A\} \vdash B$ by a deduction containing no application of generalisation to a variable that occurs free in A, then $H \vdash (A \rightarrow B)$.

(Note that generalisation *can* be used, but it must not involve a variable that is free in A.)

Proof The proof follows the same lines as in the propositional logic case. To prove the theorem we again use induction on the number of wff in a deductive sequence. We begin with the base case, where the deduction of B from H ∪ {A} requires just 1 wff in the sequence, namely B itself.

Basis step B must be an axiom or a member of the set of hypotheses, i.e. of H ∪ {A}.

Suppose B is an axiom. Then we can construct the following deduction:

$$
\begin{array}{lll}
& B & \text{Axiom} \\
& B \to (A \to B) & \text{Ax1} \\
\therefore & A \to B & \text{MP}
\end{array}
$$

Hence   H ⊢ A→B

Now suppose B ∈ H ∪ {A}. The deduction of H ⊢ A→B follows similar lines to the first case.

$$
\begin{array}{lll}
& B & \text{Hypothesis} \\
& B \to (A \to B) & \text{Ax1} \\
\therefore & A \to B & \text{MP}
\end{array}
$$

Hence   H ⊢ A→B

Induction step Let us first state our induction hypothesis:

If H ∪ {A} ⊢ B in n steps or less, and generalisation was not used on a variable free in A, then H ⊢ A→B.

Now suppose B is deduced from H ∪ {A} in n+1 steps, n > 1.

If B is an axiom or an element of H ∪ {A} then H ⊢ A→B follows as in the basis case. This, of course, is not likely in practice, because we would hardly prove in many steps what could be deduced in one. However, we include a statement about it for completeness.

Suppose then (more realistically) that B is deduced by modus ponens from two earlier formulae in the deduction sequence, say, B_j and $B_j \to B$, or by generalisation from B_j, say.

Take the modus ponens case first. Clearly, the induction hypothesis applies to both B_j and $B_j \to B$, since they were deduced in n or fewer steps. Hence we have the following:

B_j [1]

$A \to B_j$ [2]   By induction hypothesis on [1]

$B_j \to B$ [3]

$A \to (B_j \to B)$ [4]   By induction hypothesis on [3]

$$(A \rightarrow (B_j \rightarrow B)) \rightarrow ((A \rightarrow B_j) \rightarrow (A \rightarrow B)) \qquad \text{Ax2}$$

$\therefore \ (A \rightarrow B_j) \rightarrow (A \rightarrow B)$ [5]   MP using [4] and Ax2

$\therefore \ A \rightarrow B$ MP using [3] and [5]

Hence $H \vdash A \rightarrow B$

Now consider the generalisation case, i.e. the case where B is derived from B_j by generalisation, i.e. B is $(\forall x_i)B_j$. The important point to note here is that x_i cannot be free in A. Why is this? Because B involves generalisation using x_i and, by the conditions of the theorem, any use of generalisation must not involve a variable free in A. Then

$$\overset{.}{\underset{.}{B_j}} \qquad\qquad\qquad\qquad [1]$$

$A \rightarrow B_j$ [2]   By induction hypothesis

$\therefore \ (\forall x_i)(A \rightarrow B_j)$ [3]   Generalisation of [2]

$(\forall x_i)(A \rightarrow B_j) \rightarrow (A \rightarrow (\forall x_i)B_j)$ Ax5 (x_i not free in A)

$\therefore \ A \rightarrow (\forall x_i)B_j$ MP using [3] and Ax5

Hence $H \vdash A \rightarrow (\forall x_i)B_j$

i.e. $H \vdash A \rightarrow B$

By the Principle of Mathematical Induction we conclude then that in all cases in which the restriction on the use of generalisation holds

$$\text{if } H \cup \{A\} \vdash B \text{ then } H \vdash (A \rightarrow B)$$

(End)

We have two immediate corollaries.

Corollary

If A is a closed wff and if $H \cup \{A\} \vdash B$ then $H \vdash (A \rightarrow B)$

Proof The proof is immediate since whatever use of generalisation may have been involved in deriving B, it cannot have involved a variable with a free occurrence in A, since there are none. Remember a closed wff is one with no free variables.

(End)

Corollary

For *any* wff A, B, C $\{(A \rightarrow B), (B \rightarrow C)\} \vdash A \rightarrow C$

Proof The proof is the very same as in the propositional logic case.

(End)

Thus, in predicate logic we have the same useful extra rule of deduction involving the transitivity of $\rightarrow$, namely TI. Note that there is no restriction on the result, because generalisation is not used in the proof.

Let's see the usefulness of the deduction theorem in a couple of examples.

Example 7.2

$$\vdash \ (\forall x_i)(\forall x_j)A \rightarrow (\forall x_j)(\forall x_i)A$$

This is easy! We proved above that $(\forall x_i)(\forall x_j)A \vdash (\forall x_j)(\forall x_i)A$. Now we use the deduction theorem to move $(\forall x_i)(\forall x_j)A$ to the right-hand side to get our result. Note that neither x_i nor x_j is free in $(\forall x_i)(\forall x_j)A$.

Example 7.3

If x_i occurs free in $A(x_i)$ and x_j does not occur in $A(x_i)$, then

$$\vdash \ (\forall x_i)A(x_i) \rightarrow (\forall x_j)A(x_j)$$

Proof	$(\forall x_i)A(x_i)$	Hypothesis
	$(\forall x_i)A(x_i) \rightarrow A(x_j)$	Ax4 (x_j is free for x_i in A)
	$\therefore \ A(x_j)$	MP
	$\therefore \ (\forall x_j)A(x_j)$	G

Thus $\{(\forall x_i)A(x_i)\} \vdash (\forall x_j)A(x_j)$

Therefore $\vdash \ (\forall x_i)A(x_i) \rightarrow (\forall x_j)A(x_j)$ by deduction theorem, since G was used on x_j, and x_j did not occur at all in A, never mind free.

(End)

Similarly we could prove $\vdash \ (\forall x_j)A(x_j) \rightarrow (\forall x_i)A(x_i)$ whence we have

$$\vdash \ (\forall x_j)A(x_j) \leftrightarrow (\forall x_i)A(x_i)$$

Example 7.4

$$\vdash \ (\forall x_i)\neg A \rightarrow \neg(\forall x_i)A$$

Proof This is a little more subtle. We use the fact that $\neg A$ is $A \rightarrow \bot$, and aim towards a proof by contradiction. Thus we try to show that $\bot$ can be derived from $(\forall x_i)\neg A$ and $(\forall x_i)A$. The result then follows feasily. So

$(\forall x_i)\neg A$	Hypothesis
$(\forall x_i)\neg A \rightarrow \neg A$	Ax4
$\therefore \ \neg A$	MP
$(\forall x_i)A$	Hypothesis
$(\forall x_i)A \rightarrow A$	Ax4
$\therefore \ A$	MP
$\neg A \rightarrow (A \rightarrow \bot)$	Theorem carried over from AL
$\therefore \ \bot$	MP twice

Hence $\{(\forall x_i)\neg A, (\forall x_i)A\} \vdash \bot$

Therefore $\{(\forall x_i)\neg A\} \vdash (\forall x_i)A \rightarrow \bot$ by deduction theorerm, G is not used

i.e. $\{(\forall x_i)\neg A\} \vdash \neg(\forall x_i)A$

Therefore $\vdash (\forall x_i)\neg A \rightarrow \neg(\forall x_i)A$ by deduction theorerm, G is not used.

(End)

Exercise

7.1 Prove the following theorems in FOPL:

(i) $\vdash (\forall x_i)(A(x_i)\rightarrow A(x_i))$

(ii) $\{A, (\forall x_i)A\rightarrow B\} \vdash (\forall x_i)B$

(iii) $\vdash (\forall x_i)(\forall x_j)(\forall x_k)A\rightarrow(\forall x_k)(\forall x_j)(\forall x_i)A$

(iv) $\vdash (\forall x_i)(A\rightarrow B) \rightarrow ((\forall x_i)A\rightarrow(\forall x_i)B)$

(v) $\vdash (\forall x_i)A\rightarrow\neg(\forall x_i)\neg A$

7.2.2 Further proofs

To deepen our understanding of the axiomatic approach to first order predicate logic and to hone our skills in constructing proofs, let us study a number of further examples. Some of these results are important in their own right.

Example 7.5

$$\vdash (\forall x_i)(A\rightarrow B) \rightarrow ((\exists x_i)A\rightarrow(\exists x_i)B)$$

Proof Remember that $(\exists x_i)A \equiv \neg(\forall x_i)\neg A$. So we have to prove

$$\vdash (\forall x_i)(A\rightarrow B) \rightarrow (\neg(\forall x_i)\neg A \rightarrow \neg(\forall x_i)\neg B)$$

It seems reasonable to start with the assumption $(\forall x_i)(A\rightarrow B)$. Let us do that and see where it leads.

$(\forall x_i)(A\rightarrow B)$	Hypothesis
$(\forall x_i)(A\rightarrow B) \rightarrow (A\rightarrow B)$	Ax4
$\therefore\ A\rightarrow B$	MP

Where do we go from here? The next most reasonable hypothesis would appear to be $\neg(\forall x_i)\neg A$, in the hope of then deriving $\neg(\forall x_i)\neg B$. But what use can we make of $\neg(\forall x_i)\neg A$? None that seems obvious. The initial $\neg$ blocks further progress.

Well, we remember from Chapter 4 that if it is difficult to prove $\neg A\rightarrow\neg B$ maybe it is worth trying to prove $B\rightarrow A$. So let us look at the possibility of proving $(\forall x_i)\neg B\rightarrow(\forall x_i)\neg A$, from which we can get our result.

We continue

$(\forall x_i)\neg B$	Hypothesis
$(\forall x_i)\neg B\rightarrow \neg B$	Ax4
$\therefore\ \neg B$	MP

Now, mindful of the third line above we have

$(A\rightarrow B) \rightarrow (\neg B\rightarrow\neg A)$	Theorem (originally proved in AL)
$\therefore\ \neg B\rightarrow\neg A$	MP, from third and last line
$\therefore\ \neg A$	MP, from last line and three lines back
$\therefore\ (\forall x_i)\neg A$	G

So now we have $\{(\forall x_i)(A{\rightarrow}B), (\forall x_i)\neg B\} \vdash (\forall x_i)\neg A$

As G(eneralisation) was used with x_i, which is not free in $(\forall x_i)\neg B$ we can bring $(\forall x_i)\neg B$ to the right-hand side by the deduction theorem.

Thus $\{(\forall x_i)(A{\rightarrow}B)\} \vdash (\forall x_i)\neg B{\rightarrow}(\forall x_i)\neg A$

But $((\forall x_i)\neg B{\rightarrow}(\forall x_i)\neg A) \rightarrow (\neg(\forall x_i)\neg A{\rightarrow}\neg(\forall x_i)\neg B)$ Theorem of AL

Therefore $\{(\forall x_i)(A{\rightarrow}B)\} \vdash (\neg(\forall x_i)\neg A{\rightarrow}\neg(\forall x_i)\neg B)$ MP

Therefore $\vdash (\forall x_i)(A{\rightarrow}B) \rightarrow (\neg(\forall x_i)\neg A{\rightarrow}\neg(\forall x_i)\neg B)$ Deduction theorem, x_i not free in $(\forall x_i)(A{\rightarrow}B)$

i.e. $\vdash (\forall x_i)(A{\rightarrow}B) \rightarrow ((\exists x_i)A{\rightarrow}(\exists x_i)B)$

(End)

Example 7.6

If x_i does not have a free occurrence in A then
$$\vdash (\exists x_i)(A{\rightarrow}B) \rightarrow (A{\rightarrow}(\exists x_i)B)$$

Proof The obvious starting assumption is $(\exists x_i)(A{\rightarrow}B)$, but it does not appear as if we can make any progress from it. Even if we add the assumption A to it, there does not seem to be any clear continuation. So we need to be a little more subtle. Maybe we should swap things around a bit. Remember that if $\vdash A \rightarrow (B{\rightarrow}C)$ then $\vdash B \rightarrow (A{\rightarrow}C)$.

Let us look then at the possibilities in
$$A \rightarrow ((\exists x_i)(A{\rightarrow}B) \rightarrow (\exists x_i)B),$$
i.e. $A \rightarrow (\neg(\forall x_i)\neg(A{\rightarrow}B) \rightarrow \neg(\forall x_i)\neg B)$.

The obvious assumptions are A and $\neg(\forall x_i)\neg(A{\rightarrow}B)$, but again the initial $\neg$ makes progress difficult.

So (finally) let us look at
$$A \rightarrow ((\forall x_i)\neg B \rightarrow (\forall x_i)\neg(A{\rightarrow}B))$$
where we are again thinking of $(\neg A{\rightarrow}\neg B) \rightarrow (B{\rightarrow}A)$

A	[1]	Hypothesis
$(\forall x_i)\neg B$	[2]	Hypothesis
$(\forall x_i)\neg B{\rightarrow}\neg B$		Ax4
$\therefore \neg B$	[3]	MP on [2] and Ax4
$A \rightarrow (\neg B \rightarrow \neg(A{\rightarrow}B))$	[4]	Theorem (see Theorem 4.10)
$\therefore \neg(A{\rightarrow}B)$	[5]	MP twice, on [1], [3] and [4]
$\therefore (\forall x_i)(\neg(A{\rightarrow}B))$		G of [5]

So $\{A, (\forall x_i)\neg B\} \vdash (\forall x_i)(\neg(A{\rightarrow}B))$

Therefore $\{A\} \vdash (\forall x_i)\neg B \rightarrow (\forall x_i)(\neg(A{\rightarrow}B))$ Deduction theorem, x_i not free in $(\forall x_i)\neg B$

Therefore $\{A\} \vdash (\neg(\forall x_i)\neg(A{\rightarrow}B) \rightarrow \neg(\forall x_i)\neg B)$ Theorem and MP

i.e. $\{A\} \vdash ((\exists x_i)(A \rightarrow B) \rightarrow (\exists x_i)B)$

Therefore $\{A, (\exists x_i)(A{\rightarrow}B)\} \vdash ((\exists x_i)B)$ Converse of deduction theorem

Therefore $\{(\exists x_i)(A{\rightarrow}B)\} \vdash (A{\rightarrow}(\exists x_i)B)$ Deduction theorem, x_i not free in A

Thus $\vdash (\exists x_i)(A{\to}B) \to (A \to (\exists x_i)B)$ Ded Th, x_i not free in $(\exists x_i)(A{\to}B)$

(End)

You may like to go over this theorem again carefully. It is a compact, yet eloquent example of how reshaping a problem may render it more tractable.

Example 7.7

If x_i does not have a free occurrence in B then
$$\vdash (\exists x_i)(A{\to}B) \to ((\forall x_i)A{\to}B)$$

Proof The proof here follows the same strategic lines as the last example. We reshape $(\exists x_i)(A{\to}B) \to ((\forall x_i)A{\to}B)$

to $\quad (\exists x_i)(A{\to}B) \to (\neg B{\to}\neg(\forall x_i)A)$

to $\quad \neg B \to ((\exists x_i)(A{\to}B) \to \neg(\forall x_i)A)$

i.e. $\qquad \neg B \to (\neg(\forall x_i)\neg(A{\to}B) \to \neg(\forall x_i)A)$

to $\quad \neg B \to ((\forall x_i)A \to (\forall x_i)\neg(A{\to}B))$

and we consider using $\neg B$ and $(\forall x_i)A$ as our assumptions.

Hence

$\neg B$	[1]	Hypothesis
$(\forall x_i)A$	[2]	Hypothesis
$(\forall x_i)A \to A$		Ax4
$\therefore\ A$	[3]	MP on [2] and Ax4
$A \to (\neg B \to \neg(A{\to}B))$	[4]	Theorem 4.10
$\therefore\ \neg(A \to B)$	[5]	MP twice on [1], [3] and [4]
$\therefore\ (\forall x_i)(\neg(A{\to}B))$		G of [5]

So $\{\neg B, (\forall x_i)A\} \vdash (\forall x_i)(\neg(A{\to}B))$

Therefore $\{\neg B\} \vdash (\forall x_i)A \to (\forall x_i)(\neg(A{\to}B))$ Deduction theorem, x_i not free in $(\forall x_i)A$

Therefore $\{\neg B\} \vdash (\neg(\forall x_i)\neg(A{\to}B) \to \neg(\forall x_i)A)$ Theorem and MP

i.e. $\{\neg B\} \vdash ((\exists x_i)(A{\to}B) \to \neg(\forall x_i)A)$

Therefore $\{\neg B, (\exists x_i)(A{\to}B)\} \vdash \neg(\forall x_i)A$ Converse of deduction theorem

Therefore $\{(\exists x_i)(A{\to}B)\} \vdash (\neg B \to \neg(\forall x_i)A)$ Deduction theorem, x_i not free in $\neg B$

Therefore $\{(\exists x_i)(A{\to}B)\} \vdash ((\forall x_i)A{\to}B)$ Theorem

Thus $\vdash (\exists x_i)(A{\to}B) \to ((\forall x_i)A{\to}B)$ Deduction theorem, x_i not free in $(\exists x_i)(A{\to}B)$

(End)

You can see for yourself how closely the proof Example 7.7 mirrors 7.6. Let's look at one final example.

Example 7.8

If x_i does not have a free occurrence in B then

$$\vdash (\forall x_i)(A \rightarrow B) \rightarrow ((\exists x_i)A \rightarrow B)$$

Proof This is a little easier. Nevertheless, some reshaping is useful, after which the lines of the proof should be clear.

Think of $(\neg B \rightarrow \neg (\exists x_i)A)$, i.e. $(\neg B \rightarrow (\forall x_i) \neg A)$ instead of $((\exists x_i)A \rightarrow B)$.

$(\forall x_i)(A \rightarrow B)$	Hypothesis
$(\forall x_i)(A \rightarrow B) \rightarrow (A \rightarrow B)$	Ax4
$\therefore\ A \rightarrow B$	MP
$(A \rightarrow B) \rightarrow (\neg B \rightarrow \neg A)$	Theorem
$\therefore\ \neg B \rightarrow \neg A$	MP
$\neg B$	Hypothesis
$\therefore\ \neg A$	MP
$\therefore\ (\forall x_i) \neg A$	G

So $\{(\forall x_i)(A \rightarrow B),\ \neg B\} \vdash (\forall x_i) \neg A$

Therefore $\{(\forall x_i)(A \rightarrow B)\} \vdash (\neg B \rightarrow (\forall x_i) \neg A)$ Deduction theorem, x_i not free in $\neg B$

Therefore $\{(\forall x_i)(A \rightarrow B)\} \vdash (\neg(\forall x_i) \neg A \rightarrow B)$ \qquad Theorem and MP

i.e. $\{(\forall x_i)(A \rightarrow B)\} \vdash ((\exists x_i)A \rightarrow B)$

Thus $\vdash (\forall x_i)(A \rightarrow B) \rightarrow ((\exists x_i)A \rightarrow B)$ Deduction theorem, x_i not free in $(\forall x_i)(A \rightarrow B)$

(End)

Exercises

7.2 Prove the following theorems in FOPL:

(i) $\vdash (\forall x_i) \neg A \rightarrow \neg(\exists x_i)A$

(ii) $\vdash \neg(\exists x_i)A \rightarrow (\forall x_i) \neg A$

(iii) $\vdash (\exists x_i) \neg A \rightarrow \neg(\forall x_i)A$

(iv) $\vdash (A \rightarrow (\forall x_i)B) \rightarrow (\forall x_i)(A \rightarrow B)$ if x_i does not occur free in A

(v) $\vdash (A \rightarrow (\exists x_i)B) \rightarrow (\exists x_i)(A \rightarrow B)$ if x_i does not occur free in A

(vi) $\vdash ((\exists x_i)A \rightarrow B) \rightarrow (\forall x_i)(A \rightarrow B)$ if x_i does not occur free in B

(vii) $\vdash ((\forall x_i)A \rightarrow B) \rightarrow (\exists x_i)(A \rightarrow B)$ if x_i does not occur free in B

7.3 Prove that if x_j does not occur in $A(x_i)$ then

$$\vdash (\exists x_i)A(x_i) \leftrightarrow (\exists x_j)A(x_j)$$

7.3 Soundness and Completeness

Clearly, it is highly desirable that FOPL be both sound and complete. That is, we would like all the theorems of FOPL to be logically valid (soundness), and all logically valid wff of L to be provable. Though we won't do so here, it can be proved that FOPL has these properties (see e.g. Hamilton, 1978).

The proof of soundness is fairly straightforward. It involves establishing that each instance of the axioms is valid, that the two rules of deduction, MP and G, preserve validity, and then using induction to carry through the proof of validity for all the theorems. In fact, we have already established the validity of some of the axioms in the last chapter. In addition, we have shown that if A and A→B are valid then so is B, and that if A is valid so is $(\forall x_i)A$. So we are really well on our way to establishing the soundness of FOPL. You might like to test your understanding and skills by carrying through the proof completely.

Exercise

7.4.   Prove the soundness of FOPL.

The proof of completeness is much more involved, and we will not attempt it in this first book on logic. The theorem was first proved by Gödel in 1929. Later, other, simpler proofs were developed.

Historical Note

Kurt Gödel (1906 – 1978)
Gödel, perhaps the most outstanding logician of the 20th century, was born in Brno, now in the Czech Republic, on 28th April 1906. He was a first class student at school, in spite of frequent absences occasioned by ill health. Unfortunately, poor health and bouts of depression dogged him all through his life and in his later years he became a severe hypochondriac.

Gödel worked for his Ph.D. at the University of Vienna and in his doctoral dissertation, submitted in 1929, he proved the completeness theorem for the predicate calculus. In 1931 he published a paper in which he proved two of the most famous theorems in all of mathematical logic – the celebrated first and second incompleteness theorems. Essentially he showed that any formal system rich enough to describe the arithmetic of natural numbers is either incomplete or inconsistent. This effectively shattered a long-standing mathematicians' dream of bringing all of mathematics within an axiomatic formal system and established Gödel's reputation in the front rank of logicians.

Gödel emigrated to the US in 1940 and never returned to Europe. He worked at the Institute for Advanced Study at Princeton and after his death on 14th January 1978 of 'malnutrition and inanition' was buried at Princeton Cemetery.

7.4 Decidability

We saw in Chapter 4 that the formal system, AL, of propositional logic was decidable, i.e. there is a mechanical procedure for determining whether or not a given wff is a theorem of AL. Unfortunately, there is no such algorithmic or mechanical method for first order logic. It can be proved that there is no effectively computable method for deciding if any given wff is logically valid. This, of course, means that there is no effective method for deciding in general if a wff is a theorem or not. There are some first order theories which are decidable, but the general problem for predicate logic is unsolvable.

7.5 Proper Axioms and Theories

The axioms we have been studying in this chapter are the *logical axioms* sufficient to form a sound and complete foundation for all of first order predicate logic. The theory which emerges from them, through the use of the rules of deduction – MP and G – is the theory of valid wff of a first order language. Various interpretations are possible, in all of which the valid wff will, of course, be valid, but in which other wff may or may not be satisfied, or may or may not be true. In order to distinguish between different interpretations, and in order to investigate specific systems, specialised, distinguishing properties need to be identified. This may be done by enunciating *proper axioms*, i.e. axioms peculiar to a specific system.

For example, we might propose axioms which would define the arithmetic of natural numbers, or the theory of abelian groups, or the theory of identity. An interesting question is whether the axioms which we identify as defining, say, first order arithmetic, do so exclusively, i.e. whether or not they admit of models which are different in some essential respect from the natural numbers. In other words, with regard to proper axioms, do they, in each case, identify a particular system categorically, i.e. up to isomorphism? This is a question which is too advanced for us here. However, we will take a look at a simple example in order to see proper axioms at work.

A theory may be described as the set of deductive consequences, using sound rules of deduction, of a set of of axioms. Thus, if A is a set of axioms, then the theory

$$T(A) = \{F \mid A \vdash F\}$$

7.5.1 First Order Theory of Identity

Perhaps the most basic first order theory is that of equality, or identity. We often interpret the predicate P_1^2 as equality, but in order to get an actual theory of equality we need to specify that P_1^2 has certain properties. Thus, we get the following proper axioms:

$(\forall x_i)P_1^2(x_i, x_i)$
$(\forall x_i)(\forall x_j)(P_1^2(x_i, x_j) \rightarrow (A(x_i, x_i) \rightarrow A(x_i, x_j)))$, where A represents any wff
$(\forall x_i)(\forall x_j)(P_1^2(x_i, x_j) \rightarrow P_1^2(f(x_i), f(x_j)))$, where f represents any function

The notation $A(x_i, x_i) \rightarrow A(x_i, x_j)$ indicates that zero or more occurrences of x_i may be replaced by x_j.

We usually use = (in infix fashion), rather than P_1^2, for equality, and then we get a more perspicuous statement of the identity axioms as follows:

EAx1 $(\forall x_i)(x_i = x_i)$
EAx2 $(\forall x_i)(\forall x_j)(x_i = x_j \rightarrow (A(x_i, x_i) \rightarrow A(x_i, x_j)))$
EAx3 $(\forall x_i)(\forall x_j)(x_i = x_j \rightarrow f(x_i) = f(x_j))$

We can now prove some recognisably familiar properties of equality.

Example 7.9

We can prove that any term is equal to itself, i.e. $\vdash t = t$.
Proof

$(\forall x_i)(x_i = x_i)$	EAx1
$(\forall x_i)(x_i = x_i) \rightarrow t = t$	Ax4, where we assume t does not contain x_i; if it does then simply rename variables
$\therefore$ $t = t$	MP

(End)

Example 7.10

We can prove the symmetry of equality, i.e. $\vdash t_1 = t_2 \rightarrow t_2 = t_1$
Proof Let $A(x_i, x_j)$ be interpreted as $x_j = x_i$. Then

$(\forall x_i)(\forall x_j)(x_i = x_j \rightarrow (x_i = x_i \rightarrow x_j = x_i))$ EAx2
$(\forall x_i)(\forall x_j)(x_i = x_j \rightarrow (x_i = x_i \rightarrow x_j = x_i)) \rightarrow (\forall x_j)(t_1 = x_j \rightarrow (t_1 = t_1 \rightarrow x_j = t_1))$
   Ax4, where we assume t_1 does not contain x_j; if it does then simply rename variables.
$\therefore$ $(\forall x_j)(t_1 = x_j \rightarrow (t_1 = t_1 \rightarrow x_j = t_1))$ MP
$(\forall x_j)(t_1 = x_j \rightarrow (t_1 = t_1 \rightarrow x_j = t_1)) \rightarrow (t_1 = t_2 \rightarrow (t_1 = t_1 \rightarrow t_2 = t_1))$
   Ax4
$\therefore$ $t_1 = t_2 \rightarrow (t_1 = t_1 \rightarrow t_2 = t_1)$ MP
$(t_1 = t_2 \rightarrow (t_1 = t_1 \rightarrow t_2 = t_1)) \rightarrow (t_1 = t_1 \rightarrow (t_1 = t_2 \rightarrow t_2 = t_1))$
   Theorem $(A \rightarrow (B \rightarrow C)) \rightarrow (B \rightarrow (A \rightarrow C))$
$\therefore$ $t_1 = t_1 \rightarrow (t_1 = t_2 \rightarrow t_2 = t_1)$ MP
$t_1 = t_1$ Theorem (just proved)
$\therefore$ $t_1 = t_2 \rightarrow t_2 = t_1$ MP

(End)

Exercise

7.5 Given the axioms of equality (in addition to the logical axioms) prove the following:

(i) $\vdash t_1 = t_2 \rightarrow f(t_1) = f(t_2))$

(ii) $\vdash (\forall x_i)(A(x_i) \rightarrow (\forall x_j)(x_i = x_j \rightarrow A(x_j)))$
    if x_j does not occur in $A(x_i)$

(iii) $\vdash (\forall x_i)((\forall x_j)(x_i = x_j \rightarrow A(x_j)) \rightarrow A(x_i))$
    if x_j does not occur in $A(x_i)$

(iv) $\vdash t_1 = t_2 \rightarrow (t_2 = t_3 \rightarrow t_1 = t_3)$

(v) $\{t_1 = t_2, t_2 = t_3\} \vdash t_1 = t_3$

(vi) $\{t_1 = t_2, t_1 = t_3\} \vdash t_2 = t_3$

(vii) $\{t_1 = t_2, t_1 = t_3, t_2 = t_4\} \vdash t_3 = t_4$

7.6 Axiomatic Semantics and Programming

In chapter 6 we saw how logic can be applied to the formalisation of software by using first order predicates to characterise sets of program states and treating the assignment instruction as a function from a set of states to a set of states. We also saw how that formalism can be used to assist in the construction of correct programs. We continue here with that theme and describe the formal semantics of a simple (but non-trivial) programming language – similar to Pascal.

Recall that we used an in inductive assertion to define the semantics of the assignment instruction. Our inductive assertions took the form

$$\{P(X_1, X_2, ..., X_n)\} \; s \; \{Q(X_1, X_2, ..., X_n)\}$$

where P and Q are first order predicates, s is a statement in our pseudocode and X_1, X_2, ..., X_n represent variables in the program – usually those specifically referenced by statement s. This notation can easily be expressed in a more familiar first order predicate form as

$$(\forall X_1)(\forall X_2) ... (\forall X_n) \, (P(X_1, X_2, ..., X_n) \rightarrow Q(f(X_1), (X_2), ..., (X_n)))$$

where f is interpreted as a function representing the transformation of a variable due to the statement s.

Using an inductive assertion we defined the assignment instruction as

$$\{P(X)[e\backslash X]\} \; x := e \; \{P(X)\}$$

This instruction is the basic mechanism for changing the state of the computer. However, single assignments alone cannot do very much in the way of computation. What we need is to be able to combine assignements in useful ways to produce program statements.

The simplest technique is *sequential composition* – assignments carried out in sequence. The sequential composition of two statements can be written

s1 ; s2

where we use ';' to indicate the composition. The behaviour of the computer on execution of such a statement can be defined using inductive assertions as follows:

$$\text{if} \quad \{P\} \, s1 \, \{R\}$$
$$\text{and} \quad \{R\} \, s2 \, \{Q\}$$
$$\text{then} \quad \{P\} \, s1 \, ; \, s2 \, \{Q\}$$

This asserts that if a statement, s1, starting in state $\{P\}$ establishes state $\{R\}$ and another statement, s2, starting in state $\{R\}$ establishes state $\{Q\}$, then the two can be combined and the compound statement s1 ; s2, starting in state $\{P\}$ will establish state $\{Q\}$.

Example 7.11

$\{((X > 0) \wedge (Y = 10))\} \, x := y{-}1 \, ; \, y := x \, \{((X = 9) \wedge (Y = 9))\}$
is the composition of the two assertions
$\{((X > 0) \wedge (y = 10))\} \, x := y{-}1 \, \{((X = 9) \wedge (Y = 10))\}$
$\{((X = 9) \wedge (Y = 10))\} \, y := x \, \{((X = 9) \wedge (Y = 9))\}$

Example 7.12

Given the two assertions

$$\{(Z = N!)\} \, z := z{\times}(n{+}1) \, \{(Z = (N{+}1)!)\}$$
and $\quad \{(Z = (N{+}1)!)\} \, n := n{+}1 \, \{(Z = N!)\}$

(where X! means the factorial of X), we compose them to obtain

$$\{(Z = N!)\} \, z := z{\times}(n{+}1) \, ; \, n := n{+}1 \, \{(Z = N!)\}$$

Thus, we have widened our repertoire of statements to include not only assignments but also sequential compositions of statements themselves. Naturally, we can sequentially compose statements that are themselves sequential compositions.

Example 7.13

Given the two assertions
$\{((X > 0) \wedge (Y = 10))\} \, x := y{-}1 \, ; \, y := x \, \{((X = 9) \wedge (Y = 9))\}$
and $\quad \{((X = 9) \wedge (Y = 9))\} \, x := y{\times}2 \, \{((X = 18) \wedge (Y = 9))\}$
we can combine them to obtain
$\{((X > 0) \wedge (Y = 10))\}$
$x := y{-}1 \, ; \, y := x \, ; \, x := y{\times}2$
$\{((X = 18) \wedge (Y = 9))\}$
(We split the assertion across three lines for convenience.)

A second technique for combining statements is the so-called *alternative statement*, in which one of two statements are executed depending on the value of a Boolean expression. It is written as
      if *le* then s1 else s2 endif

and is executed as follows: logical expression *le* is evaluated, if it is true then statement s1 is executed, otherwise statement s2 is executed.

The semantics can be described as follows:

$$\text{if} \quad \{P \land le\} \text{ s1 } \{Q\}$$
$$\text{and } \{P \land \neg le\} \text{ s2 } \{Q\}$$
$$\text{then} \quad \{P\} \text{ if } le \text{ then s1 else s2 endif } \{Q\}.$$

Example 7.14

Let |Y| represent the absolute value of the variable y. Given the two assertions

$$\{(Y > 0) \land (Z = 7)\} \; x := y \; \{(X = |Y|) \land (Z = 7)\}$$
$$\text{and} \quad \{(Y < 0) \land (Z = 7)\} \; x := -y \; \{(X = |Y|) \land (Z = 7)\}$$

we can combine them to get

$$\{(Z = 7)\} \text{ if } y > 0 \text{ then } x := y \text{ else } x := -y \; \{(X = |Y|)\}$$

Example 7.15

Let max(X,Y) represent the maximum of the two values X and Y such that if X ≥ Y, max(X,Y) is X otherwise it is Y. Given the two assertions

$$\{(X >= Y)\} \; z := x \; \{(Z = \max(X,Y))\}$$
$$\text{and} \quad \{(Y > X)\} \; z := y \; \{(Z = \max(X,Y))\}$$

we can combine them to get

$$\{(\text{true})\} \text{ if } x \geq y \text{ then } z := x \text{ else } z := y \; \{(Z = \max(X,Y))\}$$

Our final technique for combining statements is a very powerful one. It allows us to cause many state changes with a relatively small amount of code. It is the so-called *repetitive* or *loop* statement, which causes the repeated execution of a statement (or combination of statements) until a certain condition is fulfilled. The loop statement is written

while *le* do statement endwhile

and is executed as follows: if the logical expression *le* is false then the loop statement terminates, otherwise execute the statement and repeat the process. Its semantics can be described by

$$\text{if} \quad \{P \land le\} \text{ s } \{P\}$$
$$\text{then} \quad \{P\} \text{ while } le \text{ do s endwhile } \{P \land \neg le\}.$$

Example 7.16

In example 7.12 we described the assertion

$$\{(Z = N!)\} \; z := z \times (n+1) \; ; \; n := n+1 \; \{(Z = N!)\}$$

We can now use this as the basis of a loop as follows

$$\{(Z = N!) \land (N < 10)\}$$
$$\text{while } n < 10 \text{ do } z := z \times (n+1) \; ; \; n := n+1$$
$$\{(Z = N!) \land (N = 10)\}$$

The postcondition can be shown to be equivalent to $\{(Z = 10!)\}$.

7.6.1 An Axiomatic System for Programming

We are, finally, in a position to formalise properly the 'art' of programming by describing a *theory of program construction.*

Our theory of program construction will consist of

Axioms
- All theorems from the theories describing the domains of the program variables.
- The assignment axiom, PAx1

$$P(e)\} \ x := e \ \{P(X)\}, \text{ where } P(e) = P(X)[e/X]$$

Rules of deduction.

1. Composition

   $$\{P\} \ s1 \ \{R\}, \ \{R\} \ s2 \ \{Q\} \vdash \ \{P\} \ s1; s2 \ \{Q\}$$

2. Alternation

   $$\{P \land le \ \} \ s1 \ \{Q\}, \ \{P \land \neg le \ \} \ s2 \ \{Q\} \vdash$$
   $$\{P\} \ \underline{if} \ le \ \underline{then} \ s1 \ \underline{else} \ s2 \ \underline{endif} \ \{Q\}$$

3. Repetition

   $$\{P \land le\} \ s \ \{P\} \vdash \ \{P\} \ \underline{while} \ le \ \underline{do} \ s \ \underline{endwhile} \ \{P \land \neg le\}$$

4. Precondition rule

   $$P \to R, \ \{R\} \ s \ \{Q\} \vdash \ \{P\} \ s \ \{Q\}$$

5. Postcondition rule

   $$R \to Q, \ \{P\} \ s \ \{R\} \vdash \ \{P\} \ s \ \{Q\}$$

The last two rules allow us to manipulate characteristic predicates by shrinking or expanding them during program construction and proving. They allow us to 'forget' about part of a characteristic predicate that is not relevant for a certain statement, and re-introduce parts that become relevant. While this is not necessary, it makes the task a little easier.

It can be shown that each of our rules of deduction is sound. For the purposes of this example we will not prove this but the reader is referred to *Mathematical Logic for Computer Science* by M. Ben-Ari (1993). Alternatively, the reader is invited to prove the soundness of the rules of deduction.

Exercise

7.6 Prove the soundness of the rules of deduction for the theory of program construction given.

We will now demonstrate how our formal axiomatic system can be used, by proving the correctness of the following program for computing the factorial of the maximum of two given input values:

$$\underline{if} \ (\ a \geq b \ ) \ \underline{then} \ x := a \ \underline{else} \ x := b \ \underline{endif};$$
$$y := 0;$$
$$z := 1;$$
$$\underline{while} \ (y <> x \ ) \ \underline{do} \ z := z \times (y+1) \ ; \ y := y+1 \ \underline{endwhile}$$

where a and b are some specific integer values. We can prove the correctness of this program with respect to the initial states characterised by the predicate

$$((a > 0) \land (b > 0))$$

and final states characterised by the predicate

$$((Z = X!) \land (X = \max (a, b))).$$

We will take each statement in turn and use the axioms and rules of deduction to calculate the states throughout the program.

1. $(a = \max(a,b)) \rightarrow a \geq b$ Theorem of natural numbers

2. $\{(a > 0) \land (b > 0) \land (X = \max(a,b))[a\backslash X]\}$
   x := a
   $\{(a > 0) \land (b > 0) \land (X = \max(a,b))\}$ PAx1

3. $(b = \max(a,b)) \rightarrow a < b$ Theorem of natural numbers

4. $\{(a > 0) \land (b > 0) \land (X = \max(a,b))[b\backslash X]\}$
   x := b
   $\{(a > 0) \land (b > 0) \land (X = \max(a,b))\}$ PAx1

5. $\{(a > 0) \land (b > 0) \land (X \geq b)[a\backslash X]\}$
   x := a
   $\{(a > 0) \land (b > 0) \land (X = \max(a,b))\}$ Precondition on 1 and 2

6. $\{(a > 0) \land (b > 0) \land (X > a)[b \backslash X]\}$
   x := b
   $\{(a > 0) \land (b > 0) \land (X = \max(a,b))\}$ Precondition on 3 and 4

7. $\{(a > 0) \land (b > 0)\}$
   if $(a \geq b)$ then x := a else x := b endif
   $\{(a > 0) \land (b > 0) \land (X = \max(a,b))\}$ Alternation on 5 and 6

8. $(a > 0) \land (b > 0) \land (X = \max(a,b)) \rightarrow$
           $(a > 0) \land (b > 0) \land (X = \max(a,b)) \land (Y=0)[0\backslash Y]$
                         As 0=0 is true and A $\land$ true $\equiv$ A

9. $\{(a > 0) \land (b > 0) \land (X = \max(a,b) \land (Y=0)[0\backslash Y]\}$
   y := 0
   $\{(a > 0) \land (b > 0) \land (X = \max(a,b)) \land (Y = 0)\}$ PAx1

10. $\{(a > 0) \land (b > 0) \land (X = \max(a,b)\}$
    y := 0
    $\{(a > 0) \land (b > 0) \land (X = \max(a,b)) \land (Y=0)\}$ Precondition on 8 and 9

11. $\{(a > 0) \land (b > 0)\}$
    if $(a \geq b)$ then x := a else x := b endif ; y := 0
    $\{(a > 0) \land (b > 0) \land (X = \max(a, b)) \land (Y = 0)\}$
                            Composition on 9 and 10

To this point we have been very rigorous. We will continue at a slightly brisker pace by passing over the more obvious steps.

12. $\{(a > 0) \wedge (b > 0)\}$
   $\underline{if}$ $(a \geq b)$ $\underline{then}$ x := a $\underline{else}$ x := b $\underline{endif}$; y := 0 ; z := 1
   $\{(X = max(a,b)) \wedge (Y = 0) \wedge (Z = 1)\}$ Composition on PAx1 and 11

13. $((X = max(a,b)) \wedge (Y = 0) \wedge (Z = 1)) \rightarrow (Z = Y!)$

   Theorem of natural numbers

14. $\{(X = max(a,b)) \wedge (Z = Y!) \wedge (Y <> X)\}$
   $\underline{while}$ $(y <> x$ $)$ $\underline{do}$ z := z×(y+1) ; y := y+1 $\underline{endwhile}$
   $\{(X = max(a,b)) \wedge (Z = Y!) \wedge (Y = X)\}$ From Example 7.16

Finally, we can bring the whole lot together using composition (and some precondition and postcondition rules) on 12, 13 and 14 to get

> $\{(a > 0) \wedge (b > 0)\}$
> $\underline{if}$ $(a \geq b)$ $\underline{then}$ x := a $\underline{else}$ x := b $\underline{endif}$;
> y := 0;
> z := 1;
> $\underline{while}$ $(y <> x$ $)$ $\underline{do}$ z := z×(y+1) ; y := y+1 $\underline{endwhile}$
> $\{(X = max(a,b)) \wedge (Z = Y!) \wedge (Y = X)\}$

A further postcondition rule on the last postcondition will give us the characteristic predicate $((Z = X!) \wedge (X = max (a, b)))$. Thus, we have proven the correctness of the program with respect to the precondition and postcondition.

In the course of this example we have made some serious assumptions about the first order theories underlying the domains of interpretation of the variables of the program. If any of the necessary theorems cannot be proven (or indeed can be proven false) then our own theory of program development fails. However, when applying logic to the formalisation of program development and correctness proving, 'common-sense' decisions are quite appropriate provided they can ultimately be backed up if necessary.

Using logic as part of the programming process can significantly increase our confidence in the correctness of our programs. Much research effort has been spent developing more practical techniques than above for using logic as a tool in the construction of correct programs. Although the uptake of formal methods by industry has been slow more and more examples of its successful use are being reported.

7.7 Summary

- Our formal system of first order predicate logic, FOPL, has the axiom schemas:

  Ax1 $A \rightarrow (B \rightarrow A)$

  Ax2 $(A \rightarrow (B \rightarrow C)) \rightarrow ((A \rightarrow B) \rightarrow (A \rightarrow C))$

  Ax3 $(\neg A \rightarrow \neg B) \rightarrow (B \rightarrow A)$

  Ax4 $(\forall x_i)A(x_i) \rightarrow A(t)$, where t is free for x_i in A

  Ax5 $(\forall x_i)(A \rightarrow B) \rightarrow (A \rightarrow (\forall x_i)B)$, where A contains no free occurrences of x_i

  and the rules of deduction:

  (i) modus ponens – from A and $A \rightarrow B$, B can be derived, where A and B are any well-formed formulae.

  (ii) generalisation – from A, $(\forall x_i)A$ can be derived, where A is any wff and x_i is *any* variable.

- A deduction in FOPL is a sequence of wff $F_1, F_2, ..., F_n$, such that for each i $(1 \leq i \leq n)$

  (a) F_i is an axiom

  or (b) F_i is a hypothesis

  or (c) F_i is derived by modus ponens from F_j, F_k, where j,k < i.

  or (d) F_i is derived by generalisation from F_j, where j < i.

- The deduction theorem for predicate logic is:

  If $H \cup \{A\} \vdash B$ by a deduction containing no application of generalisation to a variable that occurs free in A, then $H \vdash (A \rightarrow B)$.

- FOPL is sound, i.e. $\vdash A \Rightarrow \models A$.

- FOPL is complete, i.e. $\models A \Rightarrow \vdash A$.

- FOPL is undecidable.

- Proper axioms (added to FOPL) are used to define logical structures with specific properties.

- Proper axioms for the theory of identity are:

  EAx1 $(\forall x_i)(x_i = x_i)$

  EAx2 $(\forall x_i)(\forall x_j)(x_i = x_j \rightarrow (A(x_i, x_i) \rightarrow A(x_i, x_j)))$

  EAx3 $(\forall x_i)(\forall x_j)(x_i = x_j \rightarrow f(x_i) = f(x_j))$

- A theory of program development consists of appropriate proper axioms and rules of deduction for constructing program statements.

In this chapter we have

(1) studied an axiomatic approach, FOPL, to first order systems.

(2) proved some theorems in FOPL.

(3) noted that FOPL is sound and complete, but not decidable.

(4) examined briefly how proper axioms are used to define specific theories.

(5) looked briefly at the first order theory of identity.

(6) looked briefly at a first order theory of program development and proved the correctness of a simple program.

In the next chapter we extend our treatment of semantic tableaux to deal with problems in first order logic.

Miscellaneous Exercises

1. Prove the following theorems in FOPL:

    (i) $\vdash (\forall x_i)((A(x_i) \wedge B(x_i)) \rightarrow B(x_i))$

    (ii) $\vdash (\forall x_i)(A(x_i) \rightarrow (A(x_i) \vee A(x_i)))$

    (iii) $\vdash (\forall x_i)((A(x_i) \rightarrow (A(x_i) \rightarrow B(x_i))) \rightarrow ((A(x_i) \rightarrow A(x_i)) \rightarrow (A(x_i) \rightarrow B(x_i))))$

    (iv) $\vdash (\forall x_k)(A(x_i) \rightarrow A(x_i))$

    (v) $\vdash (\forall x_i)(A(x_i) \rightarrow (\neg A(x_i) \rightarrow B(x_i)))$

    (vi) $\{A \rightarrow B\} \vdash (\forall x_j)A \rightarrow (\forall x_j)B$

    (vii) $\{A \rightarrow B\} \vdash (\exists x_i)A \rightarrow (\exists x_i)B$

    (viii) $\vdash (\forall x_i)(\forall x_j)(\neg(A(x_i) \rightarrow \neg B(x_j)) \rightarrow A(x_i))$

    (ix) $\vdash ((\forall x_i)A(x_i) \rightarrow (\forall x_j)(\exists x_k)B(x_j, x_k)) \leftrightarrow (\exists x_i)(\forall x_j)(\exists x_k)(A(x_i) \rightarrow B(x_j, x_k))$

2. A first order logic system is consistent if $\perp$ is not a theorem of S. Suppose A is a closed wff which is not a theorem of a consistent first order system S, and T is the first order system consisting of S together with $\neg$A as an additional axiom. Prove that T is consistent.

CHAPTER 8

Semantic Tableaux in Predicate Logic

Chapter Aims

(1) To study the rules for semantic tableaux in first order logic.
(2) To prove a number of theorems using semantic tableaux.
(3) To apply semantic tableaux to problems involving objects and quantifiers.

At the end of this chapter you should
(a) know the rules for constructing semantic tableaux in first order predicate logic.
(b) understand the reasons for the rules.
(c) be able to construct semantic tableaux for first order formulae.
(d) be able to resolve arguments through the use of semantic tableaux.

8.1 Introduction

In this chapter we return to the semantic tableaux method of developing derivations, which, you will probably agree, was the method that was easiest to manage in propositional logic. Recall that the use of semantic tableaux is based on the strategy of negating the conclusion of an argument and checking if the result is inconsistent with the premises, i.e. a refutation strategy. Although the construction of tableaux can be looked at from a purely formal point of view, they are essentially semantically 'rooted' and the rules of construction draw their justification from considerations of truth and compatibility. They are more intuitively plausible and acceptable than the frugal axioms and rules of deduction of the classical axiomatic approach.

8.2 Semantic Tableaux

Semantic tableaux in predicate logic are basically the same as in propositional logic, i.e. a sequence of well-formed formulae constructed according to certain rules, and usually laid out in the form of a tree. The well-formed formulae here, of course, are those formed within a first order language, L, as detailed in the last two chapters. We will again make use of the 'relaxed' notation without subscripts and superscripts, as outlined there, i.e. letters like x and y for variables, a and v for constants, f and g for functions and uppercase letters for predicates and general wff.

The rules that were used in propositional logic are used again in predicate logic, and these are supplemented by some rules involving the quantifiers.

For completeness, we repeat here the rules formulated for propositional logic.

Rule (1): A∧B

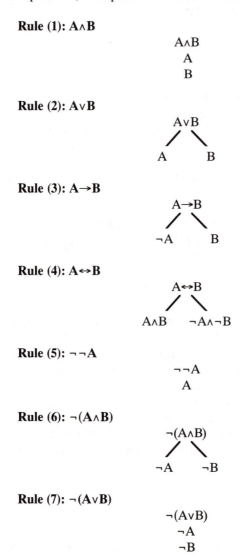

Rule (2): A∨B

Rule (3): A→B

Rule (4): A↔B

Rule (5): ¬¬A

Rule (6): ¬(A∧B)

Rule (7): ¬(A∨B)

Rule (8): ¬(A→B)

$$\begin{array}{c} \neg(A{\rightarrow}B) \\ A \\ \neg B \end{array}$$

Rule (9): ¬(A↔B)

$$\neg(A{\leftrightarrow}B)$$

$$A{\wedge}\neg B \qquad \neg A{\wedge}B$$

Let us now state the rules involving quantifiers.

Rule (10): ∀

$$\begin{array}{c} (\forall x)A(x) \\ A(t) \end{array}$$

where t is a term.

This rule is known as universal instantiation (UI). The substitution of t for x can occur whether A is a property (a unary relation) or an n-ary relation, with x as one component of an n-tuple.

Rule (11): ∃

$$\begin{array}{c} (\exists x)A(x) \\ A(t) \end{array}$$

where t is a term which has *not* been used in the derivation so far.

This rule is known as existential instantiation (EI). A 'standard' constant 'a' is often used for t (this constant is sometimes called the 'witness').

Rule (12): ¬∀

$$\begin{array}{c} \neg(\forall x)A(x) \\ (\exists x)\neg A(x) \end{array}$$

Rule (13): ¬∃

$$\begin{array}{c} \neg(\exists x)A(x) \\ (\forall x)\neg A(x) \end{array}$$

Rules (12) and (13) are seen to reflect results deduced in the last chapter.

Rule (14): Finally, we again have the rule that whenever a wff A and its negation ¬A appear in a branch of a tableau, an inconsistency is indicated in that branch and it is *closed*, i.e. it is not further extended.

As in propositional logic, if all the branches of a semantic tableau are closed then the logical expressions from which the tableau was 'grown' are mutually inconsistent.

Before we engage in an attempt to justify Rules (10) and (11) let us look at a couple of examples of semantic tablaux for predicate logic.

Example 8.1

Prove $(\forall x)(\forall y)R(x,y) \rightarrow R(a,a)$.

As usual we negate the 'conclusion' and list it along with the premises. There are no premises here, so we simply list the negation of the conclusion.

1.	$\neg((\forall x)(\forall y)R(x,y) \rightarrow R(a,a))$	
2.	$(\forall x)(\forall y)R(x,y)$	Rule (8) applied to line 1
3.	$\neg R(a,a)$	Rule (8) applied to line 1
4.	$(\forall y)R(a,y)$	Rule (10) applied to line 2
5.	$\underline{R(a,a)}$	Rule (10) applied to line 4
	Closed	

The tableau is closed because of lines 3 and 5. So the result is proved.

Example 8.2

Prove $(\forall x)A(x) \rightarrow (\exists y)A(y)$.

We start with the negation of the conclusion.

1.	$\neg((\forall x)A(x) \rightarrow (\exists y)A(y))$	
2.	$(\forall x)A(x)$	Rule (8) applied to line 1
3.	$\neg(\exists y)A(y)$	Rule (8) applied to line 1
4.	$(\forall y)\neg A(y)$	Rule (13) applied to line 3
5.	$\neg A(a)$	Rule (10) applied to line 4
6.	$\underline{A(a)}$	Rule (10) applied to line 2
	Closed	

The tableau is closed because of lines 5 and 6. So the result is proved.

Note carefully that when using the rule of universal instantiation we can make use of the same term more than once, cf. use of constant a above.

In order to show why the use of a term in Rule (11) is conditional on its *not* having been used before, let us look at the following *wrong* 'deduction'.

Example 8.3

Prove $(\exists x)(\exists y)R(x, y) \rightarrow R(a, a)$

1.   ¬((∃x)(∃y)R(x, y)→R(a, a))
2.   (∃x)(∃y)R(x, y)   Rule (8) applied to line 1
3.   ¬R(a, a)   Rule (8) applied to line 1
4.   (∃y)R(a, y)   Rule (11) applied to line 2
5.   R(a, a)   Rule (11) applied to line 4
              Closed ?

The tableau is now closed because of lines 3 and 5. So the result is proved!?

But, if this is a correct proof it could cause us serious grief. As in propositional logic, we would like our theorems to be valid. This result, however, is far from valid. Consider, for example, an interpretation over the natural numbers where R(x, y) is interpreted as x < y. Then, (∃x)(∃y)R(x, y) is satisfiable, but R(a, a) is not. Hence (∃x)(∃y)R(x, y)→R(a, a) is not satisfiable in this interpretation, much less valid!

Of course, the purported proof is not valid either. What has gone wrong? Clearly, using Rule (11) on line 5 has violated the condition imposed on the correct use of the rule. Term a was already used and cannot be used again. Thus, we cannot write down R(a,a), so we cannot close the tableau.

In fact, if we look more closely we will see that we cannot use a in line 4 either. a is already in use in line 3 and cannot be used again for existential instantiation. The fact that it was 'given' makes no difference. So remember that, no matter how a term makes its first appearance in a semantic tableau, it cannot be used a second time for existential instantiation. It can, of course, be used many times for universal instantiation.

Example 8.4

Prove (∀x)(A(x)∧B(x)) → (∀x)A(x)
1.   ¬((∀x)(A(x)∧B(x)) → (∀x)A(x))
2.   (∀x)(A(x)∧B(x))   Rule (8) on line 1
3.   ¬(∀x)A(x)   Rule (8) on line 1
4.   (∃x)¬A(x)   Rule (12) on line 3
5.   ¬A(a)   Rule (11) on line 4
6.   A(a) ∧ B(a)   Rule (10) on line 2
7.   A(a)   Rule (1) on line 6
8.   B(a)   Rule (1) on line 6
             Closed

The tableau is closed because of lines 5 and 7. Therefore the result is proved.

Note carefully that we used existential quantification in line 5 before using universal instantiation to get line 6 from line 2. By this means we were free to use the term a again. If we had used universal instantiation first we would not have been able to do this. From this hint comes a useful heuristic.

Heuristic for applying EI and UI in a semantic tableau

When developing a semantic tableau in first order predicate logic, use the existential instantiation rule before the universal instantiation rule.

Exercise

8.1 Decide which of the following are theorems in first order predicate logic and use semantic tableaux to prove your answers.

(i) $(\exists x)A(x) \rightarrow (\forall y)A(y)$

(ii) $(\exists x)A(x) \rightarrow (\exists y)A(y)$

(iii) $(\forall x)(A(x) \wedge B(x)) \rightarrow (\exists x)B(x)$

(iv) $(\forall x)((A(x) \wedge B(x)) \rightarrow A(x))$

(v) $(\forall x)((A(x) \vee B(x)) \rightarrow A(x))$

(vi) $(\forall x)(A(x) \rightarrow (A(x) \vee B(x)))$

(vii) $(\forall x)(A(x) \rightarrow (\neg A(x) \rightarrow B(x)))$

8.3 Instantiation Rules

It is not too difficult to see that the rule of universal instantiation is a valid principle. If $(\forall x)A(x)$ holds in some interpretation then every object in the domain has the 'property' A. Since terms 'stand for' objects, clearly we can substitute any term t for x to get the correct assertion A(t). The same applies when A symbolises an n-ary relation, and x is one of the components of an n-tuple.

In the existential case, $(\exists x)A(x)$, A is asserted to hold of some object. When we substitute t for c in existential instantiation we are essentially using t to name that object: t is then 'committed'. That is why it cannot be used again for existential instantiation. The reader can convince herself of the sense of this if she considers a homely example. Suppose $(\exists x)(\exists y)M(x, y)$ stands for 'some x is married to some y', and $(\exists x)H(x, Mary)$ stands for 'somebody is Mary's husband'. Then if we instantiate x to 'John' and y to 'Lillian' in $(\exists x)(\exists y)M(x, y)$ to get M(John, Lillian), it would clearly be a mistake to instantiate x to 'John' in $(\exists x)H(x, Mary)$ to get H(John, Mary). After all, John is committed to Lillian (undying love, 'till death do them part', etc.) and cannot bring himself to develop the same affection for Mary. Even if, in this case, John is a wretched bigamist, we could not depend on this kind of over-commital in general. So, a term which appears once at any stage of a semantic tableau cannot be used again for existential instantiation.

We move on now to prove a number of important results in first order predicate logic. We will dignify them by calling them theorems.

Note that the basic concept involved in the use of *semantic* tableaux is *semantic* entailment and so we should use the sign ⊨ to indicate the drawing of conclusions from premises, or the drawing of conclusions simpliciter. However, for the present we think of the rules of derivation used in semantic tableaux as formal syntactic rules and so we will use the theorem sign ⊢ . Later, when we turn to problem-solving, we will revert to the ⊨ sign.

Theorem 8.1

$$\vdash (\forall x)A(x) \to (\exists y)A(y)$$

Proof Already proved above.

(End)

Theorem 8.2

$$\vdash (\forall x)(A(x) \to (B(x) \to A(x)))$$

Proof

1.	$\neg(\forall x)(A(x) \to (B(x) \to A(x)))$	
2.	$(\exists x)\neg(A(x) \to (B(x) \to A(x)))$	Rule (12) on line 1
3.	$\neg(A(a) \to (B(a) \to A(a)))$	Rule (11) on line 2
4.	$A(a)$	Rule (8) on line 3
5.	$\neg(B(a) \to A(a))$	Rule (8) on line 3
6.	$B(a)$	Rule (8) on line 5
7.	$\neg A(a)$	Rule (8) on line 5
	Closed	

(End)

So far all our tableaux have been 'straight line' tableaux. The next theorem reveals an example of branching.

Theorem 8.3

$$\vdash (\forall x)((A(x) \to (B(x) \to C(x))) \to ((A(x) \to B(x)) \to (A(x) \to C(x))))$$

Proof

1.　　$\neg(\forall x)((A(x) \to (B(x) \to C(x))) \to ((A(x) \to B(x)) \to (A(x) \to C(x))))$
2.　　$(\exists x)\neg((A(x) \to (B(x) \to C(x))) \to ((A(x) \to B(x)) \to (A(x) \to C(x))))$
　　　　　　　　　　　　　　　　　　　　　Rule (12) on line 1
3.　　　$\neg((A(a) \to (B(a) \to C(a))) \to ((A(a) \to B(a)) \to (A(a) \to C(a))))$
　　　　　　　　　　　　　　　　　　　　　Rule (11) on line 2
4.　　　　　　　　$A(a) \to (B(a) \to C(a))$　　　　Rule (8) on line 3
5.　　　　　$\neg((A(a) \to B(a)) \to (A(a) \to C(a)))$　　Rule (8) on line 3
6.　　　　　　　　　$A(a) \to B(a)$　　　　　　Rule (8) on line 5
7.　　　　　　　　　$\neg(A(a) \to C(a))$　　　　Rule (8) on line 5
8.　　　　　　　　　　$A(a)$　　　　　　　Rule (8) on line 7
9.　　　　　　　　　　$\neg C(a)$　　　　　　Rule (8) on line 7

10.　　　　　$\neg A(a)$　　$B(a)$　　　　Rule (3) on line 6
　　　　　　　Closed

11.　　　　　　　$\neg A(a)$　　$B(a) \to C(a)$　　Rule (3) on line 4
　　　　　　　　　Closed

12.　　　　　　　　　$\neg B(a)$　　$C(a)$　　Rule (3) on line 11
　　　　　　　　　　　Closed　　Closed　　From lines 11 and 9

　　　　　　　　　　　　　　　　　　　　　　　(End)

From now on we will omit the mentioning of a rule which justifies the development as it proceeds, unless the development is hard to follow.

Theorem 8.4

$$\vdash\ (\forall x)((\neg A(x) \to \neg B(x)) \to (B(x) \to A(x)))$$

Proof

$$\neg(\forall x)((\neg A(x) \to \neg B(x)) \to (B(x) \to A(x)))$$
$$(\exists x)\neg((\neg A(x) \to \neg B(x)) \to (B(x) \to A(x)))$$
$$\neg((\neg A(a) \to \neg B(a)) \to (B(a) \to A(a)))$$
$$\neg A(a) \to \neg B(a)$$
$$\neg(B(a) \to A(a))$$
$$B(a)$$
$$\neg A(a)$$

　　　　　$\neg\neg A(a)$　　　　$\neg B(a)$
　　　　　　Closed　　　　　　|
　　　　　　　　　　　　　　　$A(a)$
　　　　　　　　　　　　　　　Closed

　　　　　　　　　　　　　　　　　　　　　(End)

Theorem 8.5

$$\vdash ((\forall x)A(x) \lor (\forall x)B(x)) \rightarrow (\forall x)(A(x) \lor B(x))$$

Proof

$$\neg(((\forall x)A(x) \lor (\forall x)B(x)) \rightarrow (\forall x)(A(x) \lor B(x)))$$
$$(\forall x)A(x) \lor (\forall x)B(x)$$
$$\neg(\forall x)(A(x) \lor B(x))$$
$$(\exists x)\neg(A(x) \lor B(x))$$
$$\neg(A(a) \lor B(a))$$
$$\neg A(a)$$
$$\neg B(a)$$

$(\forall x)A(x)$	$(\forall x)B(x)$
A(a)	B(a)
Closed	Closed

(End)

Suppose we now try to prove the following result which is a kind of inverse of the last theorem.

$$\vdash (\forall x)(A(x) \lor B(x)) \rightarrow ((\forall x)A(x) \lor (\forall x)B(x))$$

$$\neg((\forall x)(A(x) \lor B(x)) \rightarrow ((\forall x)A(x) \lor (\forall x)B(x)))$$
$$(\forall x)(A(x) \lor B(x))$$
$$\neg((\forall x)A(x) \lor (\forall x)B(x))$$
$$\neg(\forall x)A(x)$$
$$\neg(\forall x)B(x)$$
$$(\exists x)\neg A(x)$$
$$\neg A(a)$$
$$(\exists x)\neg B(x)$$
$$\neg B(b) \qquad\qquad \text{Note, we cannot use a again here!}$$
$$A(a) \lor B(a) \qquad \text{Or we could also have } A(b) \lor B(b)$$

A(a)	B(a)
Closed	

We could go on and on (for ever!) using new and different instantiations for x – c, d, etc., but it is clear that we are going to be left with one branch open.

General considerations show that it is reasonable not to expect

$$\vdash (\forall x)(A(x) \lor B(x)) \rightarrow ((\forall x)A(x) \lor (\forall x)B(x))$$

A little thought reveals that it is possible for $(\forall x)(A(x) \lor B(x))$ to be true while at the same time $(\forall x)A(x) \lor (\forall x)B(x)$ is false – because either A or B could be true at any time without A being always true or B being always true.

The fact that the tableau is not completely closed reveals that the result is not proved. It does not, however, *prove* that the result cannot be proved. To convince the complete sceptic we might need a counterexample.

It is not too hard to find one. Consider, for example, an interpretation over the natural numbers where A is interpreted as 'is even' and B is 'is odd'.

Note how the restriction on the application of existential instantiation comes to the rescue here.

Exercises

8.2 Prove each of the following using semantic tableaux:

(i) $\vdash (\forall x)A(x) \leftrightarrow (\forall y)A(y)$, where y does not occur in A(x)

(ii) $\vdash (\forall x)(\forall y)(A(x,y) \rightarrow (B(x) \rightarrow A(x,y))$

(iii) $\vdash (\forall x)(\forall y)((A(x) \rightarrow (B(x,y) \rightarrow C(x,y))) \rightarrow ((A(x) \rightarrow B(x,y)) \rightarrow (A(x) \rightarrow C(x,y))))$

(iv) $\vdash ((\exists x)A(x) \lor (\exists x)B(x)) \rightarrow (\exists x)(A(x) \lor B(x))$

(v) $\vdash (\exists x)(A(x) \lor B(x)) \rightarrow ((\exists x)A(x) \lor (\exists x)B(x))$

(vi) $\vdash ((\forall x)A(x) \land (\forall x)B(x)) \leftrightarrow (\forall x)(A(x) \land B(x))$

(vii) $\vdash (\exists x)(A(x) \land B(x)) \rightarrow ((\exists x)(A(x) \land (\exists x)B(x))$

(viii) $\vdash (\forall x)(A(x) \rightarrow B(x)) \rightarrow ((\exists x)(A(x) \rightarrow (\exists x)B(x))$

8.3 Show that the following wff cannot be proved:

(i) $((\exists x)A(x) \rightarrow A(a)$

(ii) $((\exists x)A(x) \land (\exists x)B(x)) \rightarrow (\exists x)(A(x) \land B(x))$

8.4 Problem-solving in Predicate Logic

Let us examine briefly how semantic tableaux can help us solve problems that take us beyond the resources of propositional logic. As in the simpler cases, the problems must first be translated into a suitable symbolic form, but now we will require the apparatus of first order predicate logic rather than the meagre facilities of propositional logic.

For simplicity, we will again use our rather loose formalism and we will assume a suitable domain of interpretation in each problem. We begin with a hoary old chestnut.

Example 8.5

Is the following argument valid?

All men are mortal.

Socrates is a man.

Therefore Socrates is mortal.

Let   M(x) stand for 'x is mortal'

H(x) stand for 'x is a man'

Then the argument can be symbolised:

$$(\forall x)(H(x){\rightarrow}M(x)) \wedge H(Socrates) \vDash M(Socrates)$$

As usual we add the negation of the conclusion to the premises and try to construct a closed tableau.

$$(\forall x)(H(x){\rightarrow}M(x))$$
$$H(Socrates)$$
$$\neg M(Socrates)$$
$$H(Socrates){\rightarrow}M(Socrates) \qquad \text{UI on first line}$$

$$\neg H(Socrates) \qquad M(Socrates)$$
$$\text{Closed} \qquad\qquad \text{Closed}$$

Since the tableau is closed we conclude that the negation of the conclusion is inconsistent with the premises, and that, therefore, the conclusion follows from the premises. The argument is therefore valid.

Example 8.6

Is the following argument valid?

   All men are mortal.
   Socrates is mortal.
   Therefore Socrates is a man.

Using the same notation as before the argument can be symbolised:

$$(\forall x)(H(x) \rightarrow M(x)) \wedge M(Socrates) \vDash H(Socrates)$$

Our tableau is

$$(\forall x)(H(x){\rightarrow}M(x))$$
$$M(Socrates)$$
$$\neg H(Socrates)$$
$$H(Socrates){\rightarrow}M(Socrates) \qquad \text{UI on first line}$$

$$\neg H(Socrates) \qquad M(Socrates)$$

We see that the tableau cannot be closed, and we conclude that the argument is not valid. This is as expected, since it is fairly clear from the start that the conclusion does not follow from the premises.

Example 8.7

Is the following argument valid?

   All lecturers are determined.
   Anyone who is determined and intelligent will give satisfactory service.

Clare is an intelligent lecturer.
Therefore Clare will give satisfactory service.

Let   L(x) stand for 'x is a lecturer'
       D(x) stand for 'x is determined'
       I(x) stand for 'x is intelligent'
       S(x) stand for 'x will give satisfactory service'

We wish to show

$$(\forall x)(L(x) \rightarrow D(x)) \land (\forall x)((D(x) \land I(x)) \rightarrow S(x)) \land L(Clare) \land I(Clare) \models S(Clare)$$

The tableau is:

1.	$(\forall x)(L(x) \rightarrow D(x))$	
2.	$(\forall x)((D(x) \land I(x)) \rightarrow S(x))$	
3.	L(Clare)	
4.	I(Clare)	
5.	¬S(Clare)	
6.	L(Clare)→D(Clare)	UI on line 1
7.	(D(Clare)∧I(Clare)) → S(Clare)	UI on line 2

8.   ¬L(Clare)   D(Clare)   From line 6
      Closed   Lines 3 and 8

9. ¬(D(Clare)∧I(Clare))   S(Clare) From line 7
                           Closed   Lines 5 and 9

10. ¬D(Clare)   ¬I(Clare))   Lines 8 and 10, 4 and 10
    Closed   Closed

Since the tableau is closed we conclude that the argument is valid.

Example 8.8

Check the following argument:

All those who honour both their parents are blessed.
If anyone dislikes any of his siblings he does not honour his parents.
Jack likes his sister, Jill.
Therefore Jack is blessed.

Let   H(x,y,z) stand for 'x honours y and z'
       f(x) stand for 'x's father' – we make use of a function
       m(x) stand for 'x's mother' – again a function is used
       B(x) stand for 'x is blessed'
       L(x,y) stand for 'x likes y'
       S(x,y) stand for 'x is y's sibling'

(We could omit the predicate S(x,y) and utilise the fact that siblings have the same parents, but it would make the description more complicated.)

The argument may be expressed as follows:

$$(\forall x)(H(x, f(x), m(x))) \rightarrow B(x)) \wedge (\forall x)(\forall y)((S(y, x) \wedge \neg L(x, y)) \rightarrow$$
$$\neg H(x, f(x), m(x))) \wedge L(Jack, Jill) \models B(Jack)$$

We therefore build a tableau for

$$(\forall x)(H(x, f(x), m(x))) \rightarrow B(x)) \wedge (\forall x)(\forall y)((S(y, x) \wedge \neg L(x, y)) \rightarrow$$
$$\neg H(x, f(x), m(x))) \wedge L(Jack, Jill) \wedge \neg B(Jack)$$

1. $(\forall x)(H(x, f(x), m(x))) \rightarrow B(x))$
2. $(\forall x)(\forall y)((S(y, x) \wedge \neg L(x, y)) \rightarrow \neg H(x, f(x), m(x)))$
3.   L(Jack, Jill)
4.   ¬B(Jack)
5.   H(Jack, f(Jack), m(Jack))) → B(Jack)   UI on line 1
6.   (S(Jill, Jack) ∧ ¬L(Jack, Jill)) → ¬H(Jack, f(Jack), m(Jack)))
                                           UI (twice) on line 2

7.   ¬H(Jack, f(Jack), m(Jack))   B(Jack)   Line 5
                                 Closed   Lines 4 and 7

8.   ¬(S(Jill, Jack) ∧ ¬L(Jack, Jill))   ¬H(Jack, f(Jack), m(Jack))   Line 7

Without developing the tableau any further we can see from the last right branch that it will not close. Therefore we conclude that the argument is not valid. (Did you really think it was?)

8.5 Summary

- In this chapter we have used the straightforward 'mechanical' method of semantic tableaux to illustrate methods of proving theorems, drawing deductions and solving simple problems in first order predicate logic.
- The rules for the development of semantic tableaux are the same as for propositional logic with the addition of four extra rules to deal with quantification, namely,

     universal instantiation $(\forall x)A(x)$
                                          $A(t)$
     existential instantiation $(\exists x)A(x)$
                                          $A(t)$

where t is a term which has not been used in the derivation so far.

$$\neg\forall \qquad\qquad \neg(\forall x)A(x)$$
$$(\exists x)\neg A(x)$$
$$\neg\exists \qquad\qquad \neg(\exists x)A(x)$$
$$(\forall x)\neg A(x)$$

- In developing tableaux use existential instantiation before universal instantiation.

In this chapter we have
(1) studied the rules for semantic tableaux in first order logic.
(2) proved a number of theorems using semantic tableaux.
(3) applied semantic tableaux to problems involving objects and quantifiers.

In the next chapter we turn our attention to the application of the method of resolution to first order predicate logic.

Miscellaneous Exercises

1. Decide which of the following can be proved in first order predicate logic and use semantic tableaux to prove your answers.

(i) $\vdash (\forall x)(\exists y)A(x,y) \rightarrow (\exists y)(\forall x)A(x,y)$

(ii) $(\forall x)(\forall y)(\forall z)((P_1^2(x,y) \wedge P_1^2(y,z)) \rightarrow P_1^2(x,z)) \vdash (\forall x)(\forall z)P_1^2(x,z)$

(iii) $\vdash (\forall x)(\forall y)((A(x,y) \rightarrow \neg A(x,y)) \rightarrow \neg A(x,y))$

(iv) $(\forall x)((A(x) \vee B(x)) \rightarrow (A(x) \wedge C(x)) \vdash (\forall x)(B(x) \rightarrow C(x))$

(v) $(\exists x)((A(x) \wedge B(x)) \wedge (A(x) \vee B(x)) \rightarrow (C(x) \wedge D(x))) \vdash (\forall x)(A(x) \rightarrow D(x))$

(vi) $(\forall x)((A(x) \rightarrow (B(x) \wedge \neg C(x))) \wedge (B(x) \rightarrow (A(x) \rightarrow C(x)))) \wedge$
$(\exists x)(A(x) \wedge B(x) \wedge \neg D(x)) \vdash (\exists x)(C(x)) \wedge D(x))$

2. Determine, in each of the following cases, if the argument is valid.

   (i) All fruit is tasty if it is not cooked. This apple is not cooked. Therefore it is tasty.

   (ii) All fruit is tasty if it is not cooked. This apple is cooked. Therefore it is not tasty.

   (iii) Some fruit is tasty if it is not cooked. This apple is cooked. Therefore it is not tasty.

   (iv) Some fruit is tasty if it is not cooked. This apple is not cooked. Therefore it is tasty.

   (v) All that glistens is not gold. This pot does not glisten. Therefore it is gold.

(vi)   No lecturer who spends her time writing books on logic or who devotes herself to her students will come to the notice of the establishment. No one who does not come to the notice of the establishment will secure preferment. Therefore no lecturer who spends her time writing books on logic will secure preferment.

(vii)   Some lecturers are imaginative but poor communicators. Only good students are lecturers. Good students are not imaginative. Every artist is imaginative. Therefore not every good student is an artist.

(viii)   Dilly loves all and only those who love Milly. Milly loves all and only those who do not love Dilly. Dilly loves herself. Therefore Milly loves herself.

CHAPTER 9

Resolution in Predicate Logic

Chapter Aims

(1) To identify the differences between predicate logic and propositional logic as they affect resolution.

(2) To re-interpret the concepts of normal form, literal and clause in first order logic.

(3) To understand the terms prenex normal form, skolemisation and Herbrand universe.

(4) To introduce the notions of substitution and unification.

(5) To develop an algorithm for unification.

(6) To study the resolution rule as applied in first order logic.

(7) To examine the use of first order logic in database applications and in programming.

When you have studied this chapter you should

(a) be familiar with the notions of normal form, literal and clause in first order logic.

(b) understand the use of Skolemisation.

(c) be able to convert first order wff to clause form.

(d) be able to unify expressions through appropriate substitutions.

(e) know a mechanical procedure for unification.

(f) be able to apply resolution to problems requiring first order logic.

(g) have an appreciation of the potential of formal logic in computer applications such as databases and programming.

9.1 Introduction

In the last chapter we saw how results in first order predicate logic could be established more or less mechanically by using semantic tableaux. In Chapter 5 we studied another mechanical method of proof development, namely resolution. This is the method which is favoured for computerised logic processing systems. It involves a single rule of inference which can be proved to be sound and complete for first order predicate logic and which admits of relatively easy mechanisation. In Chapter 5, resolution was applied only to situations which fell within the compass of propositional logic. Now we wish to apply the method within first order predicate logic.

Resolution in predicate logic is based on the same principle as in propositional logic; in fact, first order wff are, more or less, 'reduced' to propositions in order to apply the method. Hence we take over the concepts of normal forms, clauses, literals, resolvents, and resolution from Chapter 5. However, as you would expect, complications arise from the extra, richer facilities of first order logic, and there is more work to be done before the resolution technique can be applied. To get a taste of what is involved consider the following two pairs of clauses:

$$(A \lor B \lor C \lor D) \text{ and } (E \lor \neg B \lor A)$$
$$(P(x) \lor Q(y, f(z)) \lor R(a, x, y) \lor T(z)) \text{ and } (U(x, z) \lor \neg Q(x, f(g(a))) \lor V(x))$$

In the first pair we can straightforwardly resolve on B and $\neg B$ to get the resolvent clause $(A \lor C \lor D \lor E)$.

In the second case we would like to be able to resolve on the predicates Q and $\neg Q$, but that cannot be done at present because the arguments are not exactly the same in the two occurrences. Before resolution can take place the two appearances of Q must be the same. We can arrange for this to happen if we make the substitutions x for y and g(a) for z to get $Q(x, f(g(a)))$ in both clauses.

It is important to realise that matters cannot be allowed to stand just there. If we do make these substitutions, they will affect not merely the Qs but some of the other entries in the clauses as well. In fact, after substitution the clauses will become

$$(P(x) \lor Q(x, f(g(a))) \lor R(a,x,x) \lor T(g(a)))$$
and $\quad (U(x,g(a)) \lor \neg Q(x, f(g(a))) \lor V(x))$

We can now 'cancel' the Qs to get the resolvent clause

$$(P(x) \lor R(a, x, x) \lor T(g(a)) \lor U(x, g(a)) \lor V(x))$$

Our task in this chapter is to learn how the ground may be prepared for the application of resolution and to study its role in solving problems.

9.2 Normal Forms

As in the case of propositional logic, wff must be converted into clausal form before resolution can be applied. Clauses in predicate logic are similar to those in propositional logic, except that in the conversion process there is the additional complication of quantifiers to be dealt with. The strategy is to move all quantifiers to the 'front' of a wff, thereby getting what is known as *prenex normal form*. For example, the first of the two following wff is in prenex form, the second is not.

$$(\forall x)(\exists y)(\forall z)(A(x, y) \rightarrow (B(x) \vee \neg C(x, z)))$$
$$(\forall x)((\exists y)A(x, y) \rightarrow (\forall z)(B(x) \vee \neg C(x, z)))$$

In general, a wff in prenex form will have the appearance

$$(Q_1 x_1)(Q_2 x_2)...(Q_n x_n)A(x_1, x_2, ..., x_n)$$

where the Q_i represents the quantifiers, either $\forall$ or $\exists$ in each case.

The part $(Q_1 x_1)(Q_2 x_2)...(Q_n x_n)$ is called the *prefix* while the remaining part, $A(x_1, x_2, ..., x_n)$, is called the *matrix*.

In order to convert an arbitrary wff to prenex form we first eliminate $\leftrightarrow$ and $\rightarrow$ in favour of $\wedge$ and $\vee$, and then make use of the following equivalences:

1. $(\forall x)A(x) \wedge B \equiv (\forall x)(A(x) \wedge B)$ ⎤
2. $(\forall x)A(x) \vee B \equiv (\forall x)(A(x) \vee B)$ ⎟
3. $(\exists x)A(x) \wedge B \equiv (\exists x)(A(x) \wedge B)$ where x does not occur in B
4. $(\exists x)A(x) \vee B \equiv (\exists x)(A(x) \vee B)$ ⎦
5. $(\forall x)A(x) \wedge (\forall x)B(x) \equiv (\forall x)(A(x) \wedge B(x))$
6. $(\exists x)A(x) \vee (\exists x)B(x) \equiv (\exists x)(A(x) \vee B(x))$
7. $(\forall x)A(x) \wedge (\forall y)B(y) \equiv (\forall x)(\forall y)(A(x) \wedge B(y))$
8. $(\forall x)A(x) \wedge (\exists y)B(y) \equiv (\forall x)(\exists y)(A(x) \wedge B(y))$
9. $(\exists x)A(x) \wedge (\forall y)B(y) \equiv (\exists x)(\forall y)(A(x) \wedge B(y))$
10. $(\exists x)A(x) \wedge (\exists y)B(y) \equiv (\exists x)(\exists y)(A(x) \wedge B(y))$

Equivalences 7 to 10 can be compactly expressed by

$$(Q_1 x)A(x) \wedge (Q_2 y)B(y) \equiv (Q_1 x)(Q_2 y)(A(x) \wedge B(y))$$

where Q_1 and Q_2 can stand for either $\forall$ or $\exists$.

11. $(\forall x)A(x) \vee (\forall y)B(y) \equiv (\forall x)(\forall y)(A(x) \vee B(y))$
12. $(\forall x)A(x) \vee (\exists y)B(y) \equiv (\forall x)(\exists y)(A(x) \vee B(y))$
13. $(\exists x)A(x) \vee (\forall y)B(y) \equiv (\exists x)(\forall y)(A(x) \vee B(y))$
14. $(\exists x)A(x) \vee (\exists y)B(y) \equiv (\exists x)(\exists y)(A(x) \vee B(y))$

Equivalences 11 to 14 can be expressed compactly by

$$(Q_1 x)A(x) \vee (Q_2 y)B(y) \equiv (Q_1 x)(Q_2 y)(A(x) \vee B(y))$$

Note that $(\forall x)A(x) \vee (\forall x)B(x)$ is not equivalent to $(\forall x)(A(x) \vee B(x))$.
Neither is $(\exists x)A(x) \wedge (\exists x)B(x)$ equivalent to $(\exists x)(A(x) \wedge B(x))$.

To deal with these situations we change the bound variable, say in the second quantifier to get, for example, $(\exists y)B(y)$, and use one of the last 8 equivalences.

Exercises

9.1 Prove, using semantic tableaux, each of the equivalences listed above. You will have dealt with some of them in the last chapter, but why not try them again for revision?

9.2 Show that $(\forall x)A(x) \lor (\forall x)B(x) \rightarrow (\forall x)(A(x) \lor B(x))$, but that it is not the case that $(\forall x)(A(x) \lor B(x)) \rightarrow (\forall x)A(x) \lor (\forall x)B(x)$.

9.3 Show that $(\exists x)(A(x) \land B(x)) \rightarrow (\exists x)A(x) \land (\exists x)B(x)$, but that it is not the case that $(\exists x)A(x) \land (\exists x)B(x) \rightarrow (\exists x)(A(x) \land B(x))$.

9.2.1 Prenex Normal Form

Let us review some of the ideas that we introduced in Chapter 5, this time placing them within the setting of the first order predicate logic.

Definition   Recall that the basic propositions (properties, relations) of which wff are composed are called atomic formulae or atoms. Again, we define a *literal* as an atom or the negation of an atom.

$P_2^1(x_1)$ is a literal.

$\neg P_2^3(x_1, x_2, x_3)$ is a literal.

A literal consisting of an atom is called a *positive literal*, e.g. $P_1^2(x_4, c_2)$.
A literal which consists of the negation of an atom is called a *negative literal*, e.g. $\neg P_2^1(x_1)$.

Definition   A wff is in *conjunctive normal form* (CNF) if it is a conjunction of disjunctions of literals, i.e. if it is in the form

$$A_1 \land A_2 \land \ldots \land A_i \land \ldots \land A_n$$

where each A_i is of the form

$$\lambda_1 \lor \lambda_2 \lor \ldots \lor \lambda_j \lor \ldots \lor \lambda_m$$

where each λ_j is a literal.

For example

$$(P_2^1(x_1) \lor P_1^1(x_3) \lor \neg P_2^3(x_1, x_2, x_3)) \land (\neg P_2^2(x_1, c_3) \lor P_2^1(x_1) \lor P_1^3(x_1, x_2, x_3)) \land$$
$$(P_3^1(x_2) \lor \neg P_2^4(x_1, x_2, x_3, x_4) \lor P_2^1(x_1) \lor \neg P_2^1(x_1) \lor P_2^3(x_1, x_2, x_5))$$

is in CNF, as are

$$(\neg P_2^4(x_1, x_2, c_3, c_4) \lor \neg P_2^1(x_1)) \land (\neg P_2^2(x_1, x_2) \lor \neg P_1^1(x_4) \lor P_5^2(x_1, x_2))$$

and

$$P_2^4(x_1, x_2, x_3, x_4)$$

(by default, as it were).

Definition   A wff is in *disjunctive normal form* (DNF) if it is a disjunction of conjunctions of literals, i.e. if it is in the form
$$A_1 \lor A_2 \lor \ldots \lor A_i \lor \ldots \lor A_n$$
where each A_i is of the form
$$\lambda_1 \land \lambda_2 \land \ldots \land \lambda_j \land \ldots \land \lambda_m$$
where each λ_j is a literal.

For example

$$(P_2^1(x_1) \land P_1^1(x_3) \land \neg P_2^3(x_1, x_2, x_3)) \lor (\neg P_2^2(x_1, c_3) \land P_2^1(x_1) \land P_1^3(x_1, x_2, x_3)) \lor$$
$$(P_3^1(x_2) \land \neg P_2^4(x_1, x_2, x_3, x_4) \land P_2^1(x_1) \land \neg P_2^1(x_1) \land P_2^3(x_1, x_2, x_5))$$

is in DNF, as are

$$(\neg P_2^4(x_1, x_2, c_3, c_4) \land \neg P_2^1(x_1)) \lor (\neg P_2^2(x_1, x_2) \land \neg P_1^1(x_4) \land P_5^2(x_1, x_2))$$

and

$$P_2^4(x_1, x_2, x_3, x_4)$$

(by default, again).

We concentrate on conjunctive normal forms, i.e. expressions of the form
$$C_1 \land C_2 \land \ldots \land C_i \land \ldots \land C_n$$
where each C_i is a disjunction of literals, i.e it is of the form
$$\lambda_1 \lor \lambda_2 \lor \ldots \lor \lambda_j \lor \ldots \lor \lambda_m$$
where each λ_j is a literal.
The C_is are called *clauses*. Thus

Definition   A *clause* is a finite disjunction of literals. A clause may consist of just a single literal, e.g. $P_2^3(x_1, x_2, x_3)$ or $\neg P_2^3(x_1, x_2, x_3)$. If so, it is called a *unit clause*.

It is convenient once again to depart from the fussy subscript, superscript notation of first order languages and just to use uppercase letters to denote wff in general and, more specifically, atoms. Note that it is usually atoms that we wish to denote. Thus, A(x, y) will usually denote an atomic binary relation between x and y, rather than a general wff with x and y as possible free variables.

9.2.2 Converting to normal form

As in propositional logic, transformation of a wff to prenex normal form is best done in stages. In the following, A, B and C stand for general wff.

Stage 1 Use the equivalence $A \leftrightarrow B \equiv (A \rightarrow B) \wedge (B \rightarrow A)$ to eliminate $\leftrightarrow$.

Stage 2 Use the equivalence $A \rightarrow B \equiv \neg A \vee B$ to eliminate $\rightarrow$.

Stage 3 Use
      (a) De Morgan's laws $\neg(A \wedge B) \equiv \neg A \vee \neg B$ and $\neg(A \vee B) \equiv \neg A \wedge \neg B$
      (b) The law of double negation $\neg \neg A \equiv A$
      (c) The laws $\neg(\forall x)A(x) \equiv (\exists x)\neg A(x)$
          and $\neg(\exists x)A(x) \equiv (\forall x)\neg A(x)$
to push the negation sign $\neg$ immediately before atomic wff.

Stage 4 Rename bound variables, if necessary.

Stage 5 Use the equivalences 1 to 14 above as required to bring all the quantifiers to the left.

Stage 6 Use the distributive law $A \vee (B \wedge C) \equiv (A \vee B) \wedge (A \vee C)$ to effect the conversion of the matrix to CNF.

The wff which emerges from these transformations is said to be in *prenex normal form*.

Example 9.1

Convert $(\exists x)A(x) \rightarrow (\forall x)B(x)$ to prenex normal form

$(\exists x)A(x) \rightarrow (\forall x)B(x)$	$\equiv \neg(\exists x)A(x) \vee (\forall x)B(x)$	Stage 2
	$\equiv (\forall x)\neg A(x) \vee (\forall x)B(x)$	Stage 3(c)
	$\equiv (\forall x)\neg A(x) \vee (\forall y)B(y)$	Stage 4
	$\equiv (\forall x)(\forall y)(\neg A(x) \vee B(y))$	Stage 5

Example 9.2

Convert $(\forall x)(\forall y)((\forall z)(A(x, y, z) \wedge B(y)) \rightarrow (\forall x)C(x, z))$ to prenex normal form

$(\forall x)(\forall y)((\forall z)(A(x, y, z) \vee B(y)) \rightarrow (\forall x)C(x, z))$

$\equiv (\forall x)(\forall y)(\neg(\forall z)(A(x, y, z) \vee B(y)) \vee (\forall x)C(x, z))$	Stage 2
$\equiv (\forall x)(\forall y)((\exists z)\neg(A(x, y, z) \vee B(y)) \vee (\forall x)C(x, z))$	Stage 3(c)
$\equiv (\forall x)(\forall y)((\exists z)(\neg A(x, y, z) \wedge \neg B(y)) \vee (\forall x)C(x, z))$	Stage 3(a)
$\equiv (\forall x)(\forall y)((\exists z)(\neg A(x, y, z) \wedge \neg B(y)) \vee (\forall u)C(u, z))$	Stage 4
$\equiv (\forall x)(\forall y)(\exists z)(\forall u)((\neg A(x, y, z) \wedge \neg B(y)) \vee C(u, z))$	Stage 5
$\equiv (\forall x)(\forall y)(\exists z)(\forall u)((\neg A(x, y, z) \vee C(u, z)) \wedge (\neg B(y) \vee C(u, z)))$	
	Stage 6

Exercise

9.4 Convert each of the following wff to prenex normal form:
    (i) $(\exists x)A(x) \rightarrow (\exists x)B(x)$
    (ii) $(\forall x)A(x) \rightarrow (\exists x)B(x)$
    (iii) $(\forall x)A(x) \rightarrow (\forall x)B(x)$
    (iv) $(\forall x)(\forall y)(A(x, y) \wedge B(y, z)) \rightarrow (\exists x)C(x, z)$

(v) $(\forall x)((\forall y)(A(x, y) \rightarrow B(y, z)) \rightarrow (\exists x)C(x, z))$

(vi) $(\forall x)(\forall y)((\exists z)A(x, y, z) \wedge ((\exists u)C(x, u) \rightarrow (\exists v)C(x, v)))$

9.2.3 Skolem Standard Form

There is a further transformation to be effected on a wff before resolution is applied. This consists in the elimination of all the existential quantifiers by a process called Skolemization, to arrive at a wff in *skolem standard form*. How is Skolemization achieved?

Consider the wff $(\exists x)P(x)$. This can be read as stating that some x has the property P. Suppose we follow this up by saying 'Let c have the property P', i.e. we name an individual (often called a *witness*) which has the property P. This, of course, is symbolised by $P(c)$.

The use of $P(c)$ suggests that we could 'drop' the existentially quantified expression $(\exists x)P(x)$ in favour of the simpler $P(c)$. In a sense, $P(c)$ appears to be more specific and to convey more information than $(\exists x)P(x)$. 'Let c have the property P' carries with it the assumption that there is something with the property P, i.e. there exists an entity with the property P. In fact $P(c)$ may not really be more specific or give any more information. 'c' is usually just an arbitrary name, brought into being for the purpose of 'simplifying' the existential commitment.

One important point must be clearly understood. The constant that is used as a name must have no prior commitment. What is meant by this? Well, consider the following scenario – 'The car was stolen in the inner city on Tuesday evening. The driver then burgled a house in the Rathmines area, sometime before midnight. Our burglar, let us call him Joe, then cooly drove past the police station and went for a meal. The following day a somewhat poorly dressed individual, let us call him Joe, offered goods stolen from the house for sale in a public house in Bray.'

Clearly, there is something wrong with using the name Joe for the two individuals mentioned in the story. It could be the case that they are one and the same person, *but it might not*. Logically, the name Joe is *committed* after the first mention and cannot be used again unless we are sure the individual involved is the same as in the first mention.

In general, then, when we remove an existential quantifier and replace the formerly quantified variable by a constant, that constant must be a *new* one, i.e. one that has not previously been committed. This is essentially the same requirement as we had for the existential instantiation rule for semantic tableaux in the last chapter.

Now, consider the following: 'Everyone has a mother'. This could be symbolised as $(\forall x)(\exists y)M(x, y)$, i.e. For every x there is a y such that the mother of x is y.

Suppose now we remove the existential quantifier and replace y by a constant c. We get $(\forall x)M(x, c)$, which, in effect says that c is the mother of all x's (to vary a theme). This, of course, is not what we want to convey. So, must we conclude that, if an existential quantifier is preceded by a universal quantifier, we cannot replace the existential quantifier as in our first example?

Well, let us think about it a little more carefully. Clearly the use of a constant is inappropriate. Why is this? Because the value of y, i.e. the variable standing for mother, varies with the value of x. Different people have different mothers (in general!). y is tied to x; y is a function of x! Using this insight, suppose we replace the existential quantifier by a function, $m(x)$, say, rather than a constant, to get $(\forall x)M(x, m(x))$.

This now reads 'For every x the relation M holds between x and some 'object', $m(x)$, dependent on x'.

Similarly, if an existential quantifier were preceded by two universal quantifiers, it would be replaceable by a function of the two quantified variables, e.g.

$$(\forall x)(\forall y)(\exists z)P(x, y, z) \text{ might yield } (\forall x)(\forall y)P(x, y, f(x, y))$$

Definition   The process of eliminating existential quantifiers and replacing the corresponding variable by either a constant (called a Skolem constant) or a function (called a Skolem function) is called *Skolemisation*.

By way of further example let us finish off the expression we considered above to produce a final Skolem standard form.

$$(\forall x)(\forall y)(\exists z)(\forall u)((\neg A(x, y, z) \vee C(u, z)) \wedge (\neg B(y) \vee C(u, z)))$$
$$\equiv (\forall x)(\forall y)(\forall u)((\neg A(x, y, f(x, y)) \vee C(u, f(x, y))) \wedge (\neg B(y) \vee C(u, f(x, y))))$$

Note that the function which replaces z does not involve u since $\forall u$ occurs to the right of $\exists z$ in the prefix.

Skolem standard form emerges from an original wff through a (possibly) long series of transformations involving a number of stages. A question that arises is 'Has the satisfiability status, or, more pertinently, the *un*satisfiability status, of the original wff been changed by this process?' In other words, if the original wff (call it D) is unsatisfiable will the Skolem standard form (call it S) be unsatisfiable, and vice versa?

It can be proved, fairly easily, that D is unsatisfiable if and only if S is unsatisfiable. This accords with our intuitions, since the operations leading to prenex form are all based on logical equivalences and, in Skolemising, we are 'merely' giving suitably non-committed names to the 'objects' asserted to exist by the existential quantifiers. If no object satisfying the conditions involved in the formula exists then we cannot give a name to it, and, conversely, if no matter what name we supply, an inconsistency arises, then there does not exist an object satisfying the conditions.

9.2.4 Sets of Clauses

In propositional logic we found it convenient to express a wff in conjunctive normal form as a set of clauses. We do the same in first order predicate logic. We also drop all the universal quantifiers! How can we get away with this? Well, we are not 'getting away' with anything. We are simply using the fact that, after Skolemisation, the only quantifiers left in a wff are universal. Consequently, we consider it unnecessary to write them explicitly and rely on an awareness that, in clause form, it is understood that all the variables are universally quantified.

Expressed as a set of clauses our last wff above is

$$\{\{\neg A(x, y, f(x, y)), C(u, f(x, y))\}, \{\neg B(y), C(u, f(x, y))\}\}$$

There are two clauses in the set. The literals in the first clause are $\neg A(x, y, f(x, y))$ and $C(u, f(x, y))$; those in the second are $\neg B(y)$ and $C(u, f(x, y))$.

Exercise

9.5 Convert each of the following wff to Skolem standard form, and then write the result as a set of clauses:

(i) $(\exists x)A(x) \rightarrow (\exists x)(\exists y)(B(x) \wedge C(x, y))$

(ii) $(\forall x)A(x) \rightarrow ((\exists x)(\exists y)(B(x) \wedge C(x, y))$

(iii) $(\forall x)(\exists y)((\exists z)(A(x, y) \wedge B(y, z)) \rightarrow (\exists x)C(x, z))$

(iv) $(\forall x)((\forall y)(A(x, y) \rightarrow (\exists z)B(y, z)) \rightarrow (\exists x)C(x, z))$

(v) $(\forall x)(\forall y)((\exists z)A(x, y, z) \vee ((\exists u)C(x, u) \rightarrow (\exists v)(C(x, v) \wedge B(v, z))))$

9.3 Herbrand Universes

You may have wondered where the constants and functions used in Skolemisation came from. Up to now we have been fairly non-committal, just as we were vague and non-committal in Chapter 6 about the presenc of a 'suitable' domain of interpretation for our examples. You may have been satisfied with this rather cavalier approach, or you may have wondered, say in the case of Skolemization, whether it could happen that the intended interpretation did not contain a suitable function for replacement of existentially quantified variables. It has no 'mother' function, for instance!

Well, with a little bit of thought we can bring ourselves to the realisation that if a given interpretation does not appear to supply us with a ready-to-hand familiar function we can generally define one. For example, suppose the domain is the set of natural numbers, and suppose for some reason we have need of a binary function whose values are the least odd number greater than or equal to the sum of the two arguments of the function. Then we simply define such a function, e.g.

$$f(x, y) = x+y \text{ if } x+y \text{ is odd}$$
$$= x+y+1 \text{ if } x+y \text{ is even.}$$

Of course, the function was already there, implicit in the structure of the interpretation – we just had not given it a name. Essentially that is what Skolemization does. It abstracts from the process of defining specific functions for specific interpretations. It deals with 'naming' in the abstract.

It is convenient to carry this abstraction further and consider, not just abstract function names, but an abstract interpretation, an interpretation that will act as a representative for all intepretations over all domains. After all, if we are to judge a wff to be unsatisfiable, we must be convinced that it will fail to be satisfied by any valuation over any domain in any interpretation. This gives rise to a concept developed by Herbrand and since called the Herbrand universe. The Herbrand universe gives us a standard abstract domain in which all questions of unsatisfiability of wff can be settled, in the sense that a set of clauses S is unsatisfiable if and only if it is unsatisfiable in any interpretation over the Herbrand universe.

What exactly is a Herbrand universe?

A Herbrand universe is defined by reference to a set of clauses, S. Essentially it consists of the constants in S and the functions of S applied to those constants.

Definition   The *Herbrand universe* H(S) of a set of clauses S may be defined inductively as follows:

If c is a constant in any member of S then $c \in H(S)$. If S contains no constants then H(S) contains the constant symbol a.

If f is an n-ary function in S and $t_1, t_2, ..., t_n$ are in H(S) then $f(t_1, t_2, ..., t_n) \in H(S)$.

For example, if S is $\{\{A(x, b), B(b), \neg C(x, y, z)\}, \{C(c, d, x), D(y)\}\}$ then H(S) = \{b, c, d\}.

If S is $\{\{A(x, y), B(x), C(x, y, z)\}, \{\neg C(x, z, x), \neg D(y)\}\}$ then H(S) = \{a\}.

If S is $\{\{\neg A(x, y, f(x, y)), C(u, f(x, y))\}, \{\neg B(y), C(u, f(x, y))\}\}$ then H(S) = \{a, f(a, a), f(a, f(a, a)), f(f(a, a), a), f(f(a, a), f(a, a)), f(f(a, f(a, a)), a), ... \}

If S is $\{\{A(a, x), \neg B(y, f(x)), C(x, g(y, z))\}, \{B(g(c, x), c)\}\}$ then H(S) = \{a, c, f(a), f(c), g(a, a), g(a, c), g(c, a), g(c, c), f(f(a)), f(f(c)), f(g(a, a)), ... \}

Notice that if there are no functions in S the Herbrand universe is finite, but, if there is even one function, H(S) is infinite!

The terms in a Herbrand universe are called *ground terms*. Thus ground terms do not involve variables – they are composed of constants and functions applied to constants. In general, expressions not involving variables are called *ground expressions*.

In the above examples it might appear that the Herbrand universes were generated in a somewhat *ad hoc* manner, by scanning the clauses and hoping not to miss any candidate constants and functions. If the set of clauses is fairly big this hope might not be fulfilled. Luckily, there is a systematic procedure for building up the Herbrand universe which may be described as follows:

Let H_0 be the set of constants appearing in clauses of S. If none appear let $H_0 = \{a\}$.

Let H_1 be H_0 together with the ground terms generated by applying functions appearing in S to the elements of H_0, i.e.
$$H_1 = H_0 \cup \{f(t_1, t_2, ..., t_n) \mid f \in S, t_i \in H_0\}$$

.
.
.

$$H_{i+1} = H_i \cup \{f(t_1, t_2, ..., t_n) \mid f \in S, t_i \in H_i\}$$

Thus, for the last example above we have

$H_0 = \{a, c\}$
$H_1 = \{a, c, f(a), f(c), g(a, a), g(a, c), g(c, a), g(c, c)\}$
$H_2 = \{a, c, f(a), f(c), g(a, a), g(a, c), g(c, a), g(c, c), f(f(a)), f(f(c)), f(g(a, a)),$
  $f(g(a, c)), f(g(c, a)), f(g(c, c)), g(f(a), f(c)), g(f(a), g(a, a)), g(f(a), g(a,$
  $c)), g(f(a), g(c, a)), g(f(a), g(c, c)), g(f(c), f(c)), g(f(c), g(a, a)), g(f(c),$
  $g(a, c)), g(f(c), g(c, a)), g(f(c), g(c, c)), g(g(a, a), f(c)), g(g(a, a), g(a,$
  $a)), g(g(a, a), g(a, c)), g(g(a, a), g(c, a)), g(g(a, a), g(c, c)), ...\}$

Exercise

9.6 Write down (a representative part of) the Herbrand universe for each of the following sets of clauses, building up from H_0 in each case:

(i) $\{\{A(x), B(x, y)\}, \{C(x, y, z), D(x, y, z, w)\}\}$
(ii) $\{\{A(x), B(x, a)\}, \{C(x, a, b), D(a, b, c, d)\}\}$
(iii) $\{\{A(a)\}, \{\neg A(f(x))\}, \{C(x, a, b), D(a, b, c, y)\}\}$
(iv) $\{\{A(x), B(x, f(x))\}, \{C(x, y, z)\}, \{D(x, y, z, w), \neg C(x, y, f(x))\}\}$
(v) $\{\{A(a), B(x, f(a)), \neg C(x, f(x), g(a, x))\}, \{A(f(g(x, y))), D(g(f(a), x))\}\}$

9.3.1 Herbrand Interpretations

Herbrand universes are used to provide domains for Herbrand interpretations.

Definition If S is a set of clauses, the collection of ground atoms forms the *Herbrand base* of S, i.e. the Herbrand base of S = $\{P_i^n(t_1, t_2, ..., t_n) \mid P_i^n \in S, t_j \in H(S)\}$.

Definition   A *ground instance* of a clause of S is a clause in which the variables, if any, have been replaced by elements of the Herbrand universe of S.

For example, let S = {{A(a, x), ¬B(y, f(x)), C(x, g(y, z))}, {B(g(c, x), c)}}. A ground instance of the clause {A(a, x), ¬B(y, f(x)), C(x, g(y, z))} would be {A(a, a), ¬B(a, f(a)), C(a, g(a, a)}. Another would be {A(a, f(a)), ¬B(a, f(g(a, f(a)))), C(f(a), g(a, f(a)))}.

A Herbrand interpretation is essentially a valuation of the ground atoms of S, i.e. an assignment of true and false to elements of the Herbrand base of S. In this manner the determination of the satisfiability of a set of clauses is 'reduced' to the determination of the truth or falsity of ground propositions as in propositional logic. To elucidate this, let us take some examples.

Example 9.3

Let S be {{A(x), ¬B(y, x)}, {¬A(y), C(c)}
H(S) = {c}
Herbrand base = {A(c), B(c, c), C(c)}
A Herbrand interpretation h is determined by
$$h(A(c)) = \text{true}$$
$$h(B(c, c)) = \text{false}$$
$$h(C(c)) = \text{true}$$
We write this as {A(c), ¬B(c, c), C(c)}. In general, we write P if P is to be interpreted as true, and ¬P if P is interpreted as false.
Another Herbrand interpretation is {A(c), B(c, c), C(c)} while yet another is {A(c), B(c, c), ¬C(c)}.
It is easy to see that S is satisfied by the first and second of these interpretations, but not by the third. Why is this?
Consider the third interpretation. Remember that {A(x), ¬B(y, x)} is to be understood as A(x) ∨ ¬B(y, x). This becomes A(c) ∨ ¬B(c, c) after assignment of c to both x and y. This clause is true under the third interpretation, since A(c) is assigned the value true. But the clause {¬A(c), C(c)} is false since both ¬A(c) and C(c) are false. Hence S is false, since S = (A(x) ∨ ¬B(y, x)) ∧ (¬A(y) ∨ C(c)), and therefore *both* clauses must be true for S to be true.

Exercise

9.7 Check that S is satisfied by the first two interpretations given above.

Example 9.4

Let S be {{A(f(x)), ¬B(y, x)}, {¬A(c), C(x)}
H(S) = {c, f(c), f(f(c)), f(f(f(c))), ... }
Herbrand base = {A(c), B(c, c), C(c), A(f(c)), B(c, f(c)), B(f(c), c), B(f(c), f(c)),
C(f(c)), A(f(f(c))), ... }
A Herbrand interpretation is {¬A(f(c)), B(c, c), C(c), ...}. This does not
satisfy S.
Another Herbrand interpretation is {¬A(c), ¬A(f(f(c))), ¬B(c, f(c)), ¬C(c),
...}. This one does satisfy S.

Example 9.5

Let S be {{A(a, x), ¬B(y, f(x)), C(x, g(y, z))}, {B(g(c, x), c)}}
H(S) = {a, c, f(a), f(c), g(a, a), g(a, c), g(c, a), g(c, c), f(f(a)), f(f(c)), f(g(a, a)),
... }
Herbrand base = {A(a, a), B(a, a), C(a, a), A(a, c), A(a, f(a)), A(a, f(c)), ...
C(f(g(a, f(a))), g(f(a), g(a, f(a)))), ...}
A Herbrand interpretation is {A(a, a), B(a, a), C(a, a), A(a, c), B(a, c), A(a,
f(a)), A(a, f(c)), ... ¬C(a, g(a, g(f(a), a))), ...}. This satisfies S.
One that doesn't is {A(a, a), B(a, a), C(a, a), A(a, c), A(a, f(a)), A(a, f(c)), ...
¬B(g(c, a), c), C(a, g(a, g(f(a), a))), ..., C(f(g(a, f(a)))), g(f(a), g(a, f(a))), ...}

The real significance of Herbrand interpretations is that a set of clauses is
unsatisfiable if and only if it is unsatisfiable over all Herbrand interpretations.
Thus, in determining the unsatisfiability of a set of clauses we can confine our
attention to Herbrand universes. Let us look at a couple of examples.

Example 9.6

Show that S = {{A(x), ¬B(x, a)}, {A(a), B(y, a)}, {¬A(y)}} is unsatisfiable.
Herbrand universe = {a}
All the possible Herbrand interpretations are :
        {A(a), B(a, a)}
        {¬A(a), B(a, a)}
        {A(a), ¬B(a, a)}
        {¬A(a), ¬B(a, a)}
It is clear that S is satisfied under none of these interpretations; the third
clause fails under the first interpretation, the first clause fails under the second
interpretation, the third clause under the third, and the second clause fails
under the fourth interpretation.

Note the similarity between listing all the possible Herbrand interpretations and
drawing up the various combinations of true and false in a truth table.

Example 9.7

Show that S = {{A(x)}, {¬A(x), B(f(x))}, {¬B(f(a))}} is unsatisfiable.
Herbrand universe = {a, f(a), f(f(a)), f(f(f(a))), ... }
Possible Herbrand interpretations are:

    {A(a), B(a), A(f(a)), B(f(a)), ... }
    {¬A(a), B(a), A(f(a)), B(f(a)), ... }
    {A(a), ¬B(a), A(f(a)), ¬B(f(a)), ... }
    {¬A(a), ¬B(a), A(f(a)), B(f(a)), ... }
    {¬A(a), ¬B(a), ¬A(f(a)), B(f(a)), ... }
    {¬A(a), ¬B(a), ¬A(f(a)), ¬B(f(a)), A(f(f(a))), ¬B(f(f(a))), ... }

On examination we discover that none of these interpretations satisfies S.
For example, the third clause fails under the first interpretation, the second
clause fails under the third interpretation, and so on. But, a problem arises in
that the number of possible interpretations is infinite. So how can we check
that S fails under all Herbrand interpretations?

We can reason as follows. In order for the third clause to be satisfied an
interpretation must contain ¬B(f(a)). If this is the case, then in order to
satisfy the second clause we would need ¬A(a). But, then the first clause
fails. We can therefore conclude that no Herbrand interpretation satisfies S,
and that therefore S is unsatisfiable.

Exercises

9.8   For each of the sets of clauses S in exercise 9.6 write down the Herbrand
base (or a portion thereof) and two Herbrand interpretations, one that
satisfies S and one that doesn't.

9.9   Show, using Herbrand interpretations, that each of the following sets of
clauses is unsatisfiable:

    (i)   {{A(x)}, {¬A(y)}}
    (ii)   {{A(x), B(x)}, {A(a)}, {¬B(y)}, {¬A(y)}}
    (iii) {{A(x), B(x)}, {A(a), ¬B(y)}, {¬A(y)}}
    (iv) {{A(x, y), B(x, c)}, {A(c, x), ¬B(y, x)}, {¬A(x, x)}}
    (v)   {{¬A(x), B(x)}, {A(b)}, {C(a, b)}, {¬B(y), ¬C(a, y)}}

9.4 Resolution

Given the complexity of first order predicate logic and the multiplicity of
possible interpretations it is good to know that we can confine our attention to
Herbrand universes when considering the possible unsatisfiability of sets of
clauses. However, our exploitation of Herbrand universes so far has been
somewhat *ad hoc*. This may be acceptable in simple cases when only a few
small clauses are involved and refutations are quickly encountered, but it is
hopeless in more complex cases when large portions of Herbrand

interpretations must be considered before unsatisfiability is established. For example, Chang & Lee (1973) give an example of a simple set of clauses

$$\{\{P(x, g(x), y, h(x, y), z, k(x, y, z))\}, \{P(u, v, e(v), w, f(v, w), x)\}\}$$

where they claim that the earliest unsatisfiable set has of the order of 10^{256} elements!

Clearly, a more uniform method of unsatisfiability seeking would be desirable. This is where the method of resolution, which we studied in its application to propositional logic in Chapter 5, becomes of interest once more. Let us review some of the concepts and definitions that we introduced in Chapter 5.

Literals λ and $\neg\lambda$ are called a *complementary pair*.

If two clauses contain a complementary pair of literals they may be *resolved* together to give a new clause called their *resolvent*. As we saw, this is a straightforward recognition process in the domain of propositional logic. For example the clauses $\{p_1, p_2, \neg p_3\}$ and $\{p_3, p_4\}$ can be resolved to give the resolvent caluse $\{p_1, p_2, p_4\}$. In the case of predicate logic it is not quite so straightforward. Simple cases do arise, but in general a certain amount of work has to be done before complementary literals can be recognised. Let us take a couple of simple cases first.

$\{A(x), B(x, y), C(y, z)\}$ and $\{\neg A(x), B(x, x)\}$
 yield resolvent $\{B(x, y), C(y, z), B(x, x)\}$
$\{A(x, y, z)\}$ and $\{\neg A(x, y, z)\}$
 resolve to give $\bot$ (the empty clause).

Definition   As in propositional logic, the resolvent of two clauses C_1 and C_2 containing the complementary literals λ and $\neg\lambda$ respectively, is defined as:
$$\text{res}(C_1, C_2) = C_1 - \{\lambda\} \cup C_2 - \{\neg\lambda\}$$

Suppose now we have the two clauses $\{\neg A(x), B(x, y)\}$ and $\{A(a), C(y)\}$. We almost have complementary literals, $\neg A(x)$ and $A(a)$, but, since they are not exactly complementary, we cannot resolve at present. However, if we replace x by a, we get the clauses

$$\{\neg A(a), B(a, y)\} \text{ and } \{A(a), C(y)\}$$

which we can then resolve to get the resolvent $\{B(a, y), C(y)\}$.

Is this process of substitution justified? What is meant by 'justified'?

The issue is: is the resolvent a logical consequence of the clauses giving rise to it, i.e. is it impossible for the resolvent not to be satisfied when the clauses are satisfied?

Consider carefully this last example. Suppose the two clauses $\{\neg A(x), B(x, y)\}$ and $\{A(a), C(y)\}$ are satisfied, and suppose A(a) is false. Then C(y) is true (for all y; remember our variables are implicitly universally quantified) and hence the resolvent {B(a, y), C(y)} is true.

Suppose A(a) is true. Then ¬A(x) is false for x = a, and hence B(x, y) is true for x = a, i.e B(a, y) is true. Again, the resolvent {B(a, y), C(y)} is true.

This example illustrates the same principle that we had in propositional logic – the Resolution Principle (Theorem 5.1): a resolvent of two clauses, C_1, C_2, is a logical consequence of $C_1 \wedge C_2$, i.e. $C_1 \wedge C_2 \vDash \text{res}(C_1, C_2)$.

Our task now is to apply the above principle to deductions. As before, we define a resolution deduction as follows.

Definition   A *(resolution) deduction* of a clause C from a set S of clauses is a finite sequence of clauses $C_1, C_2, \ldots, C_n = C$, such that each C_i is either a member of S or is a resolvent of two clauses taken from S or earlier members of the sequence.

From the resolution principle we deduce that, if S is true under some truth valuation, v, then $v(C_i) = T$ for all C_i, and in particular $v(C) = T$.

Definition   A resolution deduction of ⊥ from a set of clauses S is called a *(resolution) refutation* of S.

In essence, a deduction of ⊥ from a set of clauses S means that the clauses in S are mutually 'incompatible', i.e. S is unsatisfiable.

Before we examine the question of substitution further, let us work through a few examples.

Example 9.8

Prove $\{\{\neg A(x), \neg B(x)\}, \{C(x), B(x)\}\} \vDash \{\neg A(x), C(x)\}$

It is convenient to set out the resolution process in the form of a tree:

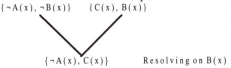

Resolving on B(x)

Example 9.9

Prove $(\forall x)(A(x) \vee B(x)) \wedge \neg B(a) \vDash A(a)$

Writing this in clause form we get $\{\{A(x), B(x)\}, \{\neg B(a)\}\} \vDash \{A(a)\}$

Using an appropriate subsitution and resolving we get

Substituting a for x and resolving on B(a)

Alternatively, we could negate the conclusion, and proceed as follows:

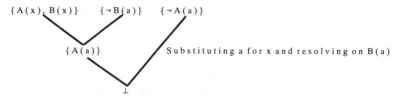

We will use the notation a/x to represent the substitution of a for x. In general, we use t/v to stand for the substition of the term t for the variable v.

Example 9.10

Prove
$$\{\{\neg A(x), B(x), C(x, f(x))\}, \{\neg A(x), B(x), D(f(x))\}, \{E(a)\}, \{A(a)\},$$
$$\{\neg C(a, y), E(y)\}, \{\neg E(x), \neg B(x)\}\} \models (\exists x)(E(x) \wedge D(x))$$

If we negate the conclusion we get
$$\neg(\exists x)(E(x) \wedge D(x)) \equiv (\forall x)\neg(E(x) \wedge D(x))$$
$$\equiv (\forall x)(\neg E(x) \vee \neg D(x))$$

which, in clause form, is $\{\neg E(x), \neg D(x)\}$.

So, we must test the following set of clauses for unsatisfiability.

1. $\{\neg A(x), B(x), C(x, f(x))\}$
2. $\{\neg A(x), B(x), D(f(x))\}$
3. $\{E(a)\}$
4. $\{A(a)\}$
5. $\{\neg C(a, y), E(y)\}$
6. $\{\neg E(x), \neg B(x)\}$
7. $\{\neg E(x), \neg D(x)\}$

The clauses are numbered for ease of reference. (It is too awkward to lay the derivation out in the form of a tree.)

Using substitution and resolution we generate the following clauses.

8. $\{\neg B(a)\}$ from 3 and 6 using a/x
9. $\{B(a), D(f(a))\}$ from 2 and 4 using a/x
10. $\{D(f(a))\}$ from 8 and 9
11. $\{B(a), C(a, f(a))\}$ from 1 and 4 using a/x
12. $\{C(a, f(a))\}$ from 8 and 11
13. $\{E(f(a))\}$ from 5 and 12 using f(a)/y
14. $\{\neg D(f(a))\}$ from 7 and 13 using f(a)/x
15. $\perp$ from 10 and 14

9.5 Unification

We are now aware that, in order to form resolvable literals, we usually have to perform substitutions. So far our approach to finding fruitful substitutions has relied on observation and insight. In general it is desirable to have a systematic method. Substitutions are designed to make occurrences of literals identical (apart from the negation sign). Substitutions which achieve this are called *unifying substitutions*, and the process is called *unification*. Although we are mainly interested in the unification of pairs of literals, we can, in general, speak about the unification of a set of expressions.

Definition   A *substitution* is a finite set of simultaneous replacements of variables by terms, i.e. a set, σ, of the form $\{t_1/v_1, t_2/v_2, ..., t_m/v_m\}$, where t_i is a term and v_i is a variable.

The formula resulting from the application of a substitution, σ, to a formula A is denoted by $A\sigma$.

For example, if $A = A(x, y, f(z))$ and $\sigma = \{a/x, g(x)/y, c/z\}$ then $A\sigma = A(a, g(x), f(c))$. If $A = B(x) \vee C(x, f(y))$ and $\sigma = \{y/x, g(a)/y\}$ then $A\sigma = B(y) \vee C(y, f(g(a)))$.

Note carefully that we make *simultaneous* substitutions for x and y. We do *not* replace y by g(a) and then replace x by g(a) to get $B(g(a)) \vee C(g(a), f(g(a)))$.

Definition   A substitution, σ, is called a *unifier* for a set $\{L_1, L_2, ..., L_n\}$ if
$$L_1\sigma = L_2\sigma = ... = L_n\sigma$$

For example, the substitution σ_1, $\{a/x, g(a)/y, a/z, f(a)/w\}$, unifies the set $\{A(x, y, f(z)), A(a, g(z), w)\}$, giving the unit set $\{A(a, g(a), f(a))\}$. The substitution σ_2, $\{a/x, g(z)/y, f(z)/w\}$, also unifies this set, giving the unit set $\{A(a, g(z), f(z))\}$. This substitution is a more general unifier than the first. In fact, we can express σ_1 as the composition of σ_2 and $\{a/z\}$, i.e. $\sigma_2 \circ \{a/z\}$.

Definition   The *composition*, $\sigma_1 \circ \sigma_2$, of two substitutions $\sigma_1 = \{t_1/x_1, t_2/x_2, ..., t_m/x_m\}$ and $\sigma_2 = \{u_1/y_1, u_2/y_2, ..., u_n/y_n\}$ is given by the set of replacements taken from
$$\{t_1\sigma_2/x_1, t_2\sigma_2/x_2, ..., t_m\sigma_2/x_m, u_1/y_1, u_2/y_2, ..., u_n/y_n\}$$
by eliminating u_i/y_i if $y_i \in \{x_1, x_2, ..., x_m\}$ and eliminating $t_i\sigma_2/x_i$ if $t_i\sigma_2 = x_i$.

For example, suppose $\sigma_1 = \{y/x, f(z)/y\}$ and $\sigma_2 = \{a/x, x/y, f(a)/z\}$. Then $\sigma_1 \circ \sigma_2$ can be constructed carefully through the following stages:

$$\{y\sigma_2/x, f(z)\sigma_2/y, a/x, x/y, f(a)/z\}$$
$$\{x/x, f(f(a))/y, a/x, x/y, f(a)/z\}$$

x/x, a/x and x/y are removed to give $\sigma_1 \circ \sigma_2 = \{f(f(a))/y, f(a)/z\}$.

Exercise
9.10 Find $\sigma_1 \circ \sigma_2$ in each of the following cases:
   (i) $\sigma_1 = \{a/x, z/y\}$, $\sigma_2 = \{a/x, c/y, y/z\}$
   (ii) $\sigma_1 = \{f(y)/x, z/y\}$, $\sigma_2 = \{a/x, c/y, y/z\}$

(iii) $\sigma_1 = \{a/x, f(z, a)/y, y/z\}$, $\sigma_2 = \{c/x, c/y, g(y)/z\}$

Definition   A *most general unifier* (mgu) σ for a set $S = \{L_1, L_2, ..., L_n\}$ is a substitution such that σ is a unifier for S, and every other unifier τ can be expressed as $\sigma \circ \lambda$, where λ is a substitution.

For example, a most general unifier σ for $S = \{A(x, y, f(z)), A(a, g(z), w)\}$ is $\{a/x, g(z)/y, f(z)/w\}$.

Exercise

9.11 Show that $\tau = \{a/x, g(b)/y, b/z, f(b)/w\}$ is a unifier for the above S, and find a substitution λ such that $\tau = \sigma \circ \lambda$.

Recall that in order to resolve clauses we usually have to unify literals. We are searching for a systematic method of performing this unification. In fact, there is a straightforward mechanical procedure for doing so. Essentially it involves scanning each of the expressions to be unified from left to right until a difference is found. If possible this difference is eliminated by means of a suitable substitution, and the scanning continues. If a difference cannot be eliminated the expressions cannot be unified.

Thus, in attempting to unify $\{A(x, y, f(z)), A(a, g(z), w)\}$, we scan from the left of the two A predicates until we encounter a difference in the third position – x occurring in the first expression, a in the second. The difference can be eliminated by replacing x by a. Continuing we see that y differs from g(z). Replacing y by g(z) eliminates this difference and we continue.

9.5.1 Unification Algorithm

This whole process of unifying a set of expressions S can be clearly presented in the form of an algorithm consisting of a succession of steps as follows.

(We use := to indicate assignment, e.g. A := v means A is assigned the value v.)

1. $S_0 := S$; $\sigma_0 := \{\}$; $i := 0$.
2. If S_i is not a unit set, find its disagreement set D_i. Otherwise we are finished, and σ_i is a most general unifier.
3. If not finished and if D_i contains a variable v_i and a term t_i such that v_i is not an element of t_i, then
$$\sigma_{i+1} := \sigma_i \circ \{t_i/v_i\}$$
$$S_{i+1} := S_i\{t_i/v_i\}$$
Otherwise finish, since S is not unifiable.
4. If not finished, $i := i + 1$; go back to step 2.

Example 9.11

Find a most general unifier for the following set:
$$S = \{A(x, z, g(x, y, f(z))), A(y, f(x), w)\}$$

Step 1	S_0	=	$\{A(x, z, g(x, y, f(z))), A(y, f(x), w)\}$; $\sigma_0 = \{\}$; $i = 0$
Step 2	D_0	=	$\{x, y\}$
Step 3	σ_1	=	$\{\} \circ \{y/x\}$ Note: we could also use $\{x/y\}$
	S_1	=	$\{A(x, z, g(x, y, f(z))), A(y, f(x), w)\}\{y/x\}$
		=	$\{A(y, z, g(y, y, f(z))), A(y, f(y), w)\}$
Step 4	i	=	$0+1 = 1$
Step 2	D_1	=	$\{z, f(y)\}$
Step 3	σ_2	=	$\{y/x\} \circ \{f(y)/z\}$
	S_2	=	$\{A(y, z, g(y, y, f(z))), A(y, f(y), w)\}\{f(y)/z\}$
		=	$\{A(y, f(y), g(y, y, f(f(y)))), A(y, f(y), w)\}$
Step 4	i	=	$1+1 = 2$
Step 2	D_2	=	$\{g(y, y, f(f(y))), w\}$
Step 3	σ_3	=	$\{y/x, f(y)/z\} \circ \{g(y, y, f(f(y)))/w\}$
	S_3	=	$\{A(y, f(y), g(y, y, f(f(y)))), A(y, f(y), w)\}\{g(y, y, f(f(y)))/w\}$
		=	$\{A(y, f(y), g(y, y, f(f(y)))), A(y, f(y), g(y, y, f(f(y))))\}$
		=	$\{A(y, f(y), g(y, y, f(f(y))))\}$

Since S_3 is a unit set we are finished and have found a most general unifier
$\sigma_3 = \{y/x, f(y)/z, g(y, y, f(f(y)))/w\}$.

Exercise

9.12 Find most general unifiers, if they exist, for each of the sets:

(i) $\{A(a, x, y, z), A(x, y, z, w)\}$

(ii) $\{A(a, x, g(f(y))), A(z, g(z), g(w))\}$

(iii) $\{A(x, f(x, y, z)), g(f(y)), A(a, g(z), g(w))\}$

(iv) $\{A(x, f(x, y, z)), g(f(y)), A(a, f(g(z), x, a), g(w))\}$

9.6 Resolution again

Now that we have seen the need for unifying literals before resolution can be effected, and studied the method of achieving unification, let us restate the definition of resolvent a little more carefully.

Re-definition If C_1 and C_2 are clauses (with no variables in common) containing literals L_1 and L_2, and if L_1 and $\neg L_2$ have a most general unifier σ, then the clause
$$(C_1\sigma - L_1\sigma) \cup (C_2\sigma - L_2\sigma)$$
is a *resolvent* of C_1 and C_2.

C_1 and C_2 in this definition are called *parent clauses*.

Example 9.12

Let $C_1 = \{A(f(y), z), B(g(y)), C(z, x, a)\}$ and $C_2 = \{A(f(a), u), \neg B(v)\}$. A most general unifier of $B(g(y))$ and $B(v)$ is $\sigma = \{g(y)/v\}$. Therefore, letting $L_1 = B(g(y))$ and $L_2 = \neg B(v)$, we have

$(C_1\sigma - L_1\sigma) \cup (C_2\sigma - L_2\sigma)$

$= (\{A(f(y), z), B(g(y)), C(z, x, a)\}\{g(y)/v\} - B(g(y))\{g(y)/v\}) \cup$
$\quad (\{A(f(y), u), \neg B(v)\}\{g(y)/v\} - \neg B(v)\{g(y)/v\})$

$= (\{A(f(y), z), B(g(y)), C(z, x, a)\} - B(g(y))) \cup (\{A(f(y), u), \neg B(g(y))\} -$
$\quad \neg B(g(y)))$

$= \{A(f(y), z), C(z, x, a)\} \cup \{A(f(y), u)\}$

$= \{A(f(y), z), C(z, x, a), A(f(y), u)\}$

9.7 Extended Examples

Let us consider two examples which bring together much of the work in this chapter.

Example 9.13

Is the following inference valid?

$(\forall x)(\forall y)(\forall z)((A(x, y)\wedge A(y, z)) \rightarrow \neg B(x, z)) \wedge (\forall x)(\forall y)(A(x, y) \leftrightarrow (B(y, x)\vee C(x, y))) \wedge (\forall x)(\exists y)A(x, y) \vDash (\forall x)A(x, x)$

Essentially we have to determine if the wff $(\forall x)A(x, x)$ is a logical consequence of the three premises

1. $(\forall x)(\forall y)(\forall z)((A(x, y)\wedge A(y, z)) \rightarrow \neg B(x, z))$
2. $(\forall x)(\forall y)(A(x, y) \leftrightarrow (B(y, x)\vee C(x, y)))$
3. $(\forall x)(\exists y)A(x, y)$

As usual we pursue a refutation procedure, i.e. we negate the conclusion and see if the negation is inconsistent with the premises. We proceed by forming a conjunction of the premises and the negation of the conclusion.

$(\forall x)(\forall y)(\forall z)((A(x, y)\wedge A(y, z)) \rightarrow \neg B(x, z)) \wedge (\forall x)(\forall y)(A(x, y) \leftrightarrow (B(y, x)\vee C(x, y))) \wedge (\forall x)(\exists y)A(x, y) \wedge \neg(\forall x)A(x, x)$

Now, we convert to clausal form by working through the various stages outlined earlier in the chapter. The relevant components at each stage are underlined below.

Eliminate $\leftrightarrow$:

$(\forall x)(\forall y)(\forall z)((A(x, y)\wedge A(y, z)) \rightarrow \neg B(x, z)) \wedge (\forall x)(\forall y)(\underline{(A(x, y) \rightarrow (B(y, x)\vee C(x, y))) \wedge ((B(y, x)\vee C(x, y)) \rightarrow A(x, y))}) \wedge (\forall x)(\exists y)A(x, y) \wedge \neg(\forall x)A(x, x)$

Eliminate $\rightarrow$:

$(\forall x)(\forall y)(\forall z)(\underline{\neg(A(x, y) \wedge A(y, z))} \vee \neg B(x, z)) \wedge (\forall x)(\forall y)((\underline{\neg A(x, y)} \vee (B(y, x) \vee C(x, y)))) \wedge (\underline{\neg(B(y, x) \vee C(x, y))} \vee A(x, y)) \wedge (\forall x)(\exists y)A(x, y) \wedge \neg(\forall x)A(x, x)$

Push $\neg$ inwards:

$(\forall x)(\forall y)(\forall z)((\underline{\neg A(x, y) \vee \neg A(y, z)}) \vee \neg B(x, z)) \wedge (\forall x)(\forall y)((\neg A(x, y) \vee (B(y, x) \vee C(x, y))) \wedge ((\underline{\neg B(y, x)} \wedge \neg C(x, y)) \vee A(x, y)) \wedge (\forall x)(\exists y)A(x, y) \wedge \underline{(\exists x) \neg A(x, x)}$

Rename variables as necessary:

$(\forall x)(\forall y)(\forall z)((\neg A(x, y) \vee \neg A(y, z)) \vee \neg B(x, z)) \wedge \underline{(\forall u)(\forall v)((\neg A(u, v)} \vee (B(v, u) \vee C(u, v))) \wedge ((\neg B(v, u) \wedge \neg C(u, v)) \vee A(u, v)) \wedge \underline{(\forall r)(\exists w)A(r, w)} \wedge \underline{(\exists s) \neg A(s, s)}$

Move quantifiers to the front:

$\underline{(\exists s)(\forall r)(\exists w)(\forall u)(\forall v)(\forall x)(\forall y)(\forall z)}((\neg A(x, y) \vee \neg A(y, z)) \vee \neg B(x, z)) \wedge ((\neg A(u, v) \vee (B(v, u) \vee C(u, v))) \wedge ((\neg B(v, u) \wedge \neg C(u, v)) \vee A(u, v)) \wedge A(r, w) \wedge \neg A(s, s)$

Note that we move existential quantifiers as far to the left as possible to reduce the need for functions when we Skolemise later. But, note also that, in the above, we cannot move $(\exists w)$ to the left of $(\forall r)$.

Distribute $\vee$ over $\wedge$ (and remove excess brackets):

$(\exists s)(\forall r)(\exists w)(\forall u)(\forall v)(\forall x)(\forall y)(\forall z)((\neg A(x, y) \vee \neg A(y, z) \vee \neg B(x, z)) \wedge (\neg A(u, v) \vee B(v, u) \vee C(u, v)) \wedge \underline{(\neg B(v, u) \vee A(u, v))} \wedge \underline{(\neg C(u, v) \vee A(u, v))} \wedge A(r, w) \wedge \neg A(s, s)$

Skolemise:

$(\forall r)(\forall u)(\forall v)(\forall x)(\forall y)(\forall z)((\neg A(x, y) \vee \neg A(y, z) \vee \neg B(x, z)) \wedge (\neg A(u, v) \vee B(v, u) \vee C(u, v)) \wedge (\neg B(v, u) \vee A(u, v)) \wedge (\neg C(u, v) \vee A(u, v)) \wedge \underline{A(r, f(r))} \wedge \underline{\neg A(a, a)}$

Drop quantifiers, $\wedge$ and $\vee$ signs, and write this as a set of clauses:

$\{\{\neg A(x, y), \neg A(y, z), \neg B(x, z)\}, \{\neg A(u, v), B(v, u), C(u, v)\}, \{\neg B(v, u), A(u, v)\}, \{\neg C(u, v), A(u, v)\}, \{A(r, f(r))\}, \{\neg A(a, a)\}\}$

Apply resolution to the set of clauses:

    1. $\{\neg A(x, y), \neg A(y, z), \neg B(x, z)\}$
    2. $\{\neg A(u, v), B(v, u), C(u, v)\}$
    3. $\{\neg B(v, u), A(u, v)\}$
    4. $\{\neg C(u, v), A(u, v)\}$
    5. $\{A(r, f(r))\}$
    6. $\{\neg A(a, a)\}$

to get:

    7. $\{B(v, u), C(u, v), \neg B(v, u)\}$ from 2 and 3

Since the clause on line 7 contains a complementary pair of literals it is a tautology. And, as this tautology was derived from the initial wff we conclude that they are mutually consistent.

Hence, we conclude that $(\forall x)A(x, x)$ was not a logical consequence of the given premises.

Example 9.14

Rather than forming a 'large' conjunction of the premises and the negation of the conclusion it is usually easier and less cluttered to convert each conjunct to clause form separately, not forgetting to rename variables, and then perform resolution. Applying this procedure to the problem in example 9.13 we get the following.

For $(\forall x)(\forall y)(\forall z)((A(x, y) \wedge A(y, z)) \rightarrow \neg B(x, z))$

Eliminate $\rightarrow$:
$(\forall x)(\forall y)(\forall z)(\neg(A(x, y) \wedge A(y, z)) \vee \neg B(x, z))$

Push $\neg$ inwards and remove excess brackets:
$(\forall x)(\forall y)(\forall z)(\neg A(x, y) \vee \neg A(y, z) \vee \neg B(x, z))$

Write as clause:
$\{\neg A(x, y), \neg A(y, z), \neg B(x, z)\}$

For $(\forall u)(\forall v)(A(u, v) \leftrightarrow (B(v, u) \vee C(u, v)))$:

Eliminate $\leftrightarrow$:
$(\forall u)(\forall v)((A(u, v) \rightarrow (B(v, u) \vee C(u, v))) \wedge ((B(v, u) \vee C(u, v)) \rightarrow A(u, v)))$

Eliminate $\rightarrow$:
$(\forall u)(\forall v)((\neg A(u, v) \vee (B(v, u) \vee C(u, v))) \wedge (\neg(B(v, u) \vee C(u, v)) \vee A(u, v)))$

Push $\neg$ inwards:
$(\forall u)(\forall v)((\neg A(u, v) \vee (B(v, u) \vee C(u, v))) \wedge (\neg B(v, u) \wedge \neg C(u, v)) \vee A(u, v)))$

Distribute $\vee$ over $\wedge$ and remove excess brackets:
$(\forall u)(\forall v)((\neg A(u, v) \vee B(v, u) \vee C(u, v)) \wedge (\neg B(v, u) \vee A(u, v)) \wedge (\neg C(u, v) \vee A(u, v)))$

Write as clauses:
$\{\neg A(u, v), B(v, u), C(u, v)\}, \{\neg B(v, u), A(u, v)\}, \{\neg C(u, v), A(u, v)\}$

For $(\forall r)(\exists w)A(r, w)$:

Skolemise:
$(\forall r)A(r, f(r))$

Write as clause:
$\{A(r, f(r))\}$
For $\neg(\forall s)A(s, s)$:

Push ¬ inwards:

(∃s)¬A(s, s)

Skolemise:

¬A(a, a)

Write as clause:

{¬A(a, a)}

We have now the same set of clauses as above and we apply resolution as before to reach the conclusion that (∀x)A(x, x) was not a logical consequence of the given premises.

9.8 Problem-solving using Resolution

Let us bring our deliberations on resolution in first order predicate logic to a close by studying its application to general problem-solving.

Example 9.15

Consider the following.

If one number is less than or equal to a second number, and the second number is less than or equal to a third, then the first number is not greater than the third. A number is less than or equal to a second number if and only if the second number is greater than the first or the first is equal to the second. Given any number, there is another number that it is less than or equal to. Therefore, every number is less than or equal to itself.

This is a bit of a mouthful to swallow when written in English like that. If we write it partly in more conventional mathematical symbolism, it looks a bit clearer.

> If $x \le y$ and $y \le z$ then not $x > z$
> $x \le y$ if and only if $y > x$ or $x = y$
> For every x, there is a y such that $x \le y$

Therefore $x \le x$ for every x

Now let us write in first order language notation. We will use LE for the predicate '≤', G for '>', and E for '='. Remember that the first two statements are implicitly 'universally quantified'.

$(\forall x)(\forall y)(\forall z)((LE(x, y) \wedge LE(y, z)) \rightarrow \neg G(x, z)) \wedge (\forall x)(\forall y)(LE(x, y) \leftrightarrow (G(y, x) \vee E(x, y))) \wedge (\forall x)(\exists y)LE(x, y) \models (\forall x)LE(x, x)$

Looks familiar? It should. If you look back at our last example, and replace LE by A, G by B and E by C, you will get exactly the same wff. Consequently, we know that the argument is not correct, since we have already done the technical work of bringing the representation to clause form and deploying resolution to check the soundness of the conclusion.

Example 9.16

Consider the following.

Some students attend logic lectures diligently. No student attends boring logic lectures diligently. Sean's lectures on logic are attended diligently by all students. Therefore none of Sean's logic lectures are boring.

Let   S(x) stand for 'x is a student'
L(x) stand for 'x is a logic lecture'
A(x, y) stand for 'x attends y diligently'
B(x) stand for 'x is boring'
G(x, y) stand for 'x is given by y'
s stand for 'Sean'

Then we can express the statements in first order notation as follows:

$(\exists x)(S(x) \land (\forall y)(L(y) \rightarrow A(x, y)))$
– 'There is an x who is a student and, for every y, if y is a logic lecture, then x attends y diligently.'

$(\forall x)(S(x) \rightarrow (\forall y)((L(y) \land B(y)) \rightarrow \neg A(x, y)))$
– 'For every x, if x is a student, then, for every y, if y is a lecture which is boring, then x does not attend y.'

$(\forall x)((L(x) \land G(x, s)) \rightarrow (\forall z)(S(z) \rightarrow A(z, x)))$
– 'If x is a lecture given by s then every student z attends it.'

$(\forall x)((L(x) \land G(x, s)) \rightarrow \neg B(x))$
– 'Every lecture given by s is not boring.'

In symbolic form, the argument is

$(\exists x)(S(x) \land (\forall y)(L(y) \rightarrow A(x, y))) \land (\forall x)(S(x) \rightarrow (\forall y)((L(y) \land B(y)) \rightarrow \neg A(x, y))) \land (\forall x)((L(x) \land G(x, s)) \rightarrow (\forall z)(S(z) \rightarrow A(z, x)))$
$\models (\forall x)((L(x) \land G(x, s)) \rightarrow \neg B(x))$

We negate the conclusion, and set ourselves the task of showing that the following wff is unsatisfiable:

$(\exists x)(S(x) \land (\forall y)(L(y) \rightarrow A(x, y))) \land (\forall x)(S(x) \rightarrow (\forall y)((L(y) \land B(y)) \rightarrow \neg A(x, y))) \land (\forall x)((L(x) \land G(x, s)) \rightarrow (\forall z)(S(z) \rightarrow A(z, x))) \land \neg(\forall x)((L(x) \land G(x, s)) \rightarrow \neg B(x))$

For $(\exists x)(S(x) \land (\forall y)(L(y) \rightarrow A(x, y)))$:

Eliminate $\rightarrow$:
$(\exists x)(S(x) \land (\forall y)(\neg L(y) \lor A(x, y)))$

Bring quantifiers to the front:
$(\exists x)(\forall y)(S(x) \wedge (\neg L(y) \vee A(x, y)))$

Skolemise:
$(\forall y)(S(a) \wedge (\neg L(y) \vee A(a, y)))$

Write as clauses:
$\{S(a)\}, \{\neg L(y), A(a, y)\}$

For $(\forall w)(S(w) \rightarrow (\forall u)((L(u) \wedge B(u)) \rightarrow \neg A(w, u)))$:

Eliminate $\rightarrow$:
$(\forall w)(\neg S(w) \vee (\forall u)(\neg (L(u) \wedge B(u)) \vee \neg A(w, u)))$

Move $\neg$ inwards and remove excess brackets:
$(\forall w)(\neg S(w) \vee (\forall u)(\neg L(u) \vee \neg B(u) \vee \neg A(w, u)))$

Bring quantifiers to the front (and remove excess brackets):
$(\forall w)(\forall u)(\neg S(w) \vee \neg L(u) \vee \neg B(u) \vee \neg A(w, u))$

Write as clause:
$\{\neg S(w), \neg L(u), \neg B(u), \neg A(w, u)\}$

For $(\forall v)((L(v) \wedge G(v, s)) \rightarrow (\forall z)(S(z) \rightarrow A(z, v)))$:

Eliminate $\rightarrow$:
$(\forall v)(\neg (L(v) \wedge G(v, s)) \vee (\forall z)(\neg S(z) \vee A(z, v)))$

Move $\neg$ inwards and remove excess brackets:
$(\forall v)(\neg L(v) \vee \neg G(v, s) \vee (\forall z)(\neg S(z) \vee A(z, v)))$

Bring quantifiers to the front (and remove excess brackets):
$(\forall v)(\forall z)(\neg L(v) \vee \neg G(v, s) \vee \neg S(z) \vee A(z, v))$

Write as clause:
$\{\neg L(v), \neg G(v, s), \neg S(z), A(z, v)\}$

For $\neg(\forall r)((L(r) \wedge G(r, s)) \rightarrow \neg B(r))$:

Eliminate $\rightarrow$:
$\neg(\forall r)(\neg (L(r) \wedge G(r, s)) \vee \neg B(r))$

Move $\neg$ inwards:
$(\exists r)\neg(\neg (L(r) \wedge G(r, s)) \vee \neg B(r))$

And again:
$(\exists r)(\neg \neg (L(r) \wedge G(r, s)) \wedge \neg \neg B(r))$

Remove $\neg \neg$ and excess brackets:
$(\exists r)(L(r) \wedge G(r, s) \wedge B(r))$

Skolemise:

$(L(b) \wedge G(b, s) \wedge B(b))$

Write as clauses:

$\{L(b)\}, \{G(b, s)\}, \{B(b)\}$

Apply resolution to the clauses:

1. $\{S(a)\}$
2. $\{\neg L(y), A(a, y)\}$
3. $\{\neg S(w), \neg L(u), \neg B(u), \neg A(w, u)\}$
4. $\{\neg L(v), \neg G(v, s), \neg S(z), A(z, v)\}$
5. $\{L(b)\}$
6. $\{G(b, s)\}$
7. $\{B(b)\}$

to get:

8. $\{\neg L(u), \neg B(u), \neg A(a, u)\}$ from lines 1 and 3 using $\{a/w\}$
9. $\{A(a, b)\}$ from lines 2 and 5 using $\{b/y\}$
10. $\{\neg B(b), \neg A(a, b)\}$ from lines 5 and 8 using $\{b/u\}$
11. $\{\neg A(a, b)\}$ from lines 7 and 10
12. $\perp$ from lines 9 and 11

At long last we conclude that the argument is valid.

Exercise

9.13 Are the following arguments valid?

(i)   Some students are anxious. Some students study. If a student is anxious he will not pass his examination unless he studies. Therefore no students will pass their examinations.

(ii) Some students are anxious. Some students study. If a student is anxious he will not pass his examination unless he studies. Therefore some students will pass their examinations.

(iii) Some students are anxious. All students study. If a student is anxious he will not pass his examination unless he studies. Therefore all students will pass their examinations.

(iv) All students are anxious. Some students study. If a student is anxious he will not pass his examination unless he studies. Therefore some students will pass their examinations.

9.9 Resolution as a Computing Tool

9.9.1 Deductive Databases

A database is a (usually large) collection of data organised to provide efficient storage and retrieval of information. First order logic may be considered as a potentially useful tool for the description and processing of this data. Issues such as consistency, integrity constraints (conditions which the data are expected or assumed to fulfil) and the posing and answering of queries may all be carefully and soundly handled through the language of logic. To provide a small flavour of the approach let us consider a very simple example.

Example 9.17

Suppose we have an automated library system which consists essentially of a file of information in the form of records containing

Author of book; Publisher; Title of book;
Name of borrower; Return date.

Typical records might be:

book(Kelly J, Prentice Hall, First Steps in Logic, J Doe, 1-1-1996)
book(Golding William, Penguin, Pincher Martin, nil, nil)

Some useful formulae might be:

A1. $(\forall x)(\forall y)(\forall z)(\forall u)(\forall v)((book(x, y, z, u, v) \wedge \neg(u = nil)) \rightarrow$ borrowed(z))
A2. $(\forall x)(\forall y)(\forall z)(\forall u)(\forall v)((book(x, y, z, u, v) \wedge (v > today)) \rightarrow$ overdue(z))
A3. $(\forall x)(\forall y)(\forall z)(\forall u)(\forall v)(book(x, y, z, u, v) \rightarrow author(x, z))$
A4. $(\forall x)(\forall y)(\forall z)(\forall u)(\forall v)(book(x, y, z, u, v) \rightarrow title(z))$
A5. $(\forall y)(author(Banville John, y) \rightarrow goodread(y))$

A1 to A5, along with the information about the actual books, could be considered to be proper axioms for the library system. The idea would then be to find answers to queries by a process of logical deduction. If a query Q is posed, we may treat it as a statement and then attempt to find a refutation of the formula A1∧A2∧A3∧A4∧A5∧¬Q using the 'facts' of the library system treated as instances of the predicate 'book'.

For example, suppose the query is

'Has the library any book by William Golding?'

This may be expressed as $(\exists x)author(Golding William, x)$?
We try to find a resolution refutation (for example) of

{book}∧A1∧A2∧A3∧A4∧A5∧¬$(\exists x)$author(Golding William, x)
i.e. {book}∧A1∧A2∧A3∧A4∧A5∧$(\forall x)$¬author(Golding William, x)

where {book} stands for the set of book predicates.
With a little bit of work we may transform this into the following clauses:

1. $\{\neg book(x, y, z, u, v), (u = nil), borrowed(z)\}$
2. $\{\neg book(x_1, y_1, z_1, u_1, v_1), \neg(v_1 > today), overdue(z_1)\}$
3. $\{\neg book(x_2, y_2, z_2, u_2, v_2), author(x_2, z_2)\}$

4. $\{\neg book(x_3, y_3, z_3, u_3, v_3), title(z_3)\}$
5. $\{\neg author(Banville\ John, y_4), goodread(y_4)\}$
6. $\{\neg author(Golding\ William, x_5)\}$
+ all the book statements as clauses.

Resolving we get

7. $\{\neg book(Golding\ William, y_2, x_5, u_2, v_2)\}$ using $\{Golding\ William/x_2, x_5/z_2\}$

This will resolve with the book statement given by the second record above, using $\{Penguin/y_2, Pincher\ Martin/x_5, nil/u_2, nil/v\}$ to give $\perp$.

The system concludes there is a book by William Golding in the library.

Of course in practice a person using the system would require more than a simple yes or no in answer to her query. The system would need to contain facilities for collecting information about the actual book (elicited from the unification substitutions) and also for finding alternative answers. This would be all the more so if the query were, 'What books by William Golding have you got?', i.e. find all the books by William Golding which are not out on loan. Hence, in addition to purely logical considerations other aspects of useful database systems need to be dealt with. But resolution logic could form the core of such a system.

9.9.2 Logic Programming

Programming computers usually means giving instructions to the computer to carry out various tasks. Most programming languages adopt an *imperative* approach to programming by providing means of expressing instructions. In order to use the language a special detailed syntax must be mastered and some knowledge of how the machine (actually the software system) carries out instructions is usually required.

An alternative approach which has been explored in great detail over the last twenty years or thereabouts is the so-called declarative approach. The idea is simply to state (declare) the information relevant to a given problem, ask the problem question and have the system work out the answer by using processes based on formal mathematical logic. For example, if the problem were to search a list of items to find out if a given item were contained therein, the traditional imperative programming approach would be to write a list of instructions to get the computer to search through the list until the item is found or until the end of the list is reached. Besides the actual instructions themselves, information must be given about the kind of list, the type of items in the list, the type of the search index, etc.

In an imperative language such as Pascal a suitable program might be something like the following:

```
program Search(input, output);
const Size = 1000;
var   item : string;
      L : array[1..Size] of item;
      I, N : integer;
begin
      Read(N);
      for I:= 1 to N do Read(L[I]);
      Read(item);
      I:= 0;
      repeat
            I:= I + 1
      until item = L[I] or I = N;
      if item = L[I] then Write(item, "Found")
      else Write(item, "Not Found")
end.
```

Figure 9.1

The program contains a good deal of machine-oriented information which is irrelevant as far as the actual problem is concerned. Before the actual instructions are stated various declarations about size, etc. are required. The logic programming approach can be much simpler, more direct and more general and flexible. For example, the following 'program' indicates the basic method:

X belongs to [X|_].
X belongs to [_|Rest] if X belongs to Rest.
item belongs to list?

Figure 9.2

The first two lines state what it means to belong to a list. The first says that an item X belongs to any list beginning with X. Of course! The second line says that X belongs to a list if it belongs to the rest of the list after the first item (or head of the list) is ignored. Equally obvious.

The last line simply asks if a given 'item' belongs to a given list called 'list'.

Example 9.18

To see how this works, consider the problem
    Is joann a member of the list [barbara, joann, clare, paul, stephen, john]?
This is posed as
    joann belongs to [barbara, joann, clare, paul, stephen, john]?
X is matched to (unified with) joann in the first statement above. But joann is not the head of the given list, so the first statement is not

satisfied. The second possibility is then explored, giving rise to the condition

joann belongs to [joann, clare, paul, stephen, john]?

This matches the first statement and the system returns the answer yes.

The logic program is devoid of unnecessary clutter. What is more, the list can be of different types in different instantiations of the program. It is not restricted to a pre-declared type, e.g. string, as in the Pascal program. Furthermore, the logic program can be used in different ways, not merely for searching for a specific item.

9.9.3 Logic Programming, Prolog and Resolution

Perhaps the most widely used logic programming language is Prolog. It uses a form of resolution to process information and solve problems.

A Prolog program essentially consists of well-formed formulae in clause form. When a question is put it is treated as a statement to be proved. The statement is accordingly negated and the system attempts to refute this negation. If the refutation succeeds the question is answered positively, if not the answer is in the negative. In pursuing a refutation the system is attempting to see if the statement implicit in the question is consistent with the information it already has in its clauses. We can view this as determining whether or not there is an interpretation which satisfies the question. The details of a suitable interpretation, if one is found, are made available to the questioner and essentially constitute the output of the program.

Although the Prolog system treats formulae in clause form, the programmer is not required to arrange his information in clause form. In fact she thinks in terms of facts and rules. A fact is simply a statement of a property or a relation, e.g. male(john), mother(lillian, clare).

A rule is of the form

If *condition1* and *condition2* and .... and *condition$_n$* Then *conclusion*

i.e. $C_1 \wedge C_2 \wedge \ldots \wedge C_n \rightarrow C$

In Prolog this is taken in reverse form: $C \leftarrow C_1 \wedge C_2 \wedge \ldots \wedge C_n$; and written as

$C :- C_1, C_2, \ldots, C_n$

For example, grandfather(X, Y) :- father(X, Z), parent(Z, Y).

If we convert $C_1 \wedge C_2 \wedge \ldots \wedge C_n \rightarrow C$ to clause form

$$C_1 \wedge C_2 \wedge \ldots \wedge C_n \rightarrow C \equiv \neg(C_1 \wedge C_2 \wedge \ldots \wedge C_n) \vee C$$
$$\equiv \neg C_1 \vee \neg C_2 \vee \ldots \vee \neg C_n \vee C$$
$$\equiv \{\neg C_1, \neg C_2, \ldots, \neg C_n, C\}$$

we notice that it has just one positive literal, C. Such a clause is called a *Horn clause*.

Definition   A *Horn clause* is a clause containing at most one positive literal.

A Prolog program is basically a set of Horn clauses. A fact is a unit clause, e.g. C :–, or just C. A headless Horn clause is called a *goal*, e.g. :– C_1, C_2, ..., C_n.

Resolution with Horn clauses is relatively simple and efficient and is the basis for Prolog systems.

It has to be admitted that Prolog is not a pure logic programming language, since it includes strictly imperative elements in addition to its logic elements, e.g. instructions for reading from and printing to files.

Let us finish off our brief excursion into the domain of logic programming by considering a final problem.

Example 9.19

The problem is to determine paths in graphs. Consider the graph:

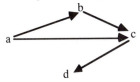

Figure 9.3

We may write a piece of Prolog program to describe paths as follows:

connected(a, b).
connected(a, c).
connected(b, c).
connected(c, d).
path(X, Y) :- connected(X, Y).
path(X, Y) :- connected(X, Z), path(Z, Y).

The second to last clause states that there is a path from node X to node Y if there is a direct connection from X to Y. The last clause states that there is a path from X to Y if there is a connection from X to some node Z, followed by a path from Z to Y. This is a recursive clause.

Let us pose the query: path(a, d)?

The first path clause is tried – X is matched to a, and Y is matched to d.

Thus, path(a, d) :- connected(a, d).

connected(a, d) fails because there is no such fact in the program.

The second path clause is tried.

path(a, d) :- connected(a, Z), path(Z, d).

A value of Z is sought to satisfy connected(a, Z). If Z is matched to b, the first fact will provide satisfaction!

We are now required to see if path(b, d) can be satisfied.

Again the first of the path clauses fails because there is no direct connection from b to d.

The second clause yields path(b, d) :- connected(b, Z), path(Z, d).

A suitable Z is c, leaving us with path(c, d) to satisfy.

This is satisfied because there is a direct path from c to d.

Hence the system concludes that there is a path from a to d.

We may lay out the journey to a solution as follows:

path(a, d) :- connected(a, Z), path(Z, d).

$$Z=b$$

connected(a, b), path(b, d) :- connected(b, Z), path(Z, d).

$$Z=c$$

connected(b, c), path(c, d) :- connected(c, d).

The successive values of Z actually give us a record of the path from a to d, namely a → b → c → d. We could have built into our Prolog program above some features to keep and print this record for us.

Notice that our treatment did not find the shortest path from a to d. This was because of the order in which we put the connected clauses. By reversing the first two clauses we would have found the path a → c → d first. But Prolog also has facilities to allow us to discover if there are alternative paths, and indeed alternative solutions to any problems.

It is instructive to examine a resolution-based solution to the above problem along the lines discussed earlier in the chapter.

The above problem may be expressed in terms of attempting to refute the following clauses:

1. {connected(a, b)}
2. {connected(a, c)}
3. {connected(b, c)}
4. {connected(c, d)}
5. {path(x, y), ¬connected(x, y)}
6. {path(w, u), ¬connected(w, z), ¬path(z, u)}
7. {¬path(a, d)}

Resolving 7 with 6 with a/w, d/u we get

8. {¬connected(a, z), ¬path(z, d)}

Resolving 8 with 1 with b/z we get

9. {¬path(b, d)}

Resolving 9 with 6 with b/w, d/u we get

10. {¬connected(b, z), ¬path(z, d)}

Resolving 10 with 3 with c/z we get

11. {¬path(c, d)}

Resolving 11 with 5 with c/x, d/y we get

12. {¬connected(c, d)}

Resolving 12 with 4 we get ⊥.

It is not too difficult to see that the progress of the Prolog program above mirrors the progress of the resolution process.

We have looked at Prolog programs from the point of view of well-formed formulae in clause form. A Prolog program can also be thought of as a form of database containing 'static' information in the form of facts together with rules to manipulate this information. Our earlier example of a library database can be handled very nicely in Prolog.

9.10 Summary

- A wff in prenex form will appear as
$$(Q_1x_1)(Q_2x_2)...(Q_nx_n)A(x_1, x_2, ..., x_n)$$
where the Q_is represent the quantifiers, either $\forall$ or $\exists$ in each case. The part $(Q_1x_1)(Q_2x_2)...(Q_nx_n)$ is called the *prefix* while the remaining part, $A(x_1, x_2, ..., x_n)$, is called the *matrix*.
- Converting a wff to prenex normal form is done in a number of stages:
  Stage 1: Use $A \leftrightarrow B \equiv (A \rightarrow B) \wedge (B \rightarrow A)$ to eliminate $\leftrightarrow$.
  Stage 2: Use $A \rightarrow B \equiv \neg A \vee B$ to eliminate $\rightarrow$.
  Stage 3: Use
    (a) De Morgan's laws $\neg(A \wedge B) \equiv \neg A \vee \neg B$ and $\neg(A \vee B) \equiv \neg A \wedge \neg B$
    (b) The law of double negation $\neg \neg A \equiv A$
    (c) The laws $\neg(\forall x)A(x) \equiv (\exists x)\neg A(x)$ and $\neg(\exists x)A(x) \equiv (\forall x)\neg A(x)$
    to push the negation sign $\neg$ immediately before atomic wff.
  Stage 4: Rename bound variables, if necessary.
  Stage 5: Use the defined equivalences of quantified formulae as required to bring all the quantifiers to the left.
  Stage 6: Use the distributive law $A \vee (B \wedge C) \equiv (A \vee B) \wedge (A \vee C)$ to affect the conversion of the matrix to CNF.
- The process of eliminating existential quantifiers and replacing the corresponding variable by either a constant (called a *Skolem constant*) or a function (called a *Skolem function*) is called *Skolemisation*.
- A wff is unsatisfiable iff its Skolem normal form is unsatisfiable.
- The *Herbrand universe*, H(S), of a wff expressed as a set of clauses S is given by the following:
    If c is a constant in any member of S then $c \in H(S)$. If S contains no constants then H(S) contains the constant symbol a.
    If f is an n-ary function in S and $t_1, t_2, ..., t_n$ are in H(S) then $f(t_1, t_2, ..., t_n) \in H(S)$.
- H(S) may be built systematically as follows:
    Let H_0 be the set of constants appearing in clauses of S. If none appear let $H_0 = \{a\}$.
    Let H_1 be H_0 together with the ground terms generated by applying functions appearing in S to the elements of H_0, i.e.

$$H_1 = H_0 \cup \{f(t_1, t_2, ..., t_n) \mid f \in S, t_i \in H_0\}$$

.

.

$$H_{i+1} = H_i \cup \{f(t_1, t_2, ... t_n) \mid f \in S, t_i \in H_i\}$$

- Expressions not involving variables are called ground expressions.
- If S is a set of clauses, the collection of ground atoms forms the Herbrand base of S.
- A Herbrand interpretation is a valuation of the ground atoms of S, i.e. an assignment of true and false to elements of the Herbrand base of S.
- A set of clauses is unsatisfiable if and only if it is unsatisfiable over all Herbrand interpretations.
- A substitution is a finite set of replacements of variables by terms, i.e. a set, σ, of the form $\{t_1/v_1, t_2/v_2, ..., t_m/v_m\}$, where t_i is a term and v_i is a variable.
- The formula resulting from the application of a substitution, σ, to a formula A is denoted by $A\sigma$.
- A substitution, σ, is called a unifier for a set $\{L_1, L_2, ..., L_n\}$ if
$$L_1\sigma = L_2\sigma = ... = L_n\sigma$$
- The composition, $\sigma_1 \circ \sigma_2$, of two substitutions
$$\sigma_1 = \{t_1/x_1, t_2/x_2, ..., t_m/x_m\} \text{ and } \sigma_2 = \{u_1/y_1, u_2/y_2, ..., u_n/y_n\}$$
is given by the set of replacements taken from
$$\{t_1\sigma_2/x_1, t_2\sigma_2/x_2, ..., t_m\sigma_2/x_m, u_1/y_1, u_2/y_2, ..., u_n/y_n\}$$
by eliminating u_i/y_i if $y_i \in \{x_1, x_2, ..., x_m\}$ and eliminating $t_i\sigma_2/x_i$ if $t_i\sigma_2 = x_i$.
- A most general unifier (mgu) σ for a set $S = \{L_1, L_2, ..., L_n\}$ is a substitution such that σ is a unifier for S, and every other unifier τ can be expressed as $\sigma \circ \lambda$, where λ is a substitution.
- An algorithm for unification is:
  1. $S_0 := S$; $\sigma_0 := \{\}$; $i := 0$.
  2. If S_i is not a unit set, find its disagreement set D_i. Otherwise we are finished, and σ_i is a most general unifier.
  3. If not finished and if D_i contains a variable v_i and a term t_i such that v_i is not an element of t_i, then
$$\sigma_{i+1} := \sigma_i \circ \{t_i/v_i\}$$
$$S_{i+1} := S_i\{t_i/v_i\}$$
     Otherwise finish, since S is not unifiable.
  4. If not finished, $i := i+1$; go to 2.
- If C_1 and C_2 are clauses (with no variables in common) containing literals L_1 and L_2, and if L_1 and $\neg L_2$ have a most general unifier σ, then the clause
$$(C_1\sigma - L_1\sigma) \cup (C_2\sigma - L_2\sigma)$$
is a resolvent of C_1 and C_2.
- Interesting applications of first order logic, and in particular resolution, include deductive databases and logic programming.

In this chapter we have
(1)   studied the concepts of normal form, literal and clause in first order logic.

(2)   examined the use of prenex normal form, Skolemisation and Herbrand universe.

(3)   introduced the notions of substitution and unification.

(4)   developed an algorithm for unification.

(5)   seen how the resolution rule is applied in first order logic.

(6)   looked briefly at how first order logic may be employed in accessing information in databases.

(7)   introduced the idea of logic programming and, in particular, the language Prolog.

And so, we have reached the end of the book. I hope you found it both enjoyable and instructive. As indicated at the beginning, this book is meant to be a general introduction to some of the topics in mathematical logic. You should now have a good understanding of the philosophy and fundamental methods of logic. Naturally, there is a lot more to learn, and there are many topics which are not even touched on in this book. Logic, however, is a very interesting and very useful discipline. The important thing to remember is that practising and applying it to more and more problems will hone your skills and enhance your ability to see new ways of using logic.

Miscellaneous Exercises

1.   Convert each of the following wff to Skolem standard form, and then write the result as a set of clauses:

(i) $(\exists x)(\exists y)(A(x, y) \rightarrow (\forall x)(B(x) \wedge C(x, y)))$

(ii) $(\forall x)A(x) \rightarrow (\exists x)(\exists y)(B(x) \vee C(x, y))$

(iii) $(\forall x)(\forall y)((\forall z)A(x, y, z) \vee ((\forall u)C(x, u) \rightarrow (\exists v)(C(x, v) \wedge B(v, z))))$

2.   Write down (a representative part of) the Herbrand universe for each of the following sets of clauses, building up from H_0 in each case:

(i) $\{\{A(x)\}, \{\neg A(f(x))\}, \{C(x, y, g(y, b)), D(a, b, c, y)\}\}$

(ii) $\{\{A(x), B(x, f(x))\}, \{C(x, f(x), f(f(x)))\}\}$

(iii) $\{\{A(x), B(x, f(a)), \neg C(x, f(x), g(y, x))\}, \{A(g(x, y)), D(g(f(a), x))\}\}$

3.   Use Herbrand interpretations to determine whether each of the following sets of clauses is satisfiable or not.

(i) $\{\{A(x, y)\}, \{\neg A(y, x)\}\}$

(ii) $\{\{A(x, f(y)), B(x, y)\}, \{A(c, x), \neg B(y, z)\}, \{\neg A(x, f(x))\}\}$

(iii) $\{\{\neg A(x), B(x)\}, \{A(y)\}, \{C(a, b)\}, \{\neg B(a), \neg C(a, y)\}\}$

4.   Find most general unifiers, if they exist, for each of the following sets:

(i) $\{A(x, f(x, g(x), y)), g(f(x, y, z)), A(a, g(z), g(w))\}$

(ii) $\{A(x, f(x), g(f(y))), A(a, f(g(z)), g(w))\}$

(iii) $\{A(f(a), y, z), A(x, f(a), z), A(x, y, f(a))\}$

5. Assess the following arguments for validity:
    (i)   Every student likes logic. If a person likes logic and studies hard she will pass all her examinations. Jo-Ann is a lover of logic who studies hard. Therefore Jo-Ann will pass her examinations.
    (ii) Some musicians are writers. Some mathematicians are not writers. Therefore some mathematicians are not musicians.
    (iii) Some people like everybody who supports the President. Everybody likes someone who supports the President. Anybody who likes somebody who supports the President, does not herself support the President. Therefore the President does not support herself.

6. Use resolution to solve the following problems.
    (i)   All fruit is tasty if it is not cooked. This apple is not cooked. Therefore it is tasty.
    (ii)   All fruit is tasty if it is not cooked. This apple is cooked. Therefore it is not tasty.
    (iii) Some fruit is tasty if it is not cooked. This apple is cooked. Therefore it is not tasty.
    (iv)   Some fruit is tasty if it is not cooked. This apple is not cooked. Therefore it is tasty.
    (v)   All that glistens is not gold. This pot does not glisten. Therefore it is gold.
    (vi)   No lecturer who spends her time writing books on logic or who devotes herself to her students will come to the notice of the establishment. No one who does not come to the notice of the establishment will secure preferment. Therefore no lecturer who spends her time writing books on logic will secure preferment.
    (vii) Some lecturers are imaginative but poor communicators. Only good students are lecturers. Good students are not imaginative. Every artist is imaginative. Therefore not every good student is an artist.
    (viii) Dilly loves all and only those who love Milly. Milly loves all and only those who do not love Dilly. Dilly loves herself. Therefore Milly loves herself.

Solutions to Selected Exercises

Chapter 1

1.1 Strictly speaking, the truth table simply defines A∧B. However, by exchanging the positions of A and B we find that B∧A = A∧B. The truth table for A∧A is

A	A	A∧A
F	F	F
T	T	T

and we conclude that A∧A = A.

1.5

A	B	A→B	B→A
F	F	T	T
F	T	T	F
T	F	F	T
T	T	T	T

Clearly, A→B is not equivalent to B→A.

A	B	C	(A→B) → C	A → (B→C)
F	F	F	F	T
F	F	T	T	T
F	T	F	F	T
F	T	T	T	T
T	F	F	T	T
T	F	T	T	T
T	T	F	F	F
T	T	T	T	T

Again, clearly (A→B)→C is not equivalent to A→(B→C).

1.6   (i), (ii), (vi), (vii) and (viii) are tautologies.
      (iii), (iv) and (v) are not tautologies.
(Use truth tables to check these answers.)

1.7   All can be easily established by using truth tables.
      As an example let us take (vi).

A	B	A∨B	¬A	¬B	¬A∧¬B	¬(¬A∧¬B)
F	F	F	T	T	T	F
F	T	T	T	F	F	T
T	F	T	F	T	F	T
T	T	T	F	F	F	T

1.9 (ii) (a) A∧A∧A∧A∧A∧A ≡ A
          since A∧A ≡ A, and associativity of ∧ allows suitable grouping of the As.

          (b) A ∧ (¬A∨B) ∨ B ∨ (A ∧ (A∨B))
              ≡ (A∧B) ∨ B ∨ (A ∧ (A∨B))
              ≡ B ∨ (A ∧ (A∨B))   {since (A∧B) ∨ B ≡ B}
              ≡ B∨A   {since A ∧ (A∨B) ≡ A}

          (c) ¬A → ¬(A→¬B)
              ≡ ¬¬A ∨ ¬(¬A∨¬B)   {since A →B ≡ ¬A ∨ B}
              ≡ A ∨ (¬¬A∧¬¬B)   {since ¬¬A ≡ A, and ¬(A∨B) ≡ ¬A∨¬B}
              ≡ A ∨ (A∧B)
              ≡ A

1.10   The circuit for Figure 1.36 is straight forward – we will go straight to the
circuit for Figure 1.37.
The function is
(¬A∧¬B∧C) ∨ (¬A∧B∧C) ∨ (A∧¬B∧C) ∨ (A∧B∧C)
      ≡ ((¬A∧C) ∧ (¬B∨B)) ∨ ((A∧C) ∧ (¬B∨B))
              by factoring out ¬A∧C and A∧C respectively
      ≡ ((¬A∧C) ∧ 1) ∨ ((A∧C) ∧ 1)
      ≡ (¬A∧C) ∨ (A∧C)
      ≡ C ∧ (¬A∨A)
      ≡ C∧1
      ≡ C
So, the circuit is simply a single line for C.

The function represented in Figure 1.38 is
(¬A∧B∧C) ∨ (A∧¬B∧C) ∨ (A∧B∧¬C) ∨ (A∧B∧C)
      ≡ ((B∧C) ∧ (¬A∨A)) ∨ A ∧ ((¬B∧C) ∨ (B∧¬C))
              by factoring out B ∧ C and A respectively.

$\equiv ((B \wedge C) \wedge 1) \vee A \wedge ((\neg B \wedge C) \vee (B \wedge \neg C))$
$\equiv (B \wedge C) \vee (A \wedge ((\neg B \wedge C) \vee (B \wedge \neg C)))$

Which gives the following circuit.

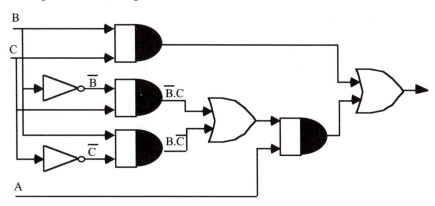

Chapter 2

2.1 (i)

$A \wedge B$
$\neg A \wedge B$
A
B
$\neg A$
B
_____
Closed

Since the tableau is closed, $A \wedge B$ and $\neg A \wedge B$ are mutually inconsistent.

(ii)

$A \wedge B$
$\neg A \vee B$
A
B

/   \
$\neg A$ B
_____
Closed

Since the tableau is not closed, $A \wedge B$ and $\neg A \vee B$ are mutually consistent, i.e. it is possible for both expressions to be true simultaneously.

(iv)

$A \rightarrow B$
$B \rightarrow A$

/   \
$\neg A$ B

/ \

¬B   A

Closed

Without going further we can see a branch that will not close, so, A→B, B→A are mutually consistent.

(vii)   (A∧B) → C

¬A→D

B∧¬C∧¬D

B

¬C

¬D

/ \

¬¬A   D

A   Closed

/ \

¬(A∧B)   C

/ \   Closed

¬A   ¬B

Closed   Closed

The expressions are mutually inconsistent.

(x)   ¬A∨B

B∧¬C

C→D

E∨¬D

A∧¬E

B

¬C

A

¬E

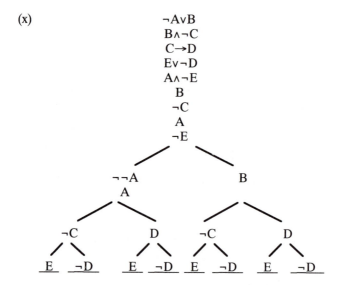

(The word 'Closed' is omitted for convenience.) We can see that all branches close. Therefore, the expressions are mutually consistent.

2.2   Let   J stand for 'John will go to the party'.
                 Y stand for 'Joyce will go to the party'.
                 C stand for 'Clare will go to the party'.
                 S stand for 'Stephen will go to the party'.
We symbolise (a) as follows:
J∨Y stands for 'John or Joyce (or both) will go to the party'.
Y → (¬S→C) stands for 'If Joyce goes to the party then Clare will go unless Stephen goes'.
J→S stands for 'Stephen will go to the party if John goes'.
Negate the conclusion, getting ¬C, and check if J∨Y, Y → (¬S→C), J→S and ¬C are mutually inconsistent.

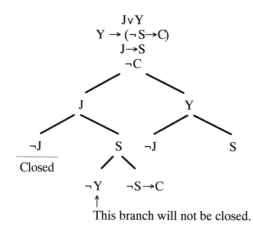

We need not expand any further, and can conclude that the argument is not valid.

Chapter 3

3.1
$$
\begin{array}{ll}
A \qquad B & \\
\hline
A{\wedge}B & {\wedge}I \\
B \to (A{\wedge}B) & \to I \\
A \to (B \to (A{\wedge}B)) & \to I
\end{array}
$$

3.4
$$
\begin{array}{ll}
A \qquad B{\wedge}C & \\
\hline
C & {\wedge}E \\
A{\to}C & \to I
\end{array}
$$

Note that we did not need to use A→ B, so effectively we have {B∧C} ⊢ A→C.
Of course it is still the case that {(A→B), (B ∧ C)} ⊢ A→C.

3.6

$$\frac{A \qquad A{\to}B}{B} \qquad \frac{A \qquad A \to (B{\to}C)}{B{\to}C} \qquad \to E$$

$$\frac{C}{} \qquad \to E$$

$$\frac{A \to C}{} \qquad \to I$$

$$\frac{(A{\to}B) \to (A{\to}C)}{} \qquad \to I$$

$$(A \to (B{\to}C)) \to ((A{\to}B) \to (A{\to}C)) \qquad \to I$$

3.7

$$\frac{A \qquad \neg A}{}$$

$$\frac{\bot}{} \qquad \text{Theorem 5}$$

$$\frac{A{\to}\bot}{} \qquad \to I$$

$$\neg A \to (A{\to}\bot) \qquad \to I$$

3.9

$$\frac{A \qquad A{\to}\bot}{}$$

$$\frac{\bot}{} \qquad \to E$$

$$\frac{\neg A}{} \qquad \text{RAA}$$

$$(A{\to}\bot) \to \neg A \qquad \to I$$

3.10

$$\frac{\neg A \qquad \neg A{\to}B}{}$$

$$\frac{B \qquad\qquad \neg B}{} \qquad \to E$$

$$\frac{\bot}{} \qquad \text{Theorem 5}$$

$$\frac{A}{} \qquad \text{RAA}$$

$$\frac{\neg B{\to}A}{} \qquad \to I$$

$$(\neg A{\to}B) \to (\neg B{\to}A) \qquad \to I$$

3.15 (ii)

$$\frac{A{\wedge}B}{}$$

$$\frac{A}{} \qquad\qquad \wedge E$$

$$A{\vee}B \qquad\qquad \vee I$$

3.15 (iii)

$$\frac{A \qquad A{\to}B}{B \qquad B{\to}C} \qquad\qquad \to E$$

$$\frac{C \qquad C{\to}D}{} \qquad\qquad \to E$$

$$\frac{D}{} \qquad\qquad \to E$$

$$\frac{A{\to}D}{} \qquad\qquad \to I$$

$$(C{\to}D) \to (A{\to}D) \qquad\qquad \to I$$

$$\frac{(B{\rightarrow}C) \rightarrow ((C{\rightarrow}D) \rightarrow (A{\rightarrow}D))}{(A{\rightarrow}B) \rightarrow ((B{\rightarrow}C) \rightarrow ((C{\rightarrow}D) \rightarrow (A{\rightarrow}D)))} \qquad \begin{array}{l} \rightarrow\text{I} \\ \rightarrow\text{I} \end{array}$$

(iv)

$$\frac{\dfrac{\bot}{\neg A} \quad \dfrac{\bot}{A}}{\dfrac{\neg A {\wedge} A}{\bot \rightarrow (\neg A {\wedge} A)}} \qquad \dfrac{\bot}{{\wedge}\text{I}} \quad \begin{array}{l} {\wedge}\text{I} \\ \\ \rightarrow\text{I} \end{array}$$

(vi)

$$\frac{\dfrac{\neg A {\wedge} A \qquad (\neg A {\wedge} A) \rightarrow \bot}{\bot}}{\neg(\neg A {\wedge} A)} \qquad \begin{array}{l} \text{Result (iv)} \\ \\ \rightarrow\text{E} \\ \\ \text{RAA} \end{array}$$

3.15   To falsify $\neg A \rightarrow (A{\rightarrow}B)$ we would need $\neg A$ to be true and $A{\rightarrow}B$ to be false. Hence we get

$$\frac{\neg A \Rightarrow A{\rightarrow}B}{\neg A \rightarrow (A{\rightarrow}B)}$$

To make $A{\rightarrow}B$ false we need A to be true and B to be false. Hence

$$\frac{\dfrac{\neg A, A \Rightarrow B}{\neg A \Rightarrow A{\rightarrow}B}}{\neg A \rightarrow (A{\rightarrow}B)}$$

Reversing the rule RT

$$\frac{\Gamma \Rightarrow \Delta}{\Gamma \Rightarrow A, \Delta}$$

allows us to drop the B to get

$$\frac{\dfrac{\dfrac{\neg A, A \Rightarrow}{\neg A, A \Rightarrow B}}{\neg A \Rightarrow A{\rightarrow}B}}{\neg A \rightarrow (A{\rightarrow}B)}$$

and reversing the rule L¬

$$\frac{\Gamma \Rightarrow A, \Delta}{\Gamma, \neg A \Rightarrow \Delta}$$

we get $A \Rightarrow A$.

Hence we now have the complete proof.

$$\frac{\dfrac{A \Rightarrow A}{\neg A, A \Rightarrow}}{\neg A, A \Rightarrow B}$$

$$\frac{\neg A \Rightarrow A \rightarrow B}{\neg A \rightarrow (A \rightarrow B)}$$

3.16 Prove each of the following sequents:
(Again, we illustrate with the first two.)

3.16 (i)

$C \Rightarrow C$	Id
$C, B \Rightarrow C$	LT
$C \Rightarrow B \rightarrow C$	R→
$C, A \Rightarrow B \rightarrow C$	LT
$C \Rightarrow A \rightarrow (B \rightarrow C)$	R→
$\Rightarrow C \rightarrow (A \rightarrow (B \rightarrow C))$	R→

(ii)

$\neg A \Rightarrow \neg A$	Id
$\neg A, \neg\neg A \Rightarrow$	L¬
$\neg\neg A \Rightarrow A$	R¬

Chapter 4

4.1 (i) This is an instance of axiom 3.

(ii)

$(\neg p_1 \rightarrow (p_3 \rightarrow \neg p_1)$	Ax1
$(\neg p_1 \rightarrow (p_3 \rightarrow \neg p_1)) \rightarrow ((\neg p_1 \rightarrow p_3) \rightarrow (\neg p_1 \rightarrow \neg p_1))$	Ax2
$\therefore\ (\neg p_1 \rightarrow p_3) \rightarrow (\neg p_1 \rightarrow \neg p_1)$	MP

(iv)

$(\neg p_2 \rightarrow \neg p_1) \rightarrow (p_1 \rightarrow p_2)$	Ax3
$((\neg p_2 \rightarrow \neg p_1) \rightarrow (p_1 \rightarrow p_2)) \rightarrow ((\neg\neg p_1 \rightarrow \neg\neg p_2) \rightarrow ((\neg p_2 \rightarrow \neg p_1) \rightarrow (p_1 \rightarrow p_2)))$	Ax1
$\therefore\ (\neg\neg p_1 \rightarrow \neg\neg p_2) \rightarrow ((\neg p_2 \rightarrow \neg p_1) \rightarrow (p_1 \rightarrow p_2))$	MP
$((\neg\neg p_1 \rightarrow \neg\neg p_2) \rightarrow ((\neg p_2 \rightarrow \neg p_1) \rightarrow (p_1 \rightarrow p_2))) \rightarrow (((\neg\neg p_1 \rightarrow \neg\neg p_2) \rightarrow (\neg p_2 \rightarrow \neg p_1)) \rightarrow ((\neg\neg p_1 \rightarrow \neg\neg p_2) \rightarrow (p_1 \rightarrow p_2)))$	Ax2
$\therefore\ ((\neg\neg p_1 \rightarrow \neg\neg p_2) \rightarrow (\neg p_2 \rightarrow \neg p_1)) \rightarrow ((\neg\neg p_1 \rightarrow \neg\neg p_2) \rightarrow (p_1 \rightarrow p_2))$	MP
$(\neg\neg p_1 \rightarrow \neg\neg p_2) \rightarrow (\neg p_2 \rightarrow \neg p_1)$	Ax3
$\therefore\ (\neg\neg p_1 \rightarrow \neg\neg p_2) \rightarrow (p_1 \rightarrow p_2)$	MP

(v)

$(p_1 \rightarrow ((p_1 \rightarrow p_1) \rightarrow p_1)$	Ax1
$(p_1 \rightarrow ((p_1 \rightarrow p_1) \rightarrow p_1) \rightarrow ((p_1 \rightarrow (p_1 \rightarrow p_1)) \rightarrow (p_1 \rightarrow p_1))$	Ax2
$\therefore \ (p_1 \rightarrow (p_1 \rightarrow p_1)) \rightarrow (p_1 \rightarrow p_1)$	MP
$p_1 \rightarrow (p_1 \rightarrow p_1)$	Ax1
$\therefore \ p_1 \rightarrow p_1$	MP

4.4 (ii) This is simply a form of axiom Ax3

(iv)

$(\neg A \rightarrow ((B \rightarrow\!\!\!\rightarrow A) \rightarrow \neg A)$	Ax1
$(\neg A \rightarrow ((B \rightarrow\!\!\!\rightarrow A) \rightarrow \neg A)) \rightarrow ((\neg A \rightarrow (B \rightarrow\!\!\!\rightarrow A)) \rightarrow (\neg A \rightarrow\!\!\!\rightarrow A))$	Ax2
$\therefore \ (\neg A \rightarrow (B \rightarrow\!\!\!\rightarrow A)) \rightarrow (\neg A \rightarrow\!\!\!\rightarrow A)$	MP
$\neg A \rightarrow (B \rightarrow\!\!\!\rightarrow A)$	Ax1
$\therefore \ \neg A \rightarrow\!\!\!\rightarrow A$	MP

(vi)

$(\neg\neg A \rightarrow\!\!\!\rightarrow \neg\neg B)$	Hypothesis
$(\neg\neg A \rightarrow\!\!\!\rightarrow \neg\neg B) \rightarrow (\neg B \rightarrow\!\!\!\rightarrow \neg A)$	Ax3
$\therefore \ \neg B \rightarrow\!\!\!\rightarrow \neg A$	MP
$(\neg B \rightarrow\!\!\!\rightarrow \neg A) \rightarrow (A \rightarrow B)$	Ax3
$\therefore \ (A \rightarrow B)$	MP

(vii) Compare Exercise 4.2 (iv) with the following.

$(\neg B \rightarrow\!\!\!\rightarrow \neg A) \rightarrow (A \rightarrow B)$	Ax3
$((\neg B \rightarrow\!\!\!\rightarrow \neg A) \rightarrow (A \rightarrow B)) \rightarrow ((\neg\neg A \rightarrow\!\!\!\rightarrow \neg\neg B) \rightarrow ((\neg B \rightarrow\!\!\!\rightarrow \neg A) \rightarrow (A \rightarrow B)))$	Ax1
$((\neg\neg A \rightarrow\!\!\!\rightarrow \neg\neg B) \rightarrow ((\neg B \rightarrow\!\!\!\rightarrow \neg A) \rightarrow (A \rightarrow B)))$	MP
$((\neg\neg A \rightarrow\!\!\!\rightarrow \neg\neg B) \rightarrow ((\neg B \rightarrow\!\!\!\rightarrow \neg A) \rightarrow (A \rightarrow B))) \rightarrow (((\neg\neg A \rightarrow\!\!\!\rightarrow \neg\neg B) \rightarrow (\neg B \rightarrow\!\!\!\rightarrow \neg A))$	
$\rightarrow ((\neg\neg A \rightarrow\!\!\!\rightarrow \neg\neg B) \rightarrow (A \rightarrow B)))$	Ax2
$\therefore \ ((\neg\neg A \rightarrow\!\!\!\rightarrow \neg\neg B) \rightarrow (\neg B \rightarrow\!\!\!\rightarrow \neg A)) \rightarrow ((\neg\neg A \rightarrow\!\!\!\rightarrow \neg\neg B) \rightarrow (A \rightarrow B))$	MP
$(\neg\neg A \rightarrow\!\!\!\rightarrow \neg\neg B) \rightarrow (\neg B \rightarrow\!\!\!\rightarrow \neg A)$	Ax3
$\therefore \ (\neg\neg A \rightarrow\!\!\!\rightarrow \neg\neg B) \rightarrow (A \rightarrow B)$	MP

A much easier proof for this exercise is possible using TI:

$(\neg\neg A \rightarrow\!\!\!\rightarrow \neg\neg B) \rightarrow (\neg B \rightarrow\!\!\!\rightarrow \neg A)$	Ax3
$(\neg B \rightarrow\!\!\!\rightarrow \neg A) \rightarrow (A \rightarrow B)$	Ax3
$\therefore \ (\neg\neg A \rightarrow\!\!\!\rightarrow \neg\neg B) \rightarrow (A \rightarrow B)$	TI

(ix)

$\neg\neg A \rightarrow (\neg\neg\neg\neg A \rightarrow\!\!\!\rightarrow \neg\neg A)$	Ax1
$(\neg\neg\neg\neg A \rightarrow\!\!\!\rightarrow \neg\neg A) \rightarrow (\neg A \rightarrow\!\!\!\rightarrow \neg\neg\neg A)$	Ax3
$\therefore \ \neg\neg A \rightarrow (\neg A \rightarrow\!\!\!\rightarrow \neg\neg\neg A)$	TI
$(\neg A \rightarrow\!\!\!\rightarrow \neg\neg\neg A) \rightarrow (\neg\neg A \rightarrow A)$	Ax3
$\therefore \ \neg\neg A \rightarrow (\neg\neg A \rightarrow A)$	TI
$(\neg\neg A \rightarrow (\neg\neg A \rightarrow A)) \rightarrow ((\neg\neg A \rightarrow\!\!\!\rightarrow \neg A) \rightarrow (\neg\neg A \rightarrow A))$	Ax2

∴ (¬¬A→¬¬A) →(¬¬A→A)   MP
   ¬¬A→¬¬A   Theorem 4.1
∴ ¬¬A→ A   MP

If we forego the use of TI, the proof is much more challenging. The following is one solution:

(¬¬¬¬A→¬¬A) → (¬A→¬¬¬A)   Ax3
((¬¬¬¬A→¬¬A) → (¬A→¬¬¬A)) → (¬¬A → ((¬¬¬¬A→¬¬A) →
(¬A→¬¬¬A)))   Ax1
∴ ¬¬A → ((¬¬¬¬A→¬¬A) → (¬A→ ¬¬A))   MP
(¬¬A → ((¬¬¬¬A→¬¬A) → (¬A→¬¬¬A))) → ((¬¬A →
(¬¬¬¬A→¬¬A)) → (¬¬A → (¬A→¬¬¬A)))   Ax2
∴ (¬¬A → (¬¬¬¬A→¬¬A)) → (¬¬A → (¬A→¬¬¬A))   MP
  ¬¬A → (¬¬¬¬A→¬¬A)   Ax1
∴ ¬¬A → (¬A→¬¬¬A)   MP

Down as far as here is essentially a repeat of the proof of ⊢ ¬A → (A→B) (Theorem 4.2), with ¬A replacing A and ¬¬¬A replacing B. The key insight is that we can switch ¬A→¬¬¬A 'around' using Ax3 to get ¬¬A→¬A, and then hope to get ¬¬A → (¬¬A→¬A), whence we can easily finish the proof. We continue as follows.

((¬A→¬¬¬A) → (¬¬A→A)) → (¬¬A → ((¬A→¬¬¬A) → (¬¬A→A)))
               Ax1
(¬A→¬¬¬A) → (¬¬A→A)   Ax3
∴ ¬¬A → ((¬A→¬¬¬A) → (¬¬A→A))   MP
(¬¬A → ((¬A→¬¬¬A) → (¬¬A→A))) → ((¬¬A → (¬A→¬¬¬A)) →
(¬¬A → (¬¬A→A)))   Ax2
∴ (¬¬A → (¬A→¬¬¬A)) → (¬¬A → (¬¬A→A))   MP
∴ ¬¬A → (¬¬A→A)   MP
(¬¬A → (¬¬A→A)) → ((¬¬A→¬A) → (¬¬A→A))   Ax2
∴ (¬¬A→¬A) →(¬¬A→A)   MP
  ¬¬A→¬¬A   Theorem 4.1, where A is any wff
∴ ¬¬A→A   MP

Exercises (x), (xi) and (xii) follow on from the last result.

4.5 (i)
     A   Hypothesis
     A → (B→C)   Hypothesis
  ∴ B→C   MP
     B   Hypothesis
  ∴ C   MP
  Hence {A, B, A → (B→C)} ⊢ C
  {B, A → (B→C)} ⊢ A→C   Deduction theorem

(iii)

$\neg\neg A \to A$	
$A \to B$	Hypothesis
$\therefore\ \neg\neg A \to B$	TI
$B \to \neg\neg B$	Already proved
$\therefore\ \neg\neg A \to \neg\neg B$	TI
$(\neg\neg A \to \neg\neg B) \to (\neg B \to \neg A)$	Ax3
$\therefore\ \neg B \to \neg A$	MP

Hence $\{A \to B\} \vdash \neg B \to \neg A$

Therefore $\vdash (A \to B) \to (\neg B \to \neg A)$ Deduction theorem

(iv)

$B \to (A \to B)$	Ax1
$(B \to (A \to B)) \to (\neg(A \to B) \to \neg B)$	(iii) above
$\therefore\ \neg(A \to B) \to \neg B$	MP

(vii)

$A \to \neg\neg A$	Already proved
$\neg\neg A \to (\neg\neg(A \to \neg A) \to \neg\neg A)$	Ax1
$\therefore\ A \to (\neg\neg(A \to \neg A) \to \neg\neg A)$	TI
$(\neg\neg(A \to \neg A) \to \neg\neg A) \to (\neg A \to \neg(A \to \neg A))$	Ax3
$\therefore\ A \to (\neg A \to \neg(A \to \neg A))$	TI
$(A \to (\neg A \to \neg(A \to \neg A))) \to ((A \to \neg A) \to (A \to \neg(A \to \neg A)))$ Ax2	
$\therefore\ (A \to \neg A) \to (A \to \neg(A \to \neg A))$	MP
$A \to \neg A$	Hypothesis
$\therefore\ A \to \neg(A \to \neg A)$	MP
$(A \to \neg(A \to \neg A)) \to ((A \to \neg A) \to \neg A)$	Prove this for yourself! (Similar to (iii) above)
$\therefore\ (A \to \neg A) \to \neg A$	MP
$\therefore\ \neg A$	MP (using hypothesis)

Hence $\{A \to \neg A\} \vdash \neg A$

Therefore $\vdash (A \to \neg A) \to \neg A$ Deduction theorem

(ix)

$\neg B$	Hypothesis
$A \to B$	Hypothesis
$(A \to B) \to (\neg B \to \neg A)$	(iii) above
$\therefore\ \neg B \to \neg A$	MP
$\therefore\ \neg A$	MP
$\neg A \to B$	Hypothesis
$\therefore\ B$	MP

Hence $\{\neg B, A \to B, \neg A \to B\} \vdash B$

$\therefore\ \{A \to B, \neg A \to B\} \vdash \neg B \to B$	Deduction theorem
But $\vdash (\neg B \to B) \to B$	Theorem 4.10
$\therefore\ \{A \to B, \neg A \to B\} \vdash B$	MP
$\therefore\ \{A \to B\} \vdash (\neg A \to B) \to B$	Deduction theorem
$\therefore\ \vdash (A \to B) \to ((\neg A \to B) \to B)$	Deduction theorem

4.6   (i) $v(\neg A) \neq v(A)$

If $v(A) = T$ then $v(\neg A) = F$, since $v(\neg A) \neq v(A)$ and there are only two possible values of v.

Similarly if $v(A) = F$ then $v(\neg A) = T$.

(ii) $v(A \rightarrow B) = F$ if and only if $v(A) = T$ and $v(B) = F$

This is obvious, since it is precisely what the truth table would tell us.

4.8   (i) $A \rightarrow A$

$v(A \rightarrow A) = F$ iff $v(A) = T$ and $v(A) = F$, which is impossible.

$\therefore$ $v(A \rightarrow A) = T$ always

(iv) $(\neg A \rightarrow A) \rightarrow A$

$v((\neg A \rightarrow A) \rightarrow A) = F$ iff $v(\neg A \rightarrow A) = T$ and $v(A) = F$,

i.e. $v(\neg A) = T$ and $v(A) = T$ and $v(A) = F$, which is impossible

or $v(\neg A) = F$ and $v(A) = F$, which is also impossible.

$\therefore$ $v((\neg A \rightarrow A) \rightarrow A) = T$ always

4.10   (i) $v(p_1) = T$, $v(p_2) = T$

Under this valuation $v(A) = T$.

Then $q_1 = p_1$, $q_2 = p_2$ and $A' = A$

Hence $\{q_1, q_2\} \vdash A'$ becomes $\{p_1, p_2\} \vdash A$.

i.e. $\{p_1, p_2\} \vdash (p_2 \rightarrow \neg p_1) \rightarrow (\neg p_1 \rightarrow p_2)$

This is proved as follows:

p_2	Hypothesis
$p_2 \rightarrow (\neg p_1 \rightarrow p_2)$	Ax1
$\therefore$ $\neg p_1 \rightarrow p_2$	MP
$(\neg p_1 \rightarrow p_2) \rightarrow ((p_2 \rightarrow \neg p_1) \rightarrow (\neg p_1 \rightarrow p_2))$	Ax1
$\therefore$ $(p_2 \rightarrow \neg p_1) \rightarrow (\neg p_1 \rightarrow p_2)$	MP

Hence $\{p_2\} \vdash (p_2 \rightarrow \neg p_1) \rightarrow (\neg p_1 \rightarrow p_2)$ with the assumption p_1 not used.

Hence $\{p_1, p_2\} \vdash (p_2 \rightarrow \neg p_1) \rightarrow (\neg p_1 \rightarrow p_2)$ adding redundant p_1 does no harm.

(iv) $v(p_1) = F$, $v(p_2) = F$

Under this valuation $v(A) = F$.

Then $q_1 = \neg p_1$, $q_2 = \neg p_2$ and $A' = \neg A$

Hence $\{q_1, q_2\} \vdash A'$ becomes $\{\neg p_1, \neg p_2\} \vdash \neg A$.

i.e. $\{\neg p_1, \neg p_2\} \vdash \neg((p_2 \rightarrow \neg p_1) \rightarrow (\neg p_1 \rightarrow p_2))$

This may be proved as follows:

$\neg p_1$	Hypothesis
$\neg p_1 \rightarrow (p_2 \rightarrow \neg p_1)$	Ax1
$\therefore$ $p_2 \rightarrow \neg p_1$	MP

$(p_2 \rightarrow \neg p_1) \rightarrow (\neg p_1 \rightarrow p_2)$ Hypothesis

$\therefore \quad \neg p_1 \rightarrow p_2$ MP

$\therefore \quad p_2$ MP

Hence $\{\neg p_1, (p_2 \rightarrow \neg p_1) \rightarrow (\neg p_1 \rightarrow p_2)\} \vdash p_2$

Hence $\{\neg p_1\} \vdash ((p_2 \rightarrow \neg p_1) \rightarrow (\neg p_1 \rightarrow p_2)) \rightarrow p_2$ Deduction theorem

But

$(((p_2 \rightarrow \neg p_1) \rightarrow (\neg p_1 \rightarrow p_2)) \rightarrow p_2) \rightarrow (\neg p_2 \rightarrow \neg ((p_2 \rightarrow \neg p_1) \rightarrow (\neg p_1 \rightarrow p_2)))$

                                          Exercise 4.4 (xii)

$\therefore \{\neg p_1\} \vdash \neg p_2 \rightarrow \neg ((p_2 \rightarrow \neg p_1) \rightarrow (\neg p_1 \rightarrow p_2))$ MP

$\therefore \{\neg p_1, \neg p_2\} \vdash \neg ((p_2 \rightarrow \neg p_1) \rightarrow (\neg p_1 \rightarrow p_2))$ Converse of deduction theorem

Chapter 5

5.2 (i) $p_1 \vee (p_2 \wedge p_3) \equiv (p_1 \vee p_2) \wedge (p_1 \vee p_3)$

(iv) $p_1 \leftrightarrow (p_2 \wedge p_3) \equiv (p_1 \rightarrow (p_2 \wedge p_3)) \wedge ((p_2 \wedge p_3) \rightarrow p_1)$

                        $\equiv (\neg p_1 \vee (p_2 \wedge p_3)) \wedge (\neg (p_2 \wedge p_3) \vee p_1)$

                        $\equiv (\neg p_1 \vee p_2) \wedge (\neg p_1 \vee p_3) \wedge (\neg p_2 \vee \neg p_3 \vee p_1)$

(ix) $(\neg p_1 \wedge (\neg p_2 \rightarrow p_3)) \rightarrow p_4 \equiv \neg (\neg p_1 \wedge (\neg \neg p_2 \vee p_3)) \vee p_4$

                                $\equiv \neg (\neg p_1 \wedge (p_2 \vee p_3)) \vee p_4$

                                $\equiv (\neg \neg p_1 \vee \neg (p_2 \vee p_3)) \vee p_4$

                                $\equiv (p_1 \vee (\neg p_2 \wedge \neg p_3)) \vee p_4$

                                $\equiv p_1 \vee p_4 \vee (\neg p_2 \wedge \neg p_3)$

                                $\equiv (p_1 \vee p_4 \vee \neg p_2) \wedge (p_1 \vee p_4 \vee \neg p_3)$

5.4   (i) $\{\{p_1, p_2, p_3\}, \{p_1, \neg p_3\}, \{\neg p_1\}, \{\neg p_2\}\}$

Resolve $\{p_1, p_2, p_3\}, \{p_1, \neg p_3\}$ using $p_3, \neg p_3$ to get $\{p_1, p_2\}$

Resolve $\{p_1, p_2\}, \{\neg p_1\}$ using $p_1, \neg p_1$ to get $\{p_2\}$

Resolve $\{p_2\}, \{\neg p_2\}$ to get $\bot$

Hence the clauses are inconsistent.

(iv) $\{\{p_1, \neg p_2, p_3, \neg p_4\}, \{p_1, \neg p_3\}, \{\neg p_1, p_2, \neg p_4\}, \{p_4\}\}$

Resolve $\{p_1, \neg p_2, p_3, \neg p_4\}, \{p_1, \neg p_3\}$ using $p_3, \neg p_3$ to get $\{p_1, \neg p_2, \neg p_4\}$

Resolve $\{p_1, \neg p_2, \neg p_4\}, \{\neg p_1, p_2, \neg p_4\}$ using $p_1, \neg p_1$ to get $\{\neg p_2, p_2, \neg p_4\}$,

which is a tautology

Hence the clauses are consistent. A satisfying valuation is $v(p_1) = T$, $v(p_2) = T$,

$v(p_4) = T$.

(v) $\{\{p_1, \neg p_2, p_3\}, \{p_1, \neg p_3\}, \{p_1, p_2\}$

It is easy to see that these clauses are consistent. If $v\{p_1\} = T$ they are all satisfied.

Chapter 6

6.1 (iv)   Everybody likes Paul: $(\forall x)L(x, p)$

    (v)   Everybody likes somebody: $(\forall x)(\exists y)L(x, y)$

    (vi)   Everybody who likes Stephen likes Paul: $(\forall x)(L(x, s) \rightarrow L(x, p))$

    (vii)   Every natural number is either even or odd: $(\forall x)(N(x) \rightarrow (E(x) \lor O(x)))$

    (viii)   No integer is both even and odd: $\neg(\exists x)(I(x) \land E(x) \land O(x))$

    (xi)   John likes anybody who does not like himself: $(\forall x)(\neg L(x, x) \rightarrow L(j, x))$

    (xiv)   If 5 numbers are arranged in descending order then the first number is at least as big as any of the others:

$$((x1 \geq x2) \land (x2 \geq x3) \land (x3 \geq x4) \land (x4 \geq x5)) \rightarrow (\forall x)(((x=x2) \lor (x=x3) \lor (x=x4) \lor (x=x5)) \rightarrow \neg L(x1, x))$$

6.2 Consider the statement 'There is not a person who is not happy'. This may be symbolised:

$\neg(\exists x)(P(x) \land \neg H(x))$

        $\equiv \neg(\exists x)\neg(\neg P(x) \lor H(x))$ De Morgan's law

        $\equiv \neg(\exists x)\neg(P(x) \rightarrow H(x))$ Equivalence of $A \rightarrow B$ and $\neg A \lor B$

        $\equiv (\forall x)(P(x) \rightarrow H(x))$ If we take $\forall x \equiv \neg(\exists x)\neg$

which may be read 'Everybody is happy'.

This is easily seen to express the same proposition as the original. So it is reasonable to take $\forall x$ as equivalent to $\neg(\exists x)\neg$.

6.5 (i)   Billy loves Jilly's sister: $L(b, s(j))$

    (ii)   Billy is afraid of Jilly's mother's sister's husband: $A(b, h(s(m(j))))$

    (v)   If the sum of two integers is greater than their product then one of the numbers must be zero:

$$(\forall x)(\forall y)(G(\text{sum}(x, y), \text{prod}(x, y)) \rightarrow ((x=0) \lor (y=0))$$

6.7 (i) $(\forall x)B(y, z)$

Scope of $(\forall x)$ is $B(y,z)$

x is bound, y and z are free.

(iv) $(\forall x)((\forall y)A(x, y, z) \rightarrow (\exists z)A(z, z, z))$

Scope of $(\forall x)$ is $((\forall y)A(x, y, z) \rightarrow (\exists z)A(z, z, z))$

Scope of $(\forall y)$ is $A(x, y, z)$

Scope of $(\exists z)$ is $A(z, z, z)$

Every occurrence of x and y is bound. The first occurrence of z is free, the other occurrences are bound.

(vi) $(\forall x)(((\forall y)A(x, y, z) \land (\forall x)B(x)) \rightarrow (\exists z)A(z, z, z))$

Scope of first $(\forall x)$ is $((\forall y)A(x, y, z) \land (\forall x)B(x)) \rightarrow (\exists z)A(z, z, z)$

Scope of $(\forall y)$ is $A(x, y, z)$

Scope of second $(\forall x)$ is $B(x)$

Scope of $(\exists z)$ is $A(z, z, z)$

Every occurrence of x and y is bound (the last two occurrences of x are bound by the second ($\forall$x)). The first occurrence of z is free, the last four are bound.

6.8 (i) $A_1^3(x_1, x_2, x_3)$
$x_1, x_2, f_1^1(x_1), f_1^2(x_2, x_5)$, are all free for x_2

(v) $(\forall x_1)(A_1^3(x_1, x_2, x_3) \rightarrow (\exists x_5)A_1^2(f_1^2(x_2, x_5), x_4))$
x_2 is free for x_2; $x_1, f_1^1(x_1)$ and $f_1^2(x_2, x_5)$ are not.

6.9 (i) 0 is the successor of 0.
$P_1^2(C_1, f_1^1(C_1))$

(ii) 0 has no successor.
$\neg(\exists x)P_1^2(x, f_1^1(C_1))$

(iv) If two numbers have the same successor they are equal.
$(\forall x)(\forall y)(P_1^2(f_1^1(x), f_1^1(y)) \rightarrow P_1^2(x, y))$

(v) The successor of the successor of any number is greater than the successor of that same number.
$(\forall x)P_2^2(f_1^1(x), f_1^1(f_1^1(x)))$

(x) If anybody is Barbara's mother then she is everybody's mother.
We need a predicate for equals; let us use P_3^2.
Then $(\exists x)P_3^2(x, f_1^1(c_1)) \rightarrow (\forall y)P_3^2(x, f_1^1(y))$

6.12 (i) $v(P_1^2(f_1^1(c_1), f_1^1(c_1)))$ is successor(0) = successor(0)   satisfied

(ii) $v(P_2^2(f_1^1(c_1), c_1))$ is successor(0) < 0   not satisfied

(v) $v((\exists x_1)(\forall x_2)P_1^2(f_1^1(x_2), x_1))$ is there a natural number such that the successor of every number is equal to it   not satisfied

(ix) $v(P_2^2(x_i, f_1^1(x_i)))$ is $v(x_i) <$ successor$(v(x_i))$ satisfied, no matter what $v(x_i)$ is

6.13 (i) $v(P_1^2(f_1^1(c_1), f_1^1(c_1)))$ is successor(0) = successor(0)   true

(ii) $v(P_2^2(f_1^1(c_1), c_1))$ is successor(0) < 0   false

(v) $v((\exists x_1)(\forall x_2)P_1^2(f_1^1(x_2), x_1))$ is there is a natural number such that the successor of every number is equal to it   false

(ix) $v(P_2^2(x_i, f_1^1(x_i)))$ is $v(x_i) < successor(v(x_i))$ true

6.17 Take any valuation v.
Suppose A is true and B is false.
v does not satisfy A→B if v satisfies A and v does not satisfy B.
But v does satisfy A, since A is true and v does not satisfy B, since B is false.
∴ v does not satisfy A→B.
But v is an arbitrary valuation.
∴ No valuation satisfies A→B.
∴ A→B is false.

Conversely, suppose A→B is false.
Then v does not satisfy A→B.
v satisfies A→B iff v does not satisfy A or v satisfies B.
∴ v satisfies A and v does not satisfy B.
But v is an arbitrary valuation.
∴ Every valuation satisfies A and no valuation satisfies B.
∴ A is true and B is false.

6.18 Suppose I ⊨ A and consider $(\forall x_n)A$.
Take any valuation v in I.
v satisfies $(\forall x_n)A$ if every valuation u which is n-equivalent to v satisfies A.
But such u do satisfy A, as A is true in I and therefore every valuation satisfies A.
∴ v satisfies $(\forall x_n)A$
But v is an arbitrary valuation.
∴ Every valuation satisfies $(\forall x_n)A$.
∴ I ⊨ $(\forall x_n)A$.
Then, similarly, I ⊨ $(\forall x_{n-1})(\forall x_n)A$
and also I ⊨ $(\forall x_1)(\forall x_2)(\forall x_3)...(\forall x_n)A$

Conversely, suppose I ⊨ $(\forall x_1)(\forall x_2)(\forall x_3)...(\forall x_n)A$.Take any valuation v in I.
Then v satisfies $(\forall x_1)(\forall x_2)(\forall x_3)....(\forall x_n)A$, since every valuation satisfies
$(\forall x_1)(\forall x_2)(\forall x_3)...(\forall x_n)A$.
∴ Every valuation which is equivalent to v apart possibly for values of $x_1, x_2, ...,$
x_n satisfies A.
But v is such a valuation itself.
∴ v satisfies A.
∴ I ⊨ A

6.20 Consider any valuation v in any interpretation I. Then v satisfies A and A→B, since they are logically valid.

Suppose v did not satisfy B.

Since v satisfies A and, by supposition, does not satisfy B, then v does not satisfy A→B.

But this contradicts logical validity of A→B.

∴ v does satisfy B.

But v is an arbitrary valuation in an arbitrary interpretation.

Therefore every valuation in every interpretation satisfies B.

Therefore B is logically valid.

6.22 Consider any valuation v in any interpretation I.

Suppose v does *not* satisfy $(\forall x_1)A$.

Then, by definition, v satisfies $(\forall x_1)A \rightarrow (\exists x_1)A$.

Suppose now that v does satisfy $(\forall x_1)A$.

Then every valuation u which is 1-equivalent to v satisfies A.

∴ There is some valuation 1-equivalent to v satisfying A (remember domains are non-empty).

∴ v satisfies $(\exists x_1)A$.

∴ v satisfies $(\forall x_1)A \rightarrow (\exists x_1)A$.

∴ In all cases v satisfies $(\forall x_1)A \rightarrow (\exists x_1)A$.

But v is an arbitrary valuation in an arbitrary interpretation.

Therefore every valuation in every interpretation satisfies $(\forall x_1)A \rightarrow (\exists x_1)A$.

Therefore $(\forall x_1)A \rightarrow (\exists x_1)A$ is logically valid.

Chapter 7

7.1 (i)

$A(x_i) \rightarrow ((A(x_i) \rightarrow A(x_i)) \rightarrow A(x_i))$	Ax1
$(A(x_i) \rightarrow ((A(x_i) \rightarrow A(x_i)) \rightarrow A(x_i))) \rightarrow ((A(x_i) \rightarrow (A(x_i) \rightarrow A(x_i))) \rightarrow (A(x_i) \rightarrow A(x_i)))$	Ax2
∴ $(A(x_i) \rightarrow (A(x_i) \rightarrow A(x_i))) \rightarrow (A(x_i) \rightarrow A(x_i))$	MP
$A(x_i) \rightarrow (A(x_i) \rightarrow A(x_i))$	Ax1
∴ $A(x_i) \rightarrow A(x_i)$	MP
∴ $(\forall x_i)(A(x_i) \rightarrow A(x_i))$	G

7.1 (iv)

$(\forall x_i)(A \rightarrow B)$	Hypothesis
$(\forall x_i)(A \rightarrow B) \rightarrow (A \rightarrow B)$	Ax4
∴ $(A \rightarrow B)$	MP
$(\forall x_i)A$	Hypothesis
$(\forall x_i)A \rightarrow A$	Ax4
∴ A	MP
∴ B	MP

$\therefore$ $(\forall x_i)B$ G

So, $\{(\forall x_i)(A \to B), (\forall x_i)A\} \vdash (\forall x_i)B)$

$\therefore$ $\vdash (\forall x_i)(A \to B) \to ((\forall x_i)A \to (\forall x_i)B)$ Deduction theorem (G was not
                                                                                                                               used on a variable free in
                                                                                                                               $(\forall x_i)(A \to B))$

7.2 (i)

$(\exists x_i)A \to \neg (\forall x_i)\neg A$ Def.

$((\exists x_i)A \to \neg (\forall x_i)\neg A) \to ((\forall x_i)\neg A \to \neg (\exists x_i)A)$ Theorem of AL

$\therefore$ $(\forall x_i)\neg A \to \neg (\exists x_i)A$ MP

(iv)

$A \to (\forall x_i)B$ Hypothesis

$(\forall x_i)B \to B$ Ax4

$\therefore$ $A \to B$ MP

$\therefore$ $(\forall x_i)(A \to B)$ G

So, $\{A \to (\forall x_i)B\} \vdash (\forall x_i)(A \to B)$

$\therefore$ $\vdash (A \to (\forall x_i)B) \to (\forall x_i)(A \to B)$ Deduction theorem (x_i is not
                                                                                                                               free in $A \to (\forall x_i)B$)

(vii)

$(\forall x_i)\neg (A \to B)$ Hypothesis

$(\forall x_i)\neg (A \to B) \to \neg (A \to B)$ Ax4

$\therefore$ $\neg (A \to B)$ MP

$B \to (A \to B)$ Ax1

$(B \to (A \to B)) \to (\neg (A \to B) \to \neg B)$ Theorem of AL

$\therefore$ $\neg (A \to B) \to \neg B$ MP

$\therefore$ $\neg B$ MP (see third line)

$\neg A \to (A \to B)$ Theorem of AL

$(\neg A \to (A \to B)) \to (\neg (A \to B) \to A)$ Theorem of AL

$\therefore$ $\neg (A \to B) \to A$ MP

$\therefore$ A MP (see third line)

$\therefore$ $(\forall x_i)A$ G

$(\forall x_i)A \to (\neg B \to \neg ((\forall x_i)A \to B)$ Theorem of AL

$\therefore$ $\neg B \to \neg ((\forall x_i)A \to B)$ MP

$\therefore$ $\neg ((\forall x_i)A \to B)$ MP (see line 7)

So, $\{(\forall x_i)\neg (A \to B)\} \vdash \neg ((\forall x_i)A \to B)$

$\therefore$ $\vdash (\forall x_i)\neg (A \to B) \to \neg ((\forall x_i)A \to B)$ Deduction theorem (x_i not free
                                                                                                                               in $(\forall x_i)\neg (A \to B)$)

$((\forall x_i)\neg (A \to B) \to \neg ((\forall x_i)A \to B)) \to (((\forall x_i)A \to B) \to \neg (\forall x_i)\neg (A \to B))$

                                                                                                                               Theorem of AL

$\therefore$ $((\forall x_i)A \to B) \to \neg (\forall x_i)\neg (A \to B))$ MP

i.e. $((\forall x_i)A \to B) \to (\exists x_i)(A \to B))$ Substitution of $(\exists x_i)$ for
                                                                                                                               $\neg (\forall x_i)\neg$

Chapter 8

8.2 (i)

1. $\neg((\forall x)A(x) \leftrightarrow (\forall y)A(y))$

2. $(\forall x)A(x) \wedge \neg(\forall y)A(y)$	$\neg(\forall x)A(x) \wedge (\forall y)A(y)$	Rule (9) on line 1
3. $(\forall x)A(x)$	$\neg(\forall x)A(x)$	Rule (1) on line 2
4. $\neg(\forall y)A(y)$	$(\forall y)A(y)$	Rule (1) on line 2
5. $(\exists y)\neg A(y)$	$(\exists x)\neg A(x)$	Rule (12) on lines 4 and 3
6. $\neg A(a)$	$\neg A(b)$	Rule (11) on line 5
7. $A(a)$	$A(b)$	Rule (10) on lines 3 and 4
Closed	Closed	

(iv)

1. $\neg(((\exists x)A(x) \vee (\exists x)B(x)) \rightarrow (\exists x)(A(x) \vee B(x)))$
2. $(\exists x)A(x) \vee (\exists x)B(x)$ Rule (8) on line 1
3. $\neg(\exists x)(A(x) \vee B(x))$ Rule (8) on line 1
4. $(\forall x)\neg(A(x) \vee B(x))$ Rule (13) on line 3

5. $(\exists x)A(x)$	$(\exists x)B(x)$	Rule (2) on line 2
6. $A(a)$	$B(b)$	Rule (11) on line 5
7. $\neg(A(a) \vee B(a))$	$\neg(A(b) \vee B(b))$	Rule (10) on line 4
8. $\neg A(a)$	$\neg A(b)$	Rule (7) on line 7
9. $\neg B(a)$	$\neg B(b)$	Rule (7) on line 7
Closed	Closed	

(viii)

1. $\neg((\forall x)(A(x) \rightarrow B(x)) \rightarrow ((\exists x)A(x) \rightarrow (\exists x)B(x)))$
2. $(\forall x)(A(x) \rightarrow B(x))$ Rule (8) on line 1
3. $\neg((\exists x)A(x) \rightarrow (\exists x)B(x))$ Rule (8) on line 1
4. $(\exists x)A(x)$ Rule (8) on line 3
5. $\neg(\exists x)B(x)$ Rule (8) on line 3
6. $(\forall x)\neg B(x)$ Rule (13) on line 5
7. $A(a)$ Rule (11) on line 4
8. $\neg B(a)$ Rule (10) on line 6
9. $A(a) \rightarrow B(a)$ Rule (10) on line 2

10. $\neg A(a)$	$B(a)$	Rule (3) on line 9
Closed	Closed	

8.3 (ii)

1. $\neg(((\exists x)A(x) \wedge (\exists x)B(x)) \rightarrow (\exists x)(A(x) \wedge B(x)))$
2. $(\exists x)A(x) \wedge (\exists x)B(x)$ Rule (8) on line 1
3. $\neg(\exists x)(A(x) \wedge B(x))$ Rule (8) on line 1

4.	$(\forall x)\neg(A(x)\wedge B(x))$	Rule (13) on line 3
5.	$(\exists x)A(x)$	Rule (1) on line 2
6.	$(\exists x)B(x)$	Rule (1) on line 2
7.	$A(a)$	Rule (11) on line 5
8.	$B(b)$	Rule (11) on line 6
9.	$\neg(A(a)\wedge B(a))$	Rule (10) on line 4

| 10. | $\neg A(a)$ $\qquad\qquad$ $\neg B(a)$ | Rule (6) on line 9 |

We cannot close the right branch!
Of course we could have used b in line 9 to give $\neg(A(b)\wedge B(b))$, but then the left branch could not be closed.

Chapter 9

9.2
$$\neg(((\forall x)A(x)\vee(\forall x)B(x)) \rightarrow (\forall x)(A(x)\vee B(x)))$$
$$(\forall x)A(x)\vee(\forall x)B(x)$$
$$\neg(\forall x)(A(x)\vee B(x))$$
$$(\exists x)\neg(A(x)\vee B(x))$$
$$\neg(A(a)\vee B(a))$$
$$\neg A(a)$$
$$\neg B(a)$$

$(\forall x)A(x)$	$(\forall x)B(x)$
$A(a)$	$B(a)$
Closed	Closed

Proved

$$\neg((\forall x)(A(x)\vee B(x)) \rightarrow ((\forall x)A(x)\vee(\forall x)B(x)))$$
$$(\forall x)(A(x)\vee B(x))$$
$$\neg((\forall x)A(x)\vee(\forall x)B(x))$$
$$\neg(\forall x)A(x)$$
$$\neg(\forall x)B(x)$$
$$(\exists x)\neg A(x)$$
$$(\exists x)\neg B(x)$$
$$\neg A(a)$$
$$\neg B(b)$$
$$A(a)\vee B(a)$$

$A(a)$	$B(a)$
Closed	

The tableau cannot be closed.

9.4 (i)

$(\exists x)A(x) \rightarrow (\exists x)B(x)$
$\quad \equiv \neg(\exists x)A(x) \vee (\exists x)B(x)$
$\quad \equiv (\forall x)\neg A(x) \vee (\exists x)B(x)$
$\quad \equiv (\forall x)\neg A(x) \vee (\exists y)B(y)$
$\quad \equiv (\forall x)(\exists y)(\neg A(x) \vee B(y))$

(vi)

$(\forall x)(\forall y)((\exists z)A(x, y, z) \wedge ((\exists u)C(x, u) \rightarrow (\exists v)C(x, v)))$
$\quad \equiv (\forall x)(\forall y)((\exists z)A(x, y, z) \wedge (\neg(\exists u)C(x, u) \vee (\exists v)C(x, v)))$
$\quad \equiv (\forall x)(\forall y)((\exists z)A(x, y, z) \wedge ((\forall u)\neg C(x, u) \vee (\exists v)C(x, v)))$
$\quad \equiv (\forall x)(\forall y)((\exists z)A(x, y, z) \wedge (\forall u)(\exists v)(\neg C(x, u) \vee C(x, v)))$
$\quad \equiv (\forall x)(\forall y)(\exists z)(\forall u)(\exists v)(A(x, y, z) \wedge (\neg C(x, u) \vee C(x, v)))$

9.5 (i)

$(\exists x)A(x) \rightarrow (\exists x)(\exists y)(B(x) \wedge C(x, y))$
$\quad \equiv \neg(\exists x)A(x) \vee (\exists x)(\exists y)(B(x) \wedge C(x, y))$
$\quad \equiv (\forall x)\neg A(x) \vee (\exists x)(\exists y)(B(x) \wedge C(x, y))$
$\quad \equiv (\forall x)\neg A(x) \vee (\exists z)(\exists y)(B(z) \wedge C(z, y))$
$\quad \equiv (\forall x)(\exists z)(\exists y)(\neg A(x) \vee (B(z) \wedge C(z, y)))$
$\quad \equiv (\forall x)(\exists z)(\exists y)((\neg A(x) \vee B(z)) \wedge (\neg A(x) \vee C(z, y)))$

which transforms to

$\quad (\forall x)((\neg A(x) \vee B(f(x))) \wedge (\neg A(x) \vee C(f(x), g(x))))$

which is written as

$\quad \{\{\neg A(x), B(f(x))\}, \{\neg A(x), C(f(x), g(x))\}\}$

(v)

$(\forall x)(\forall y)((\exists z)A(x, y, z) \vee ((\exists u)C(x, u) \rightarrow (\exists v)(C(x, v) \wedge B(v, z))))$
$\quad \equiv (\forall x)(\forall y)((\exists z)A(x, y, z) \vee (\neg(\exists u)C(x, u) \vee (\exists v)(C(x, v) \wedge B(v, z))))$
$\quad \equiv (\forall x)(\forall y)((\exists z)A(x, y, z) \vee ((\forall u)\neg C(x, u) \vee (\exists v)(C(x, v) \wedge B(v, z))))$
$\quad \equiv (\forall x)(\forall y)((\exists z)A(x, y, z) \vee (\forall u)(\exists v)(\neg C(x, u) \vee (C(x, v) \wedge B(v, z))))$
$\quad \equiv (\forall x)(\forall y)(\exists z)(\forall u)(\exists v)(A(x, y, z) \vee \neg C(x, u) \vee (C(x, v) \wedge B(v, z)))$
$\quad \equiv (\forall x)(\forall y)(\exists z)(\forall u)(\exists v)((A(x, y, z) \vee \neg C(x, u) \vee C(x, v)) \wedge (A(x, y, z) \vee \neg C(x, u)$
$\quad\quad \vee B(v, z)))$

which transforms to

$\quad (\forall x)(\forall y)(\forall u)(((A(x, y, f(x, y)) \vee \neg C(x, u) \vee C(x, g(x, y, u))) \wedge (A(x, y, f(x, y))$
$\quad\quad \vee \neg C(x, u) \vee B(g(x, y, u), f(x, y))))$

which is written as

$\quad \{\{A(x, y, f(x, y)), \neg C(x, u), C(x, g(x, y, u))\}, \{A(x, y, f(x, y)), \neg C(x, u),$
$\quad\quad B(g(x, y, u), f(x, y))\}\}$

9.9 (i) $\{\{A(x)\}, \{\neg A(y)\}\}$
Herbrand universe = $\{a\}$
Possible Herbrand interpretations are : $\{A(a)\}$ and $\{\neg A(a)\}$
The first interpretation fails to satisfy the second clause, while the second interpretation fails to satisfy the first clause.

(v) $\{\{\neg A(x), B(x)\}, \{A(b)\}, \{C(a,b)\}, \{\neg B(y), \neg C(a, y)\}\}$
Herbrand universe $= \{a, b\}$
Possible Herbrand interpretations are :

$\{A(a), A(b), B(a), B(b), C(a, a), C(a, b), C(b, a), C(b, b)\}$	4th clause fails
$\{A(a), A(b), B(a), B(b), C(a, a), C(a, b), C(b, a), \neg C(b, b)\}$	4th clause fails
$\{A(a), A(b), B(a), B(b), C(a, a), C(a, b), \neg C(b, a), C(b, b)\}$	4th clause fails
$\{A(a), A(b), B(a), B(b), C(a, a), C(a, b), \neg C(b, a), \neg C(b, b)\}$	4th clause fails
$\{A(a), A(b), B(a), B(b), C(a, a), \neg C(a, b), C(b, a), C(b, b)\}$	3rd clause fails
$\{A(a), A(b), B(a), B(b), C(a, a), \neg C(a, b), \neg C(b, a), \neg C(b, b)\}$	3rd clause fails
$\{A(a), A(b), B(a), B(b), \neg C(a, a), C(a, b), C(b, a), C(b, b)\}$	4th clause fails
$\{A(a), A(b), B(a), \neg B(b), C(a, a), C(a, b), C(b, a), C(b, b)\}$	4th clause fails

etc.

9.12 (i) $\{A(a, x, y, z), A(x, y, z, w)\}$
$S_0 = \{A(a, x, y, z), A(x, y, z, w)\}$; $\sigma_0 = \{\}$;
$D_0 = \{a, x\}$

$\sigma_1 = \{\} \circ \{a/x\} = \{a/x\}$; $S_1 = \{A(a, a, y, z), A(a, y, z, w)\}$;
$D_1 = \{a, y\}$

$\sigma_2 = \{a/x\} \circ \{a/y\} = \{a/x, a/y\}$; $S_2 = \{A(a, a, a, z), A(a, a, z, w)\}$;
$D_2 = \{a, z\}$

$\sigma_3 = \{a/x, a/y\} \circ \{a/z\} = \{a/x, a/y, a/z\}$; $S_3 = \{A(a, a, a, a), A(a, a, a, w)\}$;
$D_3 = \{a, w\}$

$\sigma_3 = \{a/x, a/y, a/z\} \circ \{a/w\} = \{a/x, a/y, a/z, a/w\}$; $S_3 = \{A(a, a, a, a)\}$;

9.13 (i)
Let $S(x)$ stand for 'x is a student'
     $A(x)$ stand for 'x is anxious'
     $T(x)$ stand for 'x studies'
     $P(x)$ stand for 'x will pass his examination'

The argument is:
$(\exists x)(S(x) \wedge A(x)) \wedge (\exists x)(S(x) \wedge T(x)) \wedge (\forall x)((S(x) \wedge A(x)) \rightarrow (\neg T(x) \rightarrow \neg P(x)))$
$\models \neg(\exists x)(S(x) \wedge P(x))$

We need to investigate whether
$(\exists x)(S(x) \wedge A(x)) \wedge (\exists x)(S(x) \wedge T(x)) \wedge (\forall x)((S(x) \wedge A(x)) \rightarrow (\neg T(x) \rightarrow \neg P(x))) \wedge$
$\neg\neg(\exists x)(S(x) \wedge P(x))$
is unsatisfiable.

Eliminate → (and ¬¬)

(∃x)(S(x)∧A(x)) ∧ (∃x)(S(x)∧T(x)) ∧ (∀x)(¬ (S(x)∧A(x)) ∨ (¬¬T(x) ∨¬P(x))) ∧
(∃x)(S(x)∧P(x))

Move ¬ inwards

(∃x)(S(x)∧A(x)) ∧ (∃x)(S(x)∧T(x)) ∧ (∀x)(¬ S(x)∨¬A(x)) ∨ (T(x)∨¬P(x))) ∧
(∃x)(S(x)∧P(x))

Rename variables

(∃x)(S(x)∧A(x)) ∧ (∃y)(S(y)∧T(y)) ∧ (∀z)(¬S(z) ∨¬A(z)) ∨ (T(z)∨¬P(z)) ∧
(∃w)(S(w)∧P(w))

Move quantifiers to the left and remove excess brackets

(∃x)(∃y)(∃w)(∀z)(S(x) ∧ A(x) ∧ S(y) ∧ T(y) ∧ (¬S(z)∨¬ A(z)∨T(z)∨¬P(z)) ∧
S(w) ∧ P(w))

Skolemise

(∀z)(S(a) ∧ A(a) ∧ S(b) ∧ T(b) ∧ (¬ S(z)∨¬A(z) ∨T(z)∨¬P(z)) ∧ S(c) ∧ P(c))

Write as set of clauses

{{S(a)}, {A(a)}, {S(b)}, {T(b)}, { ¬S(z), ¬A(z), T(z), ¬P(z)}, {S(c)}, {P(c)}}

Apply resolution to the clauses

    1. {S(a)}
    2. {A(a)}
    3. {S(b)}
    4. {T(b)}
    5. { ¬S(z), ¬A(z), T(z), ¬P(z)}
    6. {S(c)}
    7. {P(c)}

to get

    8. { ¬A(a), T(a), ¬ P(a)} using lines 1 and 5
    9. {T(a), ¬P(a)} using lines 2 and 8

Other resolutions are possible, but it is clear that ⊥ will not be derived. The
argument is, therefore, not valid.

Bibliography

Ben-Ari, M. (1993) *Mathematical Logic for Computer Science,* Prentice Hall, New York.

Chang, C-L. and Lee, R.C-T. (1973) *Symbolic Logic and Mechanical Theorem Proving,* Academic Press, New York.

Chellas, B.F. (1980) *Modal Logic: An Introduction,* Cambridge University Press, Cambridge.

Clocksin, W.F. & Mellish, C.S. (1984, 2nd Ed.) *Programming in Prolog,* Springer-Verlag, Berlin.

Frost, R.A. (1986) *Introduction to Knowledge Base Systems,* Collins, London.

Galton, A. (1990) *Logic for Information Technology,* John Wiley & Sons, Chichester.

Garey, M.R. & Johnson, D.S (1979) *Computers and Intractability: A Guide to the Theory of NP-Completeness,* W.H. Freeman & Co.., New York.

Hamilton, A.G. (1978) *Logic for Mathematicians,* Cambridge University Press, Cambridge.

Hughes, G.E. & Cresswell, M.J. (1968) *An Introduction to Modal Logic,* Methuen, London.

Jeffrey, R. (1981, 2nd Ed.) *Formal Logic: Its Scope and Limits,* McGraw-Hill, New York.

Kneale, W. and Kneale, M. (1961) *The Development of Logic,* Clarendon Press, Oxford.

Mendelson, E. (1987, 3rd Ed.) *Introduction to Mathematical Logic,* Wadsworth & Brooks/Cole, California.

Ramsay, A. (1988) *Formal Methods in Artificial Intelligence,* Cambridge University Press, Cambridge.

Reeves, S. & Clarke, M. (1990) *Logic for Computer Science,* Addison-Wesley, London.

Szabo, M.E. (ed.) (1969) *The Collected Papers of Gerhard Gentzen,* North-Holand, Amsterdam.

van Dalen, D. (1983, 2nd Ed.) *Logic and Structure,* Springer-Verlag, Berlin.

Glossary

And ($\wedge$) Conjunction connective. A conjunction $A \wedge B$ is true if and only if both conjuncts A and B are true.

Antecedent In a wff $A \rightarrow B$, A is called the antecedent. In a sequent $L \Rightarrow R$, L is called the antecedent.

Associative An operation $*$ is associative if $A*(B*C) = (A*B)*C$ for all values of A, B and C in the domain of application.

Atom A basic (non-decomposable) proposition (in propositional logic), or a predicate $P_i^n(t_1, t_2, \ldots, t_n)$ in first order logic.

Axiom A wff taken as a basis for deductions in a formal system.

Binding The association of a variable with a quantifier.

Bound variable Occurrences of the variable x in the expression (Qx)A, where Q is $\forall$ or Q is $\exists$, are said to be bound.

Clause A disjunction of literals.

Closed branch A branch of a semantic tableau containing a wff and its negation.

Commutative An operation $*$ is commutative if and only if $A*B = B*A$ for all values of A and B in the domain of application.

Completeness A formal system is complete if every valid wff is provable in the system.

Complementary literals Literals are complementary if one is the negation of the other.

Conjunctive normal form A wff F is in conjunctive normal form if it is a conjunction of disjunctions of literals, i.e. $F = C_1 \wedge C_2 \wedge \ldots \wedge C_n$, where $C_i = \lambda_{i1} \vee \lambda_{i2} \vee \ldots \vee \lambda_{im}$

Consequent In a wff $A \rightarrow B$, B is called the consequent. In a sequent $L \Rightarrow R$, R is called the consequent (sometimes succedent).

Consistency Semantic: A set of wff of propositional logic is consistent if there is a truth valuation under which all the wff are true. A set of wff of first order logic is consistent if there is a valuation in an interpretation under which all the wff are satisfied.
Syntactic: A formal system is consistent if, for any wff A, not both $\vdash$ A and $\vdash \neg$A.

Contradiction	A wff that is always false.
Cut rule	A rule of Gentzen's sequent calculus. Essentially, it states that if a wff A can be derived from a set of wff S1, and B can be derived from S2 and A, the A can be cut out and B can be derived from S1 and S2.
Decidability	A formal system is decidable if there is a mechanical procedure to determine whether or not any given wff is a theorem of the system.
Deduction	A sequence of wff of a formal system, each of which is an axiom or a hypothesis or derived from earlier wff in the sequence by a formal rule of deduction.
Deduction theorem	In propositional logic, if H, A $\vdash$ B then H $\vdash$ A→B. In first order logic, if H, A $\vdash$ B by a process not involving generalisation of a variable free in A, then H $\vdash$ A→B.
De Morgan's laws	$\neg(A \wedge B) = \neg A \vee \neg B$ and $\neg(A \vee B) = \neg A \wedge \neg B$
Disjunctive normal form	A wff F is in disjunctive normal form if it is a disjunction of conjunctions of literals, i.e. $F = C_1 \vee C_2 \ldots \vee C_n$, where $C_i = \lambda_{i1} \wedge \lambda_{i2} \wedge \ldots \wedge \lambda_{im}$.
Distributive	An operation $*$ is distributive over an operation $\oplus$ if $A*(B \oplus C) = (A*B) \oplus (A*C)$, for all values of A, B and C in the domain of application.
Equivalence	Two wff are equivalent if they always have the same truth value.
Existential quantifier ($\exists$)	Operates on a variable to state that there is at least one term satisfying a certain condition, e.g. $(\exists x)A(x)$
Falsum ($\perp$)	Symbol for a contradiction, i.e. an always false statement.
First order logic	A formal system based on a first order language.
First order language	A language where quantification occurs over variables of the alphabet, but not over predicate or function letters.
Formal axiomatic system	A system containing (1) Σ: an alphabet of symbols, used to form strings or expressions in the system (2) WF: the set of *well-formed formulae*, a subset of all the strings that can be formed using Σ, i.e. WF $\subseteq \Sigma^*$, where Σ^* is the set of all strings over the alphabet Σ (3) Ax: the set of *axioms*, a subset of WF (4) R: a set of *rules of deduction*.
Free for	A term is free for a variable x in a wff if no variable in the term becomes bound through substitution of the term for x.
Free variable	A variable which is not bound.

Function letter	An element of a first order alphabet which, in an interpretation corresponds to a mapping of tuples over a domain to elements of the domain, i.e. $I(f_i^n) = g: D^n \rightarrow D$, for some g.
Generalisation	A rule of deduction used in first order logic which licenses $(\forall x)A$ from A, i.e. if A occurs in the course of a deduction then $(\forall x)A$ may be used.
Ground atom	An atomic wff containing no variables.
Herbrand base	The Herbrand base of a set of clauses S is the set of ground atoms of S.
Herbrand universe	The Herbrand universe H(S) of set of clauses S consists of (1) The constants of S (if none, then arbitrary constant c) (2) $f(t_1, t_2, ..., t_n)$, where f is a function letter in S and $t_i \in$ H(S).
Herbrand interpretation	A Herbrand interpretation of a set of clauses S is a truth valuation of the elements of the Herbrand Base for S.
Higher order logic	A logic where quantification occurs not merely over (simple) variables, but over predicates and functions of first order and perhaps higher order.
Idempotence	An operation $*$ is idempotent if $A*A = A$ for all A.
If ... and only if ($\leftrightarrow$)	Bi-implication connective. $A \leftrightarrow B$ is true if and only if both A and B are true, or both A and B are false.
If ... then ($\rightarrow$)	Material implication connective. $A \rightarrow B$ is false if and only if A is true and B is false.
Inductive definition	A definition of a structure consisting of (1) a base part, describing the elementary parts of the structure (2) an inductive part, where the formation of more complex elements of the structure from simpler elements is described e.g. see definition of wff..
Instantiation	The replacement of a quantified variable by a constant in some semantic tableau rules.
Interpretation	An interpretation of a first order language consists of (1) a non-empty domain D (2) an association of constants, function letters and predicate letters of a first order language with elements, functions and relations in D.
Literal	An atom or the negation of an atom.
Logic gate	An electronic device which functions as a logic operator.
Meta-theorem	A theorem about the properties of a formal system.
Model	An interpretation of a set of wff with all the wff true.
Modus ponens	A rule of deduction: from A and $A \rightarrow B$ deduce B.
Natural deduction	A system of logic based on 'natural' rules of deduction, and no axioms.

Normal form	A standard pattern for a wff. See conjunctive/disjunctive normal form.
Not ($\neg$)	Negation. $\neg$A is true iff A is false.
Or ($\vee$)	Disjunction connective. A disjunction A$\vee$B is false if and only if both disjuncts A and B are false.
Predicate letter	An element of a first order language which is interpretable as a property or a relation over a domain.
Prenex normal form	A normal form where all quantifiers appear to the left of a quantifier-free expression called a matrix.
Proper axiom	An axiom which serves to restrict and define the possible interpretations of a first order language.
Proposition	An entity that can take on the value true or false.
Quantifier	See existential/universal quantifier.
Reductio ad absurdum	An argument which establishes a wff by showing that a contradiction may be derived from the negation of the wff.
Resolution	A method of deduction based on 'cancelling' complementary literals in separate clauses.
Resolution principle	A resolvent of two clauses C1, C2 is a logical consequence of C1 and C2, i.e. C1$\wedge$C2 $\models$ res(C1, C2)
Resolution refutation	A derivation of $\perp$ from a set of clauses S by means of the resolution rule of deduction. Such a derivation establishes that S is unsatisfiable.
Resolvent	The clause which results from the cancelling of complementary literals in a pair of distinct clauses.
Satisfaction	A wff is satisfied by a valuation in an interpretation if the statement corresponding to the wff is true.
Scope	The scope of the quantifier Q in the expression (Qx)A, where Q = $\forall$ or Q = $\exists$ is A.
Semantics	Meaning given in terms of interpretations.
Semantic tableau	A method of testing wff or inferences for validity by seeking refutations through the reduction of complex forms to simpler ones.
Sequent calculus	A form of natural deduction based on sequent rules.
Skolemisation	The replacement of existentially quantified variables in a prenex normal form by constants or appropriate Skolem functions, together with the dropping of the existential quantifiers.
Soundness	A formal system is said to be sound if all its theorems are tautologies (propositional logic) or valid (first order logic).
Substitution	The replacement of a variable by a term in a wff.

Syntax	'Form' as a sequence of symbols. Syntax has to do with the correct formation of strings of symbols drawn from a given alphabet. It may be distinguished from semantics, which has to do with the meaning or possible interpretations of strings of symbols.
Tautology	An always true wff of propositional logic.
Term	A constant, variable or function of a first order language.
Theorem	A wff derivable by formal rules of deduction from a set of axioms.
Theory	The set of deductive consequences of a set of axioms.
Transitivity	An operation $*$ is transitive if $A*B$ and $B*C$ implies $A*C$.
Truth function	A connective $*$ is said to be truth functional if the truth value of a complex expression formed by the use of $*$ depends only on the truth values of the components of the wff.
Truth table	A table laying out a systematic exhaustive enumeration of the possible truth values of combinations of simple propositions.
Truth valuation	An assignment v of values T and F to wff such that (1) $v(\neg A) \neq v(A)$ (2) $v(A \rightarrow B) = F$ iff $v(A) = T$ and $v(B) = F$.
Unification	The process of making different expressions the same by appropriate substitutions for variables.
Unifier	A set of substitutions which reduces a set of expressions to a single expression by unifying different expressions.
Unit clause	A clause containing a single literal.
Universal quantifier ($\forall$)	Operates on a variable to state that every term satisfies a certain condition, e.g. $(\forall x)A(x)$.
Valid argument	An argument from premises to a conclusion where the conclusion cannot be false if the premises are all true.
Valid wff	A wff which is satisfied by all valuations in all interpretations.
Valuation	An assignment of members of a domain to variables of a first order language.
Well-formed formula	Abbreviated as wff. A string formed from the symbols of an alphabet according to stated rules of formation (usually given inductively). For example, in the axiomatic system AL of propositional logic a wff is (1) a basic wff p_i for $i = 1, 2, \ldots$; or (2) $\neg A$ or $A \rightarrow B$ where A and B are wff.
XOR	Exclusive or connective. A XOR B is true if and only if A is true and B is false, or A is false and B is true.

Index